*Creating Flawless
Resumes for
Managers, Executives,
and CEOs*

Top Notch
Executive
Resumes

By

Katharine Hansen, PhD

CAREER
PRESS
Franklin Lakes, NJ

TOP NOTCH EXECUTIVE RESUMES
EDITED BY KATHRYN HENCHES
TYPESET BY EILEEN DOW MUNSON
Cover design by Rob Johnson / Johnson Design
Printed in the U.S.A. by Book-mart Press

To order this title, please call toll-free 1-800-CAREER-1 (NJ and Canada: 201-848-0310) to order using VISA or MasterCard, or for further information on books from Career Press.

The Career Press, Inc., 3 Tice Road, PO Box 687,
Franklin Lakes, NJ 07417
www.careerpress.com

Library of Congress Cataloging-in-Publication Data
Hansen, Katharine.
    Top notch executive resumes : creating flawless resumes for managers, executives, and CEOs / by Katharine Hansen.
        p. cm.
    Includes index.
    ISBN 978-1-56414-989-3
        1. Résumés (Employment) 2. Executives—Employment. I. Title.
    HF5383.H284 2008
    650.14'2—dc22
                                                                        2007052893

Acknowledgments

I thank Michael Pye of Career Press for giving me this project and agent Marilyn Allen for facilitating. Thanks to leadership of the Career Management Alliance, especially Liz Sumner, Wendy Enelow, and Deb Dib, for their invaluable assistance, and to the Alliance members who submitted samples for Chapter 3. Thank you to Carolynn Hood and Cynthia Buenger for their editorial assistance. Thanks to the many recruiters, HR professionals, and other hiring decision-makers for completing surveys about executive resumes. Many thanks to Maureen Crawford Hentz for facilitating the survey distribution. Thanks to the executives who submitted resumes for fictionalization and publication. And finally, endless thanks to my partner, Randall S. Hansen, for editorial suggestions and moral support.

 Contents

Chapter Three
Branded Career-Marketing Communication Tools to Enhance Your Resume
57

Chapter Four
The Opinions That Count: Resume Preferences and Peeves From Hiring Decision-Makers
133

Chapter Five
Your Resume and Executive Recruiters
143

Chapter Six
Case Studies
155

Chapter Seven
Resume and Cover Letter Samples for Aspiring Executives
177

Appendix
243

Index
251

About the Author
255

Introduction

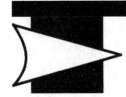

The Executive Difference

If the next step in your career is an executive, senior-level, or C-level position, this book will show you how to craft a resume that befits that upward mobility.

The next position you seek may be:

- ➤ Chief Executive Officer
- ➤ Chief Financial Officer
- ➤ Chief Information Officer
- ➤ Chief Marketing Officer
- ➤ Chief Operations Officer
- ➤ Customer Service Manager
- ➤ Director of Operations
- ➤ Director of Sales
- ➤ District Manager
- ➤ Division Manager/Director
- ➤ Executive Director
- ➤ Executive Sales Manager
- ➤ Executive VP
- ➤ First VP
- ➤ General Manager
- ➤ Human Resources Director
- ➤ Information Systems Director

- ➤ Logistics Manager
- ➤ MIS Director
- ➤ National Sales Manager
- ➤ Operations Manager
- ➤ President
- ➤ Production Manager
- ➤ Regional Manager
- ➤ Second VP
- ➤ Security Director
- ➤ Senior VP
- ➤ Telecommunications Director
- ➤ VP, Business Development
- ➤ VP, Finance
- ➤ VP, Manufacturing
- ➤ VP, Marketing
- ➤ VP, Operations
- ➤ VP, Production

If you've reached this prestigious level, chances are good that you are a mature job-seeker whose resume may have its roots in a time when resumes were very different from today's career-marketing documents. Your resume may have served you well in the past, but now you may find that it isn't working for you. Resumes have evolved, largely driven by technology, far beyond the what-I-did-and-where-and-when-I-did-it format of old. Today, resumes are keyword-driven and accomplishments-driven, especially at executive levels. The writing must be sharp, powerful, hard-hitting, and targeted.

You may be a top-level job-seeker who hasn't needed a resume for years because you've been headhunted into your jobs or found them through networking. For any number of reasons, this trend ends, and you find that you're suddenly being asked for your resume. And you probably need to start fresh with your resume rather than trying to dust off and patch up an old one.

If you're in one of these situations—or any other in which you need a resume fit for your executive or senior-level status, this book will guide you.

The first concept to master is how an executive resume differs from one for a lower-level position. An executive resume:

➤ **Positions the job-seeker within the market at a new level of seniority and prestige.** Your executive resume must show that you are ready for top-level jobs. It must distinguish you from middle managers and demonstrate that you've "arrived." It must also show growth and progression, and differentiate you from your former career incarnation. It must make a clear case for how you are qualified to move up. If you seek a top position at a public company, stockholders will have high performance expectations, and your resume must show you can meet them.

➤ **Presents the candidate in a way that clearly reveals his or her competitive advantage.** With each resume, the employer will be asking, "Why you, over any other candidate?" "What will we gain from hiring you?" Your resume must clearly answer those questions. It's not enough to be qualified for the positions you seek; you must portray yourself as the best qualified, the only logical choice, the one the organization will truly benefit form bringing on board.

➤ **Illuminates the executive's unique value proposition and return on investment (ROI).** The employer also wants to how you will add value in the open position. Especially if the employer is hiring through a search firm, the decision-makers will spend significant dollars to fill the position, so they want to know what their ROI will be.

➤ **Pointedly addresses how the candidate fits the organization's mission and can meet an employer's specific, compelling business need.** The executive resume should go beyond showing your qualifications by demonstrating that you truly understand the organization you seek to join. You comprehend its needs, its issues, its mission, its customers, its future, and more, and you can meet the needs based on your unique understanding.

➤ **Frames past accomplishments in a way that enables the employer to visualize the executive's strategic vision and industry insights, as well as what he or she can contribute going forward.** The hiring manager needs to be able to picture exactly what you can bring to the organization, and one of the best ways to evoke that picture is by vividly showing the results and accomplishments you've achieved in your past jobs. The employer needs to be able to see how you've strategically approached problems and challenges in past positions, what action you've taken, and the results you've attained. The top part of your resume also needs to show how you envision being a mover and a shaker, and making a difference for your next employer. Your full resume should convey that you can generate ideas, strategically plan their implementation, and motivate others to execute them.

Here's how this book can help you build a resume that will meet those executive requirements:

If you read nothing beyond Chapter 1 of this book, you will have learned the most important aspects of an executive resume, as encapsulated in the acronym FABUKA: *Focus, Accomplishments, Branding, Uniqueness, Keywords, Appearance.*

Chapter 2 describes each resume component—the must-includes and the optional sections—covers the details of building an effective top-level resume, and answers frequently asked questions.

In Chapter 3, you will learn about additional documents you need—from cover letters to portfolios—to market yourself.

The opinions and resume preferences that count the most—from hiring decision-makers—are covered in Chapter 4.

Chapter 5 focuses on important allies for the executive job-seeker—executive recruiters—and their resume needs.

Three case studies that highlight situations executive job-seekers frequently encounter comprise Chapter 6.

The meat of the book, 34 resume and cover-letter samples from most industry sectors, appears in Chapter 7.

The Appendix contains additional resources, including a guide for brainstorming accomplishments, along with helpful books, Websites, and information about executive resume writers.

I should note that crafting a resume is an exceedingly subjective proposition. Even among experts and veteran hiring decision-makers, you will be hard-pressed to find 100-percent agreement on any guideline on resume-writing, including those in this book. And if you show a resume—including the samples in this book—to those with hiring power, many will be attracted to it, but some won't. Add to this lack of consensus the fact that technology continues to change the concept of the resume, and it's easy to wonder which advice is authoritative. I have drawn on 18 years of experience in the career-development field, my experience as a professional resume writer, and my credentials as a Master Resume Writer in distilling the current wisdom on resume writing. More importantly, I've talked with many recruiters, human-resources directors, and other hiring decision-makers to research this book. Although consensus was hard to find, I am confident that I have reported on the range of current opinions. Ultimately, you, as the executive candidate, will have some decisions to make about your resume. It is, after all, a document that reflects your own personal tastes even as it attempts to appeal to those with the power to hire you.

Consider also experimenting. If your resume doesn't seem to be working for you, use this book to diagnose its problem or hire a professional to critique it. As discussed in Chapter 2, you will probably need several versions of your resume, but you may be able to narrow down your versions by determining which techniques are working best for you.

Though the resume is just one component in the executive job-search toolkit, it's one you are likely to need in a climate in which ExecuNet's 15th Annual Executive Job Market Intelligence Report (*www.execunet.com/r_download_intelligence.cfm?pid=ASUVX7&reflink=right_get_selected_outtakes*) notes that executives change employers every three years on average, and nearly half are currently in a job search. ExecuNet found that executive job dissatisfaction begins as early as 10 months into a job and peaks at the 14-month mark. It's also a high-opportunity environment, ExecuNet reports, in which baby boomer retirements and a shrinking candidate pool have resulted in a shortage of qualified high-level talent. Skills especially in demand, the report says, include managing and developing teams, recruiting talent, retaining key reports, growing revenue, and establishing vision and strategy.

In the face of an executive climate that has moved from pre-1990s stability, through the instability of downsizing and restructuring, and now to a restlessness that spurs greater executive mobility than ever before, executives are stepping up their responsibility for their own career management. Resumes are a big part of that.

Amid technological upheaval, job-seeking continues to evolve, with some predicting the ultimate demise of the resume. For the foreseeable future, however, the resume remains the linchpin of the job search, because it's the piece that gets the ball rolling. Sure, people get jobs without resumes, especially at the executive level, but that's a rare occurrence. And given rapid, unexpected changes, such a restructurings, mergers, and buyouts, it's wise to always have an updated resume ready at all times. Let's get started on everything you need to craft your top-notch executive resume.

Chapter One

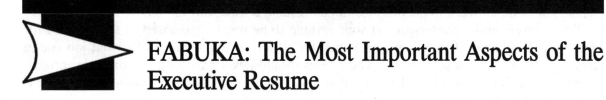

FABUKA: The Most Important Aspects of the Executive Resume

Most people find the idea of creating a resume overwhelming. Even the notion of revamping an existing resume can be daunting. Whereas Chapter 2 offers all the detailed nuts and bolts, this chapter assures you that, if you can nail six key aspects of today's executive resume, you will be off to a great start. These are the most important concepts of executive resume writing, and understanding these and the reasons behind them will enable you to undergird your resume with a firm foundation. The philosophy behind these concepts can then pervade your entire resume, making it a winner. The bottom line is that, if you read no further than this chapter, you will have mastered the ingredients of an executive resume that gets results.

If you can remember the acronym FABUKA, you can remember the key aspects of an effective executive resume.

FABUKA stands for:

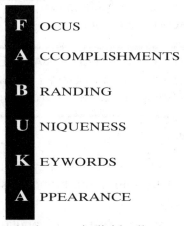

F OCUS

A CCOMPLISHMENTS

B RANDING

U NIQUENESS

K EYWORDS

A PPEARANCE

Let's look at each element individually.

Focus

Your resume must target your desired career goal with precision. Job-seekers tend to forget that employers review resumes extremely quickly—often in just a few seconds. An employer taking such a quick glance should be able to immediately grasp what you want to do and have a sense of the value you can contribute to the organization. The executive resume must focus on key strengths that position the candidate to meet a specific need and target specific jobs/employers. In other words, employers don't consider resumes that aren't focused on a job's specific requirements to be competitive, and the one-size-fits-all resume is especially ineffective at the executive level. Employers and recruiters expect your resume to be precisely tailored to the position for which you're applying. The reader should be able to tell, at a glance, exactly what job you're targeting and what need you will fill. The reader should never have to guess or wade through copious text to determine what job you want and what you'd be good at. An unfocused resume is a time-waster for the employer.

What are some ways you can sharpen your focus?

1. A headline atop your resume stating the type of job you seek, as in these examples:

ARLENE STEIN

4000 Gopher Road, Reno, NV 89511-8698 • Phone: 555-000-4497 • Cell: 555-000-6438
FAX: 555-000-4498 • E-mail: jobseeker@gol.com

EXECUTIVE SALES LEADERSHIP • MARKETING • SOURCING • STARTUPS

■

DANIELLE BANFIELD

12 Ridge Drive • Fairfax, VA 22033-4630 • Phone: 555.000.3940
E-mail: jobseeker@cs.com

**EXECUTIVE MANAGEMENT • COALITION BUILDING • LEADERSHIP
ORGANIZATIONAL STRATEGIC PLANNING**

■

MAUREY MARDER

2000 California Street, San Francisco, CA 94115
Phone: 555.000.2945 • Cell: 555.000.5981
E-mail: jobseeker@yahoo.com

MARKETING EXECUTIVE • STRATEGY • HIGH-TECH • MANAGEMENT
STRATEGIC MARKET PLANNING • LEADERSHIP • PROJECT MANAGEMENT • BRANDING
MARKETING COMMUNICATIONS • NEW PRODUCT/SERVICE DEVELOPMENT • PRODUCT LAUNCH

■

2. A branding statement that positions you for a specific job or type of job. (See the Branding section that follows.) Note that headlines and branding statements are often used in combination.

3. An objective statement. Objective statements have lost some popularity in favor of headlines and branding statements and must be effectively worded when used. (See the section on Objective Statements in Chapter 2.)

4. A Qualifications Summary or Professional Profile section. This increasingly popular resume component contains three to five bullets that represent your top selling points. Choose bullet points that directly tie your strengths to the requirements of the job you seek. (See more about these sections in Chapter 2.)

5. Use of the targeted employer's name in the foregoing resume elements. What could make your resume more focused than using the name of the employer? For example, one of the job-seekers whose resume appears as a sample in Chapter 7 seeks a position with a company called SolarBright and makes the following statement atop his resume:

   > Eager to lead innovative strategic marketing and operational initiatives that aggressively increase SolarBright's market share, sustain growth, and maximize profitability.

6. A section listing your Core Competencies/Proficiencies/Areas of Expertise. The keywords you select for this section should relate directly to the type of job you seek. (Read more in the Keywords section that follows and in Chapter 2.)

7. Strategic organization of your resume to position you for the job you seek. Remember that a resume is a marketing document that should highlight the aspects of your experience that best sell you for a particular position. In most cases, employers and recruiters want to see clear progression to where you are today. If your career path does not represent a clear trajectory to the position you seek, however, you may want to consider a non-chronological arrangement of your experience, keeping in mind that such organizational schemes can carry an element of risk (See the Organizational Formats section of Chapter 2). You may also consider placing other sections of your resume before your Experience section to showcase your best selling points. For example, do you have a newly minted MBA degree that adds value to your candidacy?

8. Bullet points describing your experience in a way that is specifically tailored to the position you seek. You've undoubtedly held jobs that encompassed a broad scope, many accountabilities, and numerous achievements. Fine-tune these to a razor-sharp list of those that are most relevant to the high-level job you seek next. Eliminate any bullet point that fails to support what you seek to do next.

9. Create multiple versions of your resume. You're probably thinking that the foregoing list means you need to craft a distinctive resume for every job for which you apply. And, yes, that's the ideal. But you can create boilerplate versions for various types of jobs and then make small changes to customize each to specific positions. One client of mine, for example, was interested in operations management, project management, and quality management, and asked me to prepare a resume for each type of position. He then had the option of tailoring each of those to specific job requirements.

Accomplishments

The executive resume must—with a future-oriented flavor—emphasize results, outcomes, and career-defining performance indicators. Using numbers, context, and meaningful metrics (for example, previous years' performance, competitors, counterparts, forecasts/projections/quotas, industry trends), the resume must paint a picture of the executive in action—meeting needs/challenges, solving problems, impacting the company's big picture, growing the business, enhancing revenue, and driving profits. This section also reveals how to mine and brainstorm accomplishments and demonstrate sought-after ethics and integrity.

Concrete, measurable accomplishments are the points that really help sell you to an employer—much more so than everyday job duties, and you can leverage your accomplishments for job-search success at all stages of the process: resume, cover letter, interview, and more.

Resume writer JoAnn Nix gave this advice in an interview on the *Guru.com* Website (*www.Guru.com*, August 2001): "A resume should be accomplishment-oriented, not responsibility-driven. The biggest mistake that I see in the resumes people send me is that they list responsibilities. That doesn't grab anybody's attention. People aren't interested in your responsibilities. They already know the general responsibilities of a position so they don't want to know what you do from day to day. They want to know that you're a mover and a shaker: How you contribute to the organization, how you show initiative, that you can be a key player. That's what they want to see."

On the *HR.com* Website (*www.hr.com*), KPMG Principal Mary Anne Davidson similarly observed, "Candidates write about what their positions entailed and not what they actually did. So they tell us their job was to do XYZ. I know what controllers do. I know what recruiters do. I need to know what accomplishments you made in your role. This makes you different than another candidate.

"In less than two sentences," Davidson continues, "I want to know the scope of your responsibilities, size of budget, geographic territory, number of team members you led or were a part of, product lines, and reporting relationship relevant to each of your roles in the last eight years."

To a great extent, if a job activity cannot be portrayed as an accomplishment, it may not be worthy of mention in your resume, cover letter, or in an interview.

If you haven't been tracking your accomplishments, start doing so today. Go through any materials you have from past jobs, such as memos and planning calendars, to see if they jog your memory about accomplishments. Talk with previous coworkers, too.

See the Appendix for a set of prompts to enable you to brainstorm all you have accomplished. Try to list some accomplishments that set you apart from other job candidates and enable the employer to picture the value you can immediately bring to his or her organization. How can you generate revenue?

Think of the "PEP Formula": Profitability, Efficiency, and Productivity. How did you contribute to profitability, through sales increase percentages? How did you contribute to efficiency, through cost reduction percentages? How did you contribute to productivity, through successfully motivating your team?

Quantify. Employers love numbers. Examples:

- Increased territory sales by 50 percent during previous year.
- Directed sales team that generated sales 20 percent higher than team for next highest territory.

"An accomplishment is defined in dollars and cents or percentages," says William M. Gaffney, recruiter and career coach for Amaxa Group (Dayton, Ohio). "Further it is expressed in revenue (income) for the company or money or time saved." Gaffney notes that accomplishments need to have a "reference point"—a standard of comparison, such as previous year's sales, another team's numbers, the performance of the previous person in your job, sales projections, or competitors' revenues.

If you describe a team accomplishment, be sure to make clear your role on the team. Give yourself appropriate credit for the team's achievement.

Use the SAR or PAR technique, in which you describe a **S**ituation or **P**roblem that existed in a given job, tell what **A**ction you took to fix the Situation or Problem, and tell what the **R**esult was. Some experts call this the CAR technique, in which **C** stands for Challenge, or the STAR technique, in which the **T** stands for **T**ask. Resume writer JoAnn Nix notes that a sales and marketing manager could employ SAR/STAR/PAR/CAR technique this way: "Joined organization to spearhead sales and marketing initiative for newly developed territory. Led the aggressive turnaround of a poorly performing district and propelled sales from one to six million in 14 months."

SAR, STAR, PAR, and CAR techniques work extremely well in resumes, indeed, throughout the job search, but given the speed in which hiring decision-makers read resumes, it's okay, indeed desirable, to give away the end of the story first. Tell the Result (R) of your Action (A) first so it catches the employer's attention. Then, ideally, describe the Situation (S), Problem (P), or Challenge (C) that your Action addressed. Quantify wherever possible.

Note in these examples of Result-Action-Situation bullet points from diverse resumes that, because of resume space limitations and employers' preference for conciseness, the Situation is not always described:

- Produced sales growth from $50K in backlog to more than $31 million in backlog in three years by building high-performance, multifunctional/multi-discipline, sales team comprised of professionals from multiple departments.

- Deflected 50-percent increase in electricity costs by designing/installing power factor correction systems.

- Reduced water usage by 80 percent by developing new cooling water temperature control system.

- Led national expansion of single-serve potato chip product—building U.S. volume +33 percent—by utilizing U.S. volume projections, international test market demands, and available capacity.

- Increased revenue by recruiting, training, and organizing efficient contract staff capable of faster processing time that optimized sales representatives' performance.

- Achieved 36-percent rating increase in customer survey scores by creating and implementing two new staff training programs that heightened levels of guest satisfaction.

- Increased sales revenue by 15 million in one year by assembling dynamic marketing team, coaching team members, and implementing highly effective marketing strategy.

- Raised $250K in one evening by coordinating 85 volunteers for school auction/dinner and through sales of 800 silent and 40 live-auction items.

- Facilitated 55-percent increase in customer satisfaction and 50-percent increase in employee job satisfaction by flattening hierarchy from 10 functional areas to just two, guiding employees to redefine their jobs, creating efficient work processes, eliminating redundancies, and eradicating paperwork in organization formerly unresponsive to clients as well as inefficient, bureaucratic, and apathetic.

- Boosted sales rate by 200 percent in first year and 400 percent over five years, successfully capturing majority of engineering specification market.

- Revived branch image, upgraded technology and equipment, and reestablished company as industry leader by increasing sales dramatically.

- Achieved 95-percent spend capture, 35-percent system operating and maintenance cost reduction, increased order visibility and leverage position, and enhanced supplier relationship management by executing successful integration of business units' procurement and payables systems and processes.

- Reduced annual consulting costs by $1.4M, streamlined development processes, facilitated rapid turnaround of customer requests, and enhanced internal application-development and application-support capabilities by developing and executing plan to in-source numerous key IT functions.

- Achieved 25-percent call-back rate, 30-percent sales increase, and a reopened revenue stream by executing direct-mail initiative to contact dormant customers to provide name recognition reminder and publish service-option details.

- Saved company $13.75 million—$1.75 million in first year and $4 million annually for three consecutive years—by conceiving, designing, and strategizing to bring branch computer maintenance in-house.

- Saved weeks in project time by instituting structured project-management methodology.

- Increased recoveries from less than 2 percent of paid, to 5.7 percent of paid, resulting in $39.6 million in increased recoverables, by creating "Third Party Recovery Recognition Templates."

- Reduced customer requests from 500 to 12 within three months by designing and implementing centralized customer task-tracking system.

- Reduced errors, saved time, achieved nearly a 100-percent paperless environment, and saved money by implementing central Web-based database that houses all client data, realizing remarkable return on equipment investment in less than a year.

Finally, a word of caution: Resist the temptation to blow your accomplishments out of proportion. Accomplishments should be measurable whenever possible and always verifiable.

Branding

Today's executive resume establishes an executive brand relevant to targeted employers. The branding expressed in your resume captures your career identity, authenticity, passion, essence, and image. "Branding is...best defined as a promise," says my partner, Randall Hansen, in an article on Quintessential Careers (*www.quintcareers.com/career_branding.html*), "...a promise of the value of the product...a promise that the product is better than all the competing products...a promise that must be delivered to be successful. Branding is the combination of tangible and intangible characteristics that make a brand unique. Branding is developing an image—with results to match."

In an executive resume, branding can be executed through at least three components:

1. The distinctive appearance of your resume, which should be carried through with all your career-marketing communications—cover letter, business cards, thank-you letters, portfolio, and much more—to package you with a consistent, branded look. Every time an employer sees this look, he or she will instantly associate it with you. (See examples in Chapter 3.)

2. A message woven throughout your resume that remains consistent and does not contradict the image you want to project. Every word and every bullet point should support the branded message you intend to convey.

3. A branding statement that defines who you are, your promise of value, and why you should be sought out. Your branding statement should encapsulate your reputation, showcase what sets you apart from others, and describe the added value you bring to a situation. Think of it as a sales pitch. Hansen suggests integrating these elements into the brief synopsis that is your branding statement:

    ➤ What makes you different?

    ➤ What qualities or characteristics make you distinctive?

    ➤ What have you accomplished?

    ➤ What is your most noteworthy personal trait?

    ➤ What benefits (problems solved) do you offer?

Here are some sample branding statements (note that some are used in combination with headlines):

SENIOR EXECUTIVE

Specialize in raising the bar, creating strategy, managing risk, and improving the quality and caliber of operations.

SENIOR PROGRAM MANAGEMENT PROFESSIONAL

Providing expertise in multi-disciplinary project management, program management, and product development. Consistently delivering integrated solutions that reap tangible bottom-line rewards while harnessing and exploiting leading-edge technologies.

DIRECTOR OF MARKETING AND RECRUITMENT

Poised to deliver to strong proficiencies in marketing, communications, recruitment, and organization to promote your campus learning environment and facilitate ongoing student success.

■

Constructing dynamic, top-producing sales organizations through proven leadership and management style, strategic partnering, design of tactical sales initiatives, and implementation of key account-management methodologies.

■

Positioned to deliver visionary leadership and strategic direction to the Chemical Engineering industry in a senior-level position in manufacturing, research and development, and knowledge exchange systems.

■

Uniquely positioned to deliver exceptional results in business-process management, solutions implementation, and service delivery, combined with expert-level technical proficiencies in a Senior Project Management capacity.

■

Positioned to provide leadership through solid foundation of accomplishments in finance, accounting, and customer service in a Director of Finance capacity on a senior-level management team.

■

Uniqueness

The executive resume must present a sales pitch that conveys the candidate's distinctiveness, passion, and unique understanding of the business environment. It must answer the employer's question: Why you over any other candidate? Clearly, uniqueness is closely related to both branding and focus. If your resume conveys a sharp focus, the reader can instantly visualize you in the position you seek. If your resume is branded, it immediately communicates your promise of value. The uniqueness factor takes your resume to the next level by portraying you as not only *in* the position but the *best person for the position*, even the *only logical choice for the position*. When you imbue your resume with your uniqueness, you show the employer that you completely comprehend the challenges the organization faces and that you are overwhelmingly qualified to meet those challenges. If you have adequately sold your uniqueness, the reader reviewing your resume should say, "This person *gets it*." Indeed, the uniqueness factor, more than any another element of the FABUKA acronym, is about selling—selling your experience, selling your success, selling your qualifications, and selling the results you've attained. If you've succeeded in conveying your uniqueness, you will have portrayed yourself as a product that the employer wants to buy. You will have communicated not just your features, but also your benefits.

A few ways to build the uniqueness factor into your resume are:

➤ Thoroughly research the employer. Go well beyond the employer's want ad or job posting. Incorporate your knowledge of such aspects as the company mission statement, needs, growth plans, and current events affecting the company into your resume.

➤ Integrate your knowledge of industry trends into the resume.

➤ Mirror the phrasing of the employer's job posting in your resume and specifically describe how you uniquely meet the needs stated.

➤ Research the competition you're likely to have for the job and describe in your resume how you are more qualified.

➤ Include testimonials from former bosses, colleagues, and clients, as in the samples on pages 83 and 86.

➤ Use unusual formats, such as those on pages 202, 204, 209, and 235, that uniquely communicate value, results, and potential.

Keywords

The majority of resumes submitted to employers today are handled by Applicant Tracking Systems (ATS's), which Wikipedia (*www.wikipedia.com*) defines as software applications "that enables the electronic handling of corporate recruitment needs." The systems store "candidate data inside a database to allow effective searching, filtering, and routing of applications." Because applicant-tracking software and keyword-searchable databases dominate today's hiring process, successful executive resumes must feature cutting-edge industry jargon.

Imagine a way to encode your resume with magical words that would virtually ensure that employers would be interested in interviewing you. But the catch is that there's a different set of magic words for every job, *and you have no way of knowing what the words are.*

Such is more or less the situation in job-hunting today, which increasingly revolves around the mysterious world of keywords. Employers' use and eventual dependence on keywords to find the job candidates they want to interview has come about in recent years because of technology. Inundated by resumes from job-seekers, employers have increasingly relied on digitizing job-seeker resumes, placing those resumes in keyword-searchable databases, and using software to search those databases for specific keywords that relate to job vacancies. Most Fortune 1000 companies, in fact, and many smaller companies, now use these technologies. In addition, many employers search the databases of third-party job-postings and resume-posting boards on the Internet. Pat Kendall, president of the National Resume Writers' Association (in an article from *http://articles.techrepublic.com*) notes that more than 80 percent of resumes are searched for job-specific keywords.

The bottom line is that if you apply for a job with a company that searches databases for keywords, and your resume doesn't have the keywords the company seeks for the person who fills that job, you are pretty much dead in the water.

Job-seekers may assume they have no way of knowing what the words are that employers are looking for when they search resume databases. That's true to some extent. But job-seekers have information and a number of tools at their disposal that can help them make educated guesses as to which keywords the employer is looking for. This section describes some of those tools and tells you how and where to use the keywords you come up with on your resume and beyond.

So, how can we figure out what the magic words are?

First, we know that in the vast majority of cases, they are nouns. Job-seekers have long been taught to emphasize action verbs in their job-search correspondence, and that advice is still valid. But the "what" that you performed the action in relation to is now just as important. In the following examples, the bold-faced nouns are the keywords that relate to the action indicated by the verbs:

- Conducted **cross-functional management** for initial and follow-up contact.
- Executed **marketing campaigns** and **promotions.**
- Directed **customer database, product updates,** and **upgrades.**
- Excelled in **project-management role.**
- Oversaw **procurement, allocation, distribution control, stock levels,** and **cost compilation/analysis.**

And what kind of nouns are sought? Those that relate to the skills and experience the employer is looking for in a candidate. More specifically, keywords can be precise "hard" skills—job-specific/profession-specific/industry-specific skills, technological terms and descriptions of technical expertise (including hardware and software in which you are proficient), job titles, certifications, names of products and services, industry buzzwords and jargon, types of degrees, names of colleges, company names, terms that tend to impress, such as *Fortune 500*, and even area codes, for narrowing down searches geographically. Awards you've won and names of professional organizations to which you belong can even be used as keywords.

There are actually a number of good ways to identify the keywords that an employer might be looking for in any given job search. But the method that career experts most commonly mention is the process of scrutinizing employment ads to see what keywords are repeatedly mentioned in association with a given job title. Later in this section, you'll see two examples of how to find keywords in want ads/job postings.

So now that we have some good ideas about how to identify keywords, how should they be used?

The prevailing wisdom for several years was that you should front-load your resume with a laundry list of keywords—a keyword summary with no context—because supposedly database search software would search no more than the first 100 words of your document. If that 100-word limitation was ever true, it doesn't seem to be anymore, and job-seekers are now advised to use keywords throughout the resume.

It still makes some sense to front-load the resume with keywords, however, partly to ensure you get as many as possible into the document, and partly for the phase of resume review in which humans will actually screen your resume (after the initial screening by the search software) and may be attracted to keywords that appear early in the document.

But, although some career experts still advise a bare-bones spewing of keywords labeled "Keyword Summary," a more accepted approach is to sprinkle keywords liberally throughout a section early in the resume labeled "Summary of Qualifications," "Professional Profile," or simply "Profile" (see Chapter 2). Instead of a mere list of words, the summary or profile section presents keywords in context, more fully describing the activities and accomplishments in which the keywords surfaced in your work. This contextual collection of keywords that describes your professional self in a nutshell will certainly hold the interest of human readers better than a list of words will. Ideally, keywords are tied to accomplishments rather than job duties, so a good way to make the leap from keyword to a nice, contextual bullet point included in a profile section is to take each keyword you've identified as critical to the job and list an accomplishment that tells how you've used the skill represented by that keyword. For example:

- Solid team-building skills, demonstrated by assembling Starwood's marketing team from the ground up to service Starwood International's 7,700 hotels worldwide.

- Savvy in e-commerce marketing concepts, having participated in design of two company Websites, and conducted a symposia series to instruct hotel executives in the value of Internet marketing.

Keywords should also appear in the rest of your resume beyond the Profile or Summary section; in fact, some hiring decision-makers surveyed for this book said they preferred to see keywords in Experience sections than isolated in their own section. Another section in which to list them is one titled Core Competencies, Areas of Expertise, or Key Proficiencies. If you are in a technical field, it's almost a given that you will list your technical skills. A reader-friendly bulleted table can be a good way to do so. (See some examples at the end of this section.)

Most applicant-search software not only looks for keywords but also ranks them on a weighted basis according to the importance of the word to the job criteria, with some keywords considered mandatory and others that are merely desirable. The keywords can also be weighted and your resume ranked according to how many times mandatory words appear in your resume. If your document contains no mandatory keywords, the keyword search obviously will overlook your resume. Those with the greatest "keyword density" will be chosen for the next round of screening, this time by a human. Generally, the more specific a keyword is to a particular job or industry, the more heavily it will be weighted. Soft skills that apply to many jobs and industries (and aren't quantifiable) tend to be less weighty.

Because you also don't know the exact form of a keyword that the employer will use as a search criterion, it makes sense to also use synonyms, various forms of your keywords, and both the spelled-out and acronym versions of common terms. For example, use both "manager" and "management;" try both CRM and Customer Relationship Management.

And remember that humans can make certain assumptions that computers can't. A commonly cited example is the concept of "cold-calling." People who read the phrase "cold-calling" in your resume will know you were in sales. But unless "cold-calling" is a specific keyword the employer is seeking in the database search, search software seeking "sales" experience may not find your resume.

To determine the keyword health of your current resume, highlight all the words in it that, based on your research of ideal positions in your field, would probably be considered keywords.

More keyword tips and cautions:

➤ The importance of keywords supports the necessity of having both a print version of your resume and a text version that you can simply paste into an e-mail message (see Delivery Methods, Chapter 2). Some employers don't want to take the extra step of opening the print version of your resume that you've sent as an e-mail attachment, and others won't do so for fear of viruses. Thus, you need a text version of your resume that can be sent to employers in the body of an e-mail message and placed directly into the employer's keyword-searchable database.

➤ If you post your resume on Internet job boards, be sure to avoid emphasizing keywords that relate to jobs you *don't* want. If you have jobs in your employment history that are unrelated to what you want to do next, go easy on loading the descriptions of those jobs with keywords. Otherwise, your resume will pop up in searches for your old career and not necessarily your new one.

➤ Some job boards have a feature that enables you to see how many times the resume you've posted has been searched. If your resume hasn't been searched many times, odds are that you lack the right keywords for the kinds of jobs you want.

➤ Keep running lists of keywords so that anytime you come across a word that's not on your resume but that employers might use as a search parameter, you'll be ready.

➤ If you've published your resume on your own Web page, keywords can boost that version, too, because employers increasingly use search "bots" and search engines to scour the Internet for candidates that meet their criteria.

➤ Use keywords in your cover letters, too. Many employers don't scan cover letters or include them in resume databases, but some do. And keywords in cover letters can be important for attracting the "human scanner." If you're answering an ad, tying specific words in your cover letter as closely as possible to the actual wording of the ad you're responding to can be a huge plus. In his book, *Don't Send a Resume*, Jeffrey Fox calls the best letters written in response to want ads "Boomerang letters" because they "fly the want ad words—the copy—back to the writer of the ad." In employing what Fox calls "a compelling sales technique," he advises letter writers to "Flatter the person who wrote the ad with your response letter. Echo the author's words and intent. Your letter should be a mirror of the ad."

➤ Want to know what keywords recruiters are searching for in a given week? Go to the Marketing-Jobs section of *The Ladders.com* for a list of the top 100 recruiter search keywords updated weekly (*http://marketing-jobs.theladders.com/toprecruiterkeywords*):

Here's a sample list of the top 10 from one week:

1. Sales	6. Tax
2. CPA	7. SAP
3. Controller	8. Software
4. Marketing	9. Recruiter
5. Human resources	10. CFO

Resources for Identifying Keywords

Although one of the best ways to identify keywords for a particular job is to scrutinize employment ads, some other ways to find keywords include:

➤ Looking for job descriptions in books and job-description software.

➤ Visiting the meetings and Websites of professional associations in your field to look and listen for current buzzwords.

➤ If you are working with a recruiter or headhunter, turning to that person as an excellent source of keyword tips.

➤ Consulting government publications such as *The Occupational Outlook Handbook* at libraries.

➤ Visiting company Websites.

➤ Imagining you were writing an ad or job description for the type of job you seek; what keywords would you use?

➤ Researching and incorporating into your keywords the company culture and values of employers you are targeting. Note especially the company's mission statement and look for ways to quote it in your resume and/or cover letter.

➤ Scrutinizing news stories in trade magazines relevant to your work and reading cutting-edge magazines, such as *Fast Company*.

➤ Joining online discussion groups and chat rooms that relate to your field and observing the words professionals are using in their discussions.

➤ Reading annual reports from the companies for which you'd like to work.

➤ Talking to human resources professionals.

➤ Using Web search engines, such as Google and Yahoo, and job meta-search engines, such as *Indeed.com*, to search for job descriptions.

➤ Consulting online dictionaries, glossaries, and encyclopedias.

➤ Visiting online specialty sites defining acronyms and technical jargon.

Samples of Keyword Tables

AREAS OF EXPERTISE

➤ Customer Development	➤ Communication	➤ Revenue Recovery
➤ Human Relations	➤ Public Relations and Event Planning	➤ Problem-Solving
➤ Research and Planning	➤ Administration and Management	➤ Training/Coaching/Mentoring
➤ Interdepartmental Liaison	➤ Administrative Decision-Making	➤ Problem Identification/Resolution
➤ Elevate Standards of Service	➤ Hiring and Workforce Supervision	➤ Scheduling/Planning/Organization
➤ Process Improvement		➤ Sales and Marketing
➤ Internal/External Customer Service		

KEY PROFICIENCIES

➤ Market Analysis	➤ Product Positioning	➤ Channel Marketing
➤ Consumer Segmentation	➤ Marketing Strategy Development	➤ Advertising and Media Strategy Development
➤ Brand Strategy	➤ Product Line Strategy	➤ P&L Management
➤ New Product Concept	➤ Product Launch Planning	➤ Cross-Functional Team Leadership
➤ Development and Testing		
➤ Consumer Market Research		

EXECUTIVE PROFICIENCIES

- Account Base Maintenance
- Account Openings & Closings
- Client Financial Data Analysis
- Assets & Liabilities
- Balance Sheet Review

- Bank Reconciliations
- Cash Dividends
- Client Investment Protection
- Client Needs Assessment
- Commodities Market
- Company Equity Valuations

- Portfolio Development
- Diversified Portfolios Setup & Management
- Divestitures
- Due Diligence
- Exchange Funds
- Financial Data Analysis

CORE COMPETENCIES

- Create/Execute Market Operating Plans
- Assess Growth Opportunities
- Key Account Plans
- Sales Process and Strategies
- Sales Pipeline Methodology
- Market Segmentation
- Market Share Growth
- Master Service Agreements
- Optimize Office Utilization
- Financial Management and Control
- Key Financial Metrics
- Manage Utilization
- Client Satisfaction
- Team-Building
- Organizational Strategic Plans
- Identify/Allocate Resources

- Multicultural Team and Customer Experience
- Coaching and Leadership
- Train and Develop Personnel
- State-of the-Art Manufacturing/ Management Methods
- Organization/Process Management
- Develop/Implement Process Control
- Validate New Processes
- Provide New Equipment Specifications
- Cost Reduction Initiatives
- Automation Systems
- Process/Product Optimization
- Meeting Parameters
- Problem-Solving
- Identify Resources
- Leading and Coordinating multicultural construction, project, and operation teams

- Oversee Maintenance, Repairs, and Equipment Modifications- Manufacturing Processes
- Scheduling and Budgetary Parameters
- Monitor/Debug New Methods and Procedures
- Design Concept Drawings
- Cost Estimates
- Recommend Changes to Process Documentation
- Interface with Manufacturing, Maintenance, and Quality Departments
- Resolve Engineering Issues
- Interface with Vendors and Outside Sales Personnel
- Evaluate, Estimate, and Select Purchases
- DMAIC

Appearance

The print version of an effective executive resume must be sleek, distinctive, and clean, yet eye-catching, reader-friendly, and upscale in appearance. The Design Tips section of Chapter 2 explains the differences and uses between a print resume and its electronic counterpart and provides more detail about the effective appearance of both, but here's a quick summary of elements that contribute to a print resume with an executive-caliber appearance:

➤ Conservative, easy-to-read fonts.

➤ Plenty of white space.

➤ A layout/design that goes beyond ordinary yet is not so far out as to turn employers off.

➤ Small blocks of text, most of which is bulleted in a reader-friendly format. Strive for no more than four lines in a paragraph or two lines in a bullet. Try to keep bullet points for any given job to no more than about seven. Large blocks of gray text are daunting for any reader and likely won't get read.

➤ Attractive graphic treatment of the elements that lend focus to your resume. If you use a headline, for example, be sure it's big and bold enough to get noticed.

➤ Graphic elements that add interest, such as rule lines, boxes, shaded areas, and tables.

➤ Elimination of clutter. Avoid having *too many* graphic elements or too much typographic variety in your resume.

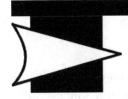

Chapter Two

Nuts and Bolts: Everything You Need to Know to Construct Your Resume

Now that you know the most important aspects of executive resumes, you can review this chapter to ensure you have all the details covered. This chapter takes you through the steps for executive-resume development, describes each standard component that employers expect on resumes, provides some wording suggestions, explains organizational formats, demystifies delivery formats (that is, how to prepare your resume on your computer for various delivery methods), and answers Frequently Asked Questions.

How to Get Started

If you are at the executive or senior level of your career, you probably have a resume. Thus, getting started on the resume that will take you to the next rung in your career ladder may be a simple matter of spiffing up your existing document, using the guidelines in this book.

Some executive and senior-level folks do have to start from square one. I sometimes hear from high-level job-seekers that they have been recruited into most of their jobs or obtained them through networking and have not needed a resume, or have one that is quite outdated. I recommend brainstorming accomplishments and results as a starting point if you do not currently have a functioning resume (See the Appendix). If you can achieve that important step, the rest will fall into place as you read this chapter and the remainder of the book.

Also consider hiring a professional resume writer, as discussed at the end of this chapter. You may at least want to have your resume critiqued by a professional. Resume critiques are usually quite inexpensive or even free, because resume writers use them as tools to promote their business.

Breakable vs. Unbreakable Resume Rules

You've likely encountered countless "rules" for resumes, and many of these guidelines in this book probably read like rules. Resumes are documents that represent job-seekers as individuals and reflect their individual tastes and approaches. As an author of a resume book, I can offer you guidelines from my own experience as well as research on current employer trends and preferences, but almost none of what appears in this book can be considered a written-in-stone "rule." Most so-called resume rules can be broken, if you have a good rationale. In my view, only two rules are unbreakable:

1. **Don't lie on your resume.**

2. **Avoid typos and misspellings.**

Resume Components

Following are the elements that most commonly appear on executive resumes in the order in which they most often appear. If you are building your resume from scratch, once you've brainstormed your accomplishments, use the following as a guideline for how to organize your material and best spotlight those results and achievements.

Name and Contact Information

Your name, of course, is a must on your resume, and use the name by which you are known professionally. If you use your middle name, for example, you can list your name one of these ways:

➤ W. Scott Carson

➤ William "Scott" Carson

The same goes for nicknames. Keep in mind that some nicknames don't exactly project professionalism, especially at the executive level, but if you are universally known by your nickname, you may want to list yourself that way on your resume.

Although studies have shown that employers rarely try reaching job-seekers using any number but land-line home phone numbers, do include your cell-phone number and any other option for reaching you, such as fax number and office phone number (if you can discreetly receive employer calls at your office). Also include your mailing address and, of course, your e-mail address(es). If you have a personal Website or Web portfolio, include the URL for it.

Branding Statement/Headline

As we saw in Chapter 1, an emerging technique for sharpening your resume's focus and grabbing the employer's attention is to use a headline, a branding statement, or a combination of the two. If you go the route of the headline, branding statement, or combination, these elements should be placed immediately following your name and contact information. Refer to Chapter 1 for more about these techniques.

Objective Statement

Although much current attention is focused on headlines and branding statements, Objective Statements are still used and are worthy of consideration. As mentioned in Chapter 1, Objective Statements have fallen somewhat out of favor. Many employers and recruiters claim they don't even read them. That's because most Objective Statements are badly written, self-serving, too vague, and not designed to do what they're supposed to do, which is to lend a sharp focus to a resume.

As we saw in Chapter 1, a sharp focus is critical resume element. Employers want resumes to show a clear match between the applicant and a job's requirements. A "general" resume that is not focused on a specific job's requirements is not seen as competitive. In a survey by *CareerBuilder.com*, 41 percent of hiring managers preferred a resume customized for the open position. Therefore, every resume should have at least some mechanism—whether it is an Objective Statement or another resume element—that tells the employer right away specifically what you bring to the employer's company. A well-crafted Objective Statement is one way to precisely sharpen your resume's focus. In her book *Resume Magic*, resume-writing guru Susan Britton Whitcomb even uses "Focus Statement" as an alternate title for the Objective Statement. Your objective can be a thematic statement that sets the scene and provides context for what is to come. Ideally, your objective should enable the reader to envision you performing the job that the employer wants to fill.

Using your objective to sharpen the focus of your resume can be especially important if your experience is diverse, or you are switching into a career not supported by the experience listed on your resume. The statement enables the career-changer to redefine his or her past and frame it in terms of the desired new career path.

To some employers, the lack of an objective signals a jobseeker who doesn't know what he or she wants. Some job-seekers think it's a plus to appear open to a wide variety of positions, but the "I'll do anything" attitude is usually a turn-off to employers; it projects an air of desperation—especially at the executive level, where candidates are expected to have a highly specific vision of what they want to do and what expertise they offer. Hiring managers simply receive too many resumes and look at them far too quickly to be able to spend time trying to read the job-seeker's mind and read between the lines to determine what kind of job you seek. They just don't have the time to figure out where the job-seeker might fit into the organization.

Numerous employers say they rarely see a well-written objective, and there's no doubt that many resume career objectives are poorly put together. Here are some common flaws:

➤ To avoid limiting themselves, too many job-seekers write objectives that are woefully vague, thus defeating the purpose of presenting an objective.

➤ Job-seekers tend to ignore the employer's need to know what the candidate can contribute, instead considering the objective as an invitation to list everything the job-seeker wants, needs, or desires from the sought-after job.

➤ Candidates make statements of the obvious, such as that they "seek a position," or, the biggest objective cliché of all, "a challenging position."

Let's look at the right way to write one.

Some effective ways to begin your Objective Statement include:

To deploy...	To contribute...	To leverage...	To improve...	To lead...
To provide...	To fill the need...	To parlay...	To create...	To influence...
To bring...	To generate...	To combine...	To deliver...	To propel...
To grow...	To engage...	To support...	To play a key role...	To maximize...
To increase...	To implement...	To augment...	To develop...	To add value...

Some effective middle and ending portions for Objective Statements include:

...will add value to operations.

...while enhancing company growth and profitability.

...while applying strategic vision to lead the organization.

...while leading a team that helps achieve your organization's success.

...and enhance your firm's profitable business opportunities.

Note that you can effectively substitute the name of the organization you're targeting for the phrases "your firm's" and "your organization's."

A specific objective is always better than a vague or general one, and you can rarely go wrong with an Objective Statement that's perfectly straightforward—simply the title of the position for which you're applying, which can be adjusted for every job for which you apply.

You can also embellish the position title with verbiage telling how you'll benefit the employer, following a formula such as these executive objectives:

Objective: To parlay extensive _____ experience into a _____ position as part of a executive team that enhances your organization's success.

Objective: To provide top-level management and creative direction in developing _____.

Objective: To analyze business needs and translate them into executable strategies for your firm in a _____ capacity.

Objective: To maximize profits in a _____ position by reducing costs and streamlining operations.

Objective: To enhance your firm's profitable business opportunities in a _____ capacity.

Objective: To boost your firm's revenues.

Objective: To propel your firm's success to new levels using finely honed _____ and _____ techniques.

Among the elements that an objective can include are:

➤ Name or title of desired position.

➤ Field or industry.

➤ Strongest skills and/or areas of experience.

➤ The job-seeker's Unique Selling Proposition: The one attribute that makes you more qualified for the job than anyone else.

➤ How/what you expect to contribute.

Guidelines for writing an Objective Statement

➤ Make it very specific, not vague, generic, or meaningless.

➤ Think of your Objective Statement as analogous to a thesis statement on a research paper or the subject line of an e-mail message: a concise phrase that captures the essence of what you can contribute to an employer and draws the reader to your resume.

➤ Objectives should reflect the employer's perspective, not the job-seeker's, and should tell what the job-seeker can contribute. An objective should demonstrate the value the candidate will add to the organization.

➤ Objectives should be as concrete and concise as possible. Generally, they should be no more than two lines in length.

➤ Because you need every possible opportunity to use keywords in your resume (see why in Chapter 1), try to use words related to your intended job field in your Objective Statement.

➤ Resumes generally should not include personal pronouns, such as "I," "me," and "my." If there is one place on the resume where an exception can be made, it's the Objective Statement. However, it's still best to avoid these pronouns if at all possible.

➤ A good Objective Statement answers questions: For what position(s) are you applying? What are your main qualifications? What can you bring to the organization? What is your professional identity?

➤ Avoid offering an "or" option in your objective, as in: "Executive management position in the plastics or specialty chemicals field." Instead, tweak the objective according to the type of job you are targeting.

➤ Any time an Objective Statement mentions "your company," "your firm," or "your organization," remember that you can substitute the specific name of an organization to target your resume to that employer.

The bottom line is that, unlike the mandatory headings on your resume (such as Education and Experience), an Objective Statement is but one option for sharpening your resume's focus. When the objective is included, it's usually the first heading after your name and contact information.

Profile/Qualifications Summary/Executive Summary

Whether or not you choose to include an Objective Statement on your resume, you may wish to present a Qualifications Summary or Profile section.

In addition to Profile and Qualifications Summary, these resume-topping sections go by numerous names: Career Summary, Summary, Executive Summary, Professional Profile, Qualifications, Strengths, Skills, Key Skills, Skills Summary, Summary of Qualifications, Background Summary, Professional Summary, and Highlights of Qualifications. All of these headings are acceptable, but my favorite is Professional Profile.

Twenty-five years ago, a Profile or Summary section was somewhat unusual on a resume. Career experts trace the use of summaries or profiles to include information about candidates' qualities beyond their credentials to the publication of the late Yana Parker's *The Damn Good Resume Guide* in 1983. For the last 20-plus years, resume writers have routinely included these sections; however, the age of electronic submissions has now caused the pendulum to swing the other way.

On one hand, electronic submission means that hiring decision-makers are inundated and overwhelmed with resumes and have less time than ever before to peruse each document. That means that many of them do not read Profile or Summary sections.

On the other hand, the age of electronic submissions, as we've seen, has increased the importance of keywords so that candidates can be found in database searches. Even some of the hiring decision-makers who don't read Profiles and Summaries advise including them as a way to ensure sufficient keywords in the resume.

A vocal contingent of decision-makers, especially among recruiters, strongly advocate for a Summary section—but one that is quite succinct: a short paragraph or single bullet point. They want to see, in a nutshell, who you are and what you can contribute.

Based on these recent trends, I recommend using the concise, single paragraph or bullet-point Summary, which I call the Thumbnail Summary, for targeting recruiters and human-resources managers. Recruiters particularly don't like you to sacrifice detail and information in your Experience section so you can have a long list of bullets in your Profile/Summary section.

For direct hiring managers, who often want to see more detail, I recommend a Full Profile or Summary section with four to five bullet points.

Many decision-makers are attracted to concise summary sections—Shawn Slevin, president of P3HRConsulting in New York City calls them "pithy and potent"—that encapsulate the candidate's top attributes. "I like profiles but *not* if they are articulating 'soft skills,'" said Maureen Crawford, manager of talent acquisition, development, and compliance at Osram Sylvania (Boston, Massachusetts), who noted that she sees the Profile section as a "three-second commercial for the resume." "I want to see three to four hard facts," Hentz said, offering as an example:

> Demonstrated ability to raise profit margins by 22 percent in a depressed market, award-winning presenter, multi-lingual CPA with international experience.

Some advantages of the Thumbnail Summary or Full Profile/Summary section include:

➤ They help to sharpen the focus of the resume. As we saw in the Chapter 1, when read by humans, resumes are scanned extremely quickly. The employer wants to know at a glance what you want to do and what you can contribute.

➤ They help to capture the reader's attention.

➤ They provide a good opportunity to front-load your resume with keywords. Although job-seekers are no longer admonished to cram keywords into the first 100 words of their resumes as they once were, it's still a good idea to use as many keywords as possible early in the resume just to make sure you get them in there.

➤ They are a way to present your Unique Selling Proposition—the selling point that distinguishes you from other candidates for the same position.

➤ They provide an opportunity to tailor your resume to a specific position or vacancy. That's an important point because those who don't write a Profile specifically tailored to the job can be eliminated. "I have managers who review them and turn candidates down because what they have listed is not what the position we have available entails—their resume substantiates what we are looking for but not the summary," notes a Washington, D.C.–area technical recruiter in the civil engineering industry.

Some employers say they don't like Summary/Profile sections because they are full of unsubstantiated fluff. Therefore, it's incumbent upon the executive job-seeker to substantiate as much of the Summary/Profile section as possible with numbers, examples, and quotes from those who know your work. Any bullet points that are not substantiated in the Summary/Profile section itself should be substantiated later in the resume. For example, Veronica Richmond, a human resources professional in Oakville, Ontario, Canada, wants to "find out exactly *how* and *when* the expertise was learned. It should *not* be unsubstantiated. A well-prepared candidate will have a relevant example for each [point] listed on the resume." Seattle-based recruiter Alice Hanson agrees that, if she sees a claim in a Profile section, "I'm going to look for the experience in the bullets when I make that second pass. If it isn't there, it undersells the claim you have that experience."

Examples of substantiated bullet points:

■ Demonstrated organizational skills at the highest level; successfully completed all projects meeting all goals and timelines, from initiating complex and sensitive operations in the United States and abroad to establishing an office in a foreign country.

■ Successfully deployed outstanding interpersonal skills during professional interactions with U.S. government personnel, representatives of Fortune 500 defense-industry corporations, and as a consultant to business groups and government employees.

If you choose a full Summary/Profile section, its first bullet point should be the Thumbnail Summary, your professional identity in a nutshell. It's the most important bullet point because it puts you into focus, characterizes who you are, and tells what you can contribute. If the reader should happen to read no further in your Summary/Profile section, he or she should at least have a sense of your essence from this first bullet point. The Thumbnail Summary will likely contain the title/functional area/level of your current position and/or position you seek, the industry you're in or seeking to be in, the number of years of your experience (no need to emphasize your age, even when the body of your resume reveals the exact number of working years; "20+ years" is a good guideline for mature candidates). Recruiter Hanson offers this shorthand for the Thumbnail Summary: "a short summary that pitches you to the hiring manager… what role do you do, how long, how big, how much, and what results can we expect if we hire you?" The Thumbnail Summary should also convey a sense of your most significant benefit to prospective employers.

Thumbnail summary examples

Dynamic MBA-level professional with more than seven years of experience in successful leadership of business and organizational turnarounds that involve multiple, complex dynamics and cross-disciplines and management levels.

■■■

PhD-level leader, change agent, and social activist who has developed broad range of programs and procedures that yielded cost effectiveness and maximum utilization of resources and accountability.

■■■

Dynamic and versatile project/program management executive with 15+ years of leadership and business management expertise gained from positions of increasing responsibility in both the U.S. Navy and the private sector.

■■■

Creative outside-the-box thinker who approaches strategic development with innovative vision, high ethical standards, unsurpassed work ethic, and ability to communicate effectively across management levels and disciplines to build highly effective cross-functional teams.

■■■

Dynamic performer with background of achievement and success in entrepreneurial and business-development roles that have catapulted bottom-line revenues.

■■■

Dynamic, multi-faceted performer with significant human-resources experience, as well as expertise in cross-functional process improvement, to integrate organizational change with business strategies, improvements, and upgrades.

■ ■ ■

Entrepreneurial, outside-the-box, critical thinker with enthusiastic mindset to deliver on front line globalization issues.

■ ■ ■

Outstanding, success-validated sales performer proven in the field as highly motivated self-starter with exceptional skill and experience in direct, persuasive interface with CEOs and senior-level marketing executives of Fortune 500, Global 2000, and NYSE companies.

■ ■ ■

Entrepreneurial business/marketing professional with more than 15 years of uncompromising accomplishment in multiple facets of building, marketing, and operating highly successful manufacturing and retail businesses.

■ ■ ■

Dynamic B2B/B2C technology marketing executive with exceptional career record of bringing products to market, precisely targeting consumer demographic while maximizing adoption and profitability.

■

Additional elements to consider including in a Full Summary/Profile are:

➤ Core competencies/areas of expertise/strengths/specialization for that field.

➤ Highlights of representative accomplishments, especially used to demonstrate skills and competencies you've used throughout your career.

➤ Top business and leadership hard skills.

➤ "Value-added" information: skills/accomplishments/experience that add to your value because they are not necessarily expected of someone with your background (for example, operations manager with deep knowledge of IT).

➤ Advanced degrees, certifications, or licenses that are integral to the type of job you seek.

➤ Language and international business skills, if relevant.

➤ Possibly affiliations if integral to the job; otherwise in a separate section.

➤ Any extremely prestigious colleges, employers, or clients.

➤ Keywords/buzzwords from ads or job postings you're responding to. (See Chapter 1.)

➤ Quantification whenever possible, using numbers for revenue generated, size of accounts, typical budgets, money saved, number of direct reports, and other quantifiable elements that characterize your job scope.

➤ Positive quotes/testimonials from supervisors, clients, taken from memos, letters, or performance evaluations. Awards you've earned can also be listed in the Summary/ Profile section to give them more up-front attention than if they were listed in their own section.

Clearly, that's a lot of potential material to cram into a four-to-five-bullet Summary/Profile section. How do you choose what to list in this section? Be primarily guided by your own unique selling points and the requirements of the job or type of job you seek.

Be sure to include bullet points from areas that:

➤ Are truly strong points for you.

➤ Are relevant to the job or type of job you seek.

➤ Can be substantiated with numbers, quotes (testimonials), or examples either in the Summary/Profile section itself or later in the resume.

If travel and/or relocation are required for a given job, it's a good idea to address those requirements in your Summary/Profile section.

■ Senior-level sales professional who offers career path reflecting progressive responsibility and sales performance, along with willingness to relocate and travel.

Parallel grammatical flow

A trick to ensure that the Summary/Profile section flows smoothly for the reader is to make it parallel, as though each bullet point is completing the same sentence. This kind of flow helps readability enormously. I imagine that each Summary/Profile bullet point I write finishes an unstated but understood sentence that begins: "I am a(n)..."

Let's see how this formula works in practice:

■ [I am a] Seasoned systems analyst with strong commitment to time and resource budgets, new-business development, strategic planning, innovation, technology trends, customer-service needs, and close collaboration with sales and marketing during development.

■ [I am a] Competent problem-solver who resolved sales and shipping issues by creating internal customer-care system and saved 20 percent on shipping; researched and delivered web conferencing service for sales that saved 30 percent of travel budgets.

■ [I am a] Visionary innovator who partnered with another programmer to create pioneering language-learning software that earned national attention; served as lead analyst for revolutionary legal document generating and tracking product.

■ [I am a] Technical guru who provided direct support for successful million-dollar negotiation with major print vendor and completed many successful major conversions from mainframe to mini-computer systems.

■ [I am a] Strong communicator who was voted best specification writer—with least number of rewrites—by programmers and their managers.

You'll note that the grammatical structure of these parallel bullet points goes like this:

[*I am a(n)*] [Adjective] [noun] [connecting words] [phrase describing skill/ strength/expertise] [supported by quote, example, numbers]

Following the suggested parallel grammatical structure, you'll see on pages 36–37 a list of adjectives that can be used to kick off your bullet points, followed by a list of nouns, followed by a list of phrases to connect the adjective-noun to verbiage that describes skills/strengths/areas of expertise.

Sample Adjectives With Which You Can Kick off Your Bullet Points

Accomplished	Diplomatic	Market-driven	Reliable
Accurate	Doctoral-level	Master's-level	Resilient
Action-driven	Dynamic	MBA-level	Resourceful
Adaptable	Efficiency-oriented	Meticulous	Respected
Analytical	Empowering	Morale-building	Results-driven
Approachable	Energetic	Motivated	Results-oriented
Articulate	Enthusiastic	Multilingual	Seasoned
Balanced	Entrepreneurial	Nonjudgmental	Self-directed
Bilingual	Excellent	Objective	Senior-level
Budget-conscious	Exceptional	Open-minded	Service-oriented
Calm	Experienced	Organized	Sharp
Candid	Fair	Outcome-focused	Skilled
Client-focused	Fast	Outstanding	Solutions-driven
Collaborative	Flexible	Perceptive	Solutions-oriented
Communicative	Focused	Persistent	Straightforward
Compassionate	Goal-driven	Personable	Strong
Competent	Goal-oriented	Persuasive	Success-driven
Competitive	Hardworking	PhD-level	Systematic
Computer-literate	High-performance	Polished	Tactful
Confident	High-performing	Priority-setting	Take-charge
Conscientious	Impartial	Proactive	Team-oriented
Consistent	Innovative	Productive	Tenacious
Creative	Insightful	Proficient	Top
Customer-driven	Inspiring	Profitability-conscious	Top-producing
Customer-focused	Intuitive	Profit-minded	Trilingual
Deadline-driven	Levelheaded	Proven	Trusted
Decisive	Loyal	Quality-focused	Versatile
Detail-oriented		Quick	Vital
Determined			

————— Sample Nouns to Anchor Your Bullet Points —————

Grammatically, these nouns would be considered the predicate nominatives in the sentences that begin with the understood "I am a(n)..."

achiever	educator	marketer	role model
change agent	executive	morale-builder	self-starter
closer	expert	motivator	solutions-provider
coach	facilitator	negotiator	specialist
coalition-builder	go-getter	performer	strategist
communicator	guru	planner	tactician
consensus-builder	implementer	presenter	team leader
conflict manager	initiator	pro	team player
consultant	innovator	problem-solver	time manager
contributor	leader	producer	technician
critical thinker	learner	professional	thinker
cultivator	listener	rapport-builder	troubleshooter
decision-maker	logical thinker	relationship-builder	visionary
diversity manager	manager	risk-taker	wizard

————— Sample Connecting Words —————

with	who can
with proven track record of	who excels at
with reputation for	whose
who is	known for

List That Functions as a Keyword Summary: Areas of Expertise/Core Competencies/Proficiencies/Strengths

To ensure that your resume is sharply focused and contains sufficient keywords, you may want to include a *keyword summary* under a heading such as Areas of Expertise, Core Competencies, Key Proficiencies, or Strengths. A keyword summary may be especially valuable if you are in a field in which many "hard skills" are required. Some employers like to see keyword sections in the top third of your resume's first page; others prefer to see them at the end of the resume. (See Chapter 1 for samples of Keyword Summaries.)

Experience

Experience information should be listed in order of importance to the reader. Therefore, in listing your jobs, what's generally most important is your title/position. So list in this preferred order: title/position, name of employer, city/state of employer, dates of employment. The element of that formula that I most often see omitted is employer location, but many hiring decision-makers want to see that information to show your record of mobility. "I think location is helpful because it allows me to see a candidate's willingness to relocate and allows me to place their experience in context," says Harlynn Goolsby of the Human Resources Department at OSRAM Sylvania (Boston, Massachusetts). Many employers and recruiters emphasize that months should be included in listings of dates, not simply years: "May 2006 to Dec. 2007" as opposed to "2006 to 2007." Melissa Holmes, senior technical recruiter at Levi, Ray & Shoup Consulting Services in Springfield, Illinois, frames the experience items she looks for similarly to journalists: "how, what, when, where, why."

I advise against the practice of tabbing information such as employer location and dates of employment to the right of the resume or isolating dates in a left column. It's better to keep all that info together so the employer can absorb it all in a quick scan.

■

Unnecessary isolation of dates (dates tabbed to right):

Development Manager, Epitome Inc., Hartland, MN   Jan. 1998 to March 2002

Unnecessary isolation of dates (dates tabbed to left):

Jan. 1998 to March 2002   Development Manager, Epitome Inc., Hartland, MN

Easier to read:

Development Manager, Epitome Inc., Hartland, MN, Jan. 1998 to March 2002

■

I often see job dates enclosed in parentheses, but there's no reason to treat dates this way, and the parentheses tend to add clutter; just set off your dates with commas.

Bullet points describing your jobs

Ensure that the bullet points you construct for your experience section are targeted to support your job goal. Craft persuasive, high-impact statements that sell your qualifications as the best candidate. Show that you speak the reader's language with industry-specific terms and relevant keywords: After scrutinizing ads, identifying keywords from them, and loading them into your resume, test your resume by comparing it to ads you want to target. If your resume doesn't include more than 50 percent of the keywords in an ad or job posting, don't expect an interview, advised Dr. John Sullivan of Dr. John Sullivan & Associates (DJS), a human-resource management advisory services and training firm (*ourworld.com/homepages/gately.pp15js83htm*).

Strike a balance with bullet points that include an appropriate amount of description to the job targeted and enough detail to substantiate the position you desire—while avoiding excessive detail.

Kick off most bullet points describing your jobs with vivid, concrete action verbs. Assuming you're still in your most recent job, verbs should be in present tense; however, using past-tense verbs for completed projects and past accomplishments within your present job may be unavoidable. Use past tense for past jobs.

Verb guidelines

➤ **Vary your verbs.** Avoid beginning consecutive bullet points with the same verb.

➤ **Keep verb forms parallel.** Generally, use simple present-tense verbs in describing your current job, not present-participle (-ing) verbs.

➤ **Watch tricky verbs, such as "lead" (present tense).** The past tense of "lead" sounds like the metal "lead," but is spelled "led."

➤ **Apply the "So what?" question.** Does each bullet point in your resume arrest the reader's attention and excite him or her? Or does it inspire the reader to ask, "So what?" To avoid a "So what?" response; use picturesque verbs.

Empowering weak verbs

Some verbs just don't pack the punch that others do. Some examples:

WEAK ➤ *Involved* in identifying pertinent documents for depositions in complex antitrust litigation.

Why it's weak: It doesn't show any initiative or accomplishment to be *involved in* an activity.

Better: *Participated in* identifying pertinent documents for depositions in complex antitrust litigation.

Even better: *Contributed to* identifying pertinent documents for depositions in complex antitrust litigation.

OR: *Identified* pertinent documents for depositions in complex antitrust litigation.

(Does it really matter that you weren't the only one doing the identifying?)

OR: *Played key role* (or *instrumental role,* or *leading role) in identifying* pertinent documents for depositions in complex antitrust litigation.

■■■

WEAK ➤ *Worked* on $1 million project and completed it on time and under budget.

Why it's weak: "*Work*" is too generalized. Everyone works. It's better to be specific.

Better: *Excelled* on $1 million project and completed it on time and under budget.

OR: *Completed* $1 million project on time and under budget.

■■■

WEAK ➤ *Worked to* achieve 15-percent reduction in operating costs in close collaboration with finance and CPA firms and partnered closely with CFO to achieve 12 percent budget reduction in three consecutive years.

Better: *Achieved* 15-percent reduction in operating costs in close collaboration with finance and CPA firms and partnered closely with CFO to achieve 12-percent budget reduction in three consecutive years.

Frequently when job-seekers use "work" in resumes and cover letters, they mean it in the sense of *working with others*. In that case, "interact" or "collaborate" are better word choices.

■■■

WEAK ➤ *Work* closely with CTO and CFO to develop financial and staffing plans.

Better: *Collaborate* closely with CTO and CFO to develop financial and staffing plans.

OR: *Partner* closely with CTO and CFO to develop financial and staffing plans.

■■■

WEAK ➤ *Received* President's Club sales award.

Why it's weak: "*Receive(d)*" doesn't give credit where it's due and suggests a passive activity.

Better: *Earned* President's Club sales award.

OR: *Won* President's Club sales award.

■■■

WEAK ➤ *Assigned* to open new branch office.

Why it's weak: "*Assigned*" fails to recognize that you were probably assigned because your supervisor knew you had the skills to do a great job.

Better: *Selected by management* to open new branch office.

OR: *Chosen by management* to open new branch office.

Even better: *Selected by management* to open new branch office based on superior performance.

■■■

WEAK ➤ *Used* technical and fundamental analysis techniques to manage and trade futures portfolio.

Why it's weak: *"Used"* is overused.

Better: *Applied* technical and fundamental analysis techniques to manage and trade futures portfolio.

Even better: *Deployed* technical and fundamental analysis techniques to manage and trade futures portfolio.

■■■

WEAK ➤ *Made* successful technical sales calls to major insurance companies by presenting firm's electronic capabilities.

Why it's weak: You can usually zero in more directly on a better verb.

Better: Successfully *called on* major insurance companies and presented firm's technical capabilities.

■■■

WEAK ➤ *Gave* persuasive sales presentations to diverse audiences.

Why it's weak: *"Gave"* is just not a very dynamic verb.

Better: *Delivered* persuasive sales presentations to diverse audiences.

OR: Persuasively *presented* sales pitch to diverse audiences.

■■■

WEAK ➤ *Was* a writer on technical documentation team.

Why it's weak: A more colorful and descriptive alternative to the verb *"to be"* is almost always available.

Better: *Wrote* effective technical documentation.

■■■

WEAK ➤ *Did* a business plan as part of new-venture startup.

Why it's weak: Again, a more colorful and descriptive alternative to the verb *"to do"* is almost always available.

Better: *Created* a business plan as part of new-venture startup.

■

Don't turn perfectly good verbs into nouns.

WEAK ➤ Collaborated in *development and implementation of* dealer Website.

Why it's weak: *"Development and implementation of"* is a wordy noun phrase.

Better: Collaborated in *developing and implementing* dealer Website.

■■■

WEAK ➤ *Provide leadership* for staff of 100.

Why it's weak: You can *"cut to the chase"* and use a more powerful verb.

Better: *Lead* staff of 100.

■■■

Don't mix noun and verb phrases when describing your jobs. Preferably, use verbs consistently.
Example:

- [verb phrase] Coordinate facilities projects, lab configuration changes, work orders and purchasing.

- [noun phrase] Compliance focal point for Environmental, Quality, Safety, and Security management systems.

■

To convert noun phrase to verb phrase:

Served as compliance focal point for Environmental, Quality, Safety, and Security management systems.

OR

Performed as compliance focal point for Environmental, Quality, Safety, and Security management systems.

OR

Excelled as compliance focal point for Environmental, Quality, Safety, and Security management systems.

Accomplishments language

Ensure that your resume is accomplishments-driven and features results. Frame most bullet points as accomplishments using the RAS, RAC, and RAP formats described in Chapter 1. Focus on accomplishments that set you apart from other job candidates. In each job, what special things did you do to set yourself apart? How did you do the job better than anyone else? What did you do to make it your own? What problems or challenges did the organization face, and what did you do to overcome the problems? What were the results of your efforts? How did the company benefit from your performance? How did you leave your employers better off than before you were there? How have you helped your employer to make money, save money, save time, make work easier, be more competitive, build relationships, expand the business, attract new customers, retain existing customers? Be sure also that the accomplishments you list support your career goals.

When writing their resumes, many job-seekers draw from the written job descriptions they've been given by their employers in current and past positions. That's a big blunder, because a job description represents the bare minimum of what a job can consist of. Employers are much more interested in your accomplishments, achievements, and results, and how you have gone above and beyond the structures of your job description.

Among the ineffective words and phrases that often spring from such job descriptions, my number-one pet peeve is any form or variation of the word "responsibility." It's a word I never want to see on a resume. I advise never to use expressions such as "Duties included," "Responsibilities included," "Accountable for," or "Responsible for." Why? Because those words and phrases comprise job-description language, not accomplishments-driven, results-oriented resume language that sells.

After all, if you were an employer seeking leaders to run your successful organization, would you look for candidates who can perform only their basic job functions, or would you want employees who can take initiative and make profitable contributions? In these days when most resumes are placed into keyword-searchable databases, you won't find employers searching resumes for words such as "responsibilities," "duties," or "responsible for."

Occasionally, "responsibility," can be used effectively, such as in this bullet point:

■ **Consistently promoted to positions of increasing responsibility.**

In the same vein, don't use words that describe mundane job duties, such as:

➤ Handled *everyday* operations.

➤ Oversaw *routine* finance tasks.

➤ Managed *day-to-day* functions.

More wording tips

The word "necessary" is rarely necessary. If a job activity were not necessary, you wouldn't have done it. Phrases such as "as necessary," "as needed," "as required," and "as assigned" also suggest job duties that you performed only because they were part of your job description—as opposed to activities you accomplished because you took the initiative. In most cases, these phrases can simply be left off your resume.

Avoid personal pronouns, particularly "I," "me," and "my." The understood grammatical subject of the bullet points in your resume is "I," though the actual pronoun is not used. Personal pronouns are, of course, used in cover letters.

Numbers on your resume will look more impressive if, instead of giving a range, you say "up to ____."

Example:

■ **Supervised 10-25 team members simultaneously.**

Clearly, 25 is a lot more impressive than 10, so why not say:

■ **Supervised up to 25 team members simultaneously.**

Similarly, instead of:

■ **Oversaw budgets ranging from $100K to $500K.**

Say:

■ **Oversaw budgets of up to $500K.**

Avoid phrases that sound like legalese, such as "including, but not limited to..." That's another phrase that comes right out of a job description. Employers use it to cover themselves in case they hire you and add job duties they had not initially thought of when they advertised your position.

For the most part, avoid articles—those little words, "a," "an," and "the." Generally speaking, resumes aren't written in sentence form, but in concise "telegraph" phrases that have become an accepted shorthand that employers understand. Articles tend to clutter up that shorthand; your resume will read in a more streamlined manner without them. You need not eliminate *every* instance of "a," "an," or "the"; occasionally, a phrase will sound better with the article left in. But do delete most articles.

Avoid jargon and acronyms that are used only in your company and are not understood outside the organization. Spell out any company-specific or industry-specific acronyms you think could be questionable, and explain any terms you think some readers of your resume might not understand. Note, however, that acronyms commonly used in your field may be among the keywords prospective employers will use to uncover applicants. But because acronyms can have varying connotations from industry to industry, it's wise to use both the acronym and spelled-out versions of these terms to cover your keyword bases.

Selected Accomplishments/Achievements

Everything on your resume should be accomplishments-driven. For that reason, many hiring decision-makers dislike isolating accomplishments in a section by themselves. Doing so suggests that the other things you did in your jobs were *not* accomplishments. Decision-makers also want to see how your accomplishments fit into your work history and particularly that they are relatively recent. "Accomplishments without context is useless," comments Goolsby. "I am not hiring a machine to go and tackle this project or reach this goal. I am bringing someone into an organization of people, teams, personalities, and work processes. I need to understand what a person has accomplished, but also how they did it." Some job-seekers, however, especially at the executive level, and even a few employers, prefer to see a separate accomplishments section.

Education and Professional Development

With rare exceptions, education should always be listed on your resume.

Education information on a resume should be listed in order of importance to the reader. Thus the preferred order is, for example:

Name of degree (spelled out: **Bachelor of Arts, Master of Business Administration, and so on**) in *name of major, name of university, city/state of university, graduation year if within the last 10 years.*

Example:

Bachelor of Arts in Communication Studies, Rutgers University, New Brunswick, NJ

Consider leaving off older graduation dates to minimize your exposure to age discrimination. List degrees in reverse chronological order, as the most recent one is usually the most important. You can also list other types of relevant training, professional development, and certification programs in the Education section (another alternative is to list them in their own section). Here, reverse chronological order gets tricky because, even though some of your training may be more recent than your degree(s), your degrees usually will still be considered the more important selling points. So, list other training after your degrees unless you feel another training-based credential sells you better than your degrees do.

Licenses/Certifications

Include licensure, certifications, and any other credentials that are *relevant* to the job you're targeting. Another option is to list these items in your Education section. Include your security clearance status if relevant and up to date.

Professional Affiliations/Memberships

In many professions, you are expected to belong to certain organizations. In others, organization affiliation can be seen as a value-added aspect of your background. Relevance should be your guide to whether to include a heading and section on Professional Affiliations/Memberships. Be sure these listings fit the job you target. Leave off old memberships from previous careers that no longer apply. Avoid listing membership in any controversial organization that could get you screened out. Remember, you are listing *professional* memberships relevant to your career.

Languages and International Travel/Experience

Languages and international experience rarely warrant a section of their own. If you are an international executive, it is assumed that you are internationally savvy and globally traveled. Your specific language fluencies and knowledge are certainly worth a mention, but, if you do not want to list a separate languages section, you can include a bullet point about languages and international background in your Profile section.

Public Speaking/Presentations

If speaking, presenting, and training are integral to your career, you may want to include a separate section listing prominent speaking engagements. Presentations can also be nicely handled in a supplemental document, as discussed in Chapter 3.

Publications

Lists of publications the job-seeker has written or co-written are particularly expected for academic jobs, as well as often for other professions, such as law, medicine, and science. Note, however, that jobs in some of these fields require a curriculum vitae rather than an executive resume. When you do use a resume, you can include a section listing publications, or as a separate document, as outlined in Chapter 3.

Military Background

Your military career is part of your experience, and one option is to include it in your Experience section, especially if the bulk of your career has been in the military. Military information you may consider listing includes length of service, branch of service, ranks, special training, medals, and discharge/reserve status. "Please tell me you are a veteran and what service," says Doreen Perri-Gynn, associate vice president of human resources at Yang Ming (America) Corp. "Rank is always good. It tells me you are a leader, can follow directions and take ownership, among other things." If your military background is dated and not especially relevant to your current career, you can list it in a separate section without dates. You could also consider leaving it off if it's not a selling point, but note that some employers want to see everything you've done since college.

Volunteer and Community Service

Showing that you are well-rounded, socially responsible, civic-minded, and community-spirited is generally advantageous on an executive resume as long as you don't get carried away. List this type of service concisely. Also consider this section as optional if you run into space constraints.

Design Tips

Today's resume exists in two worlds—a predominant world of electronic submissions, and a subset of that world in which they are viewed by the human eye. Let's call the resumes for these two worlds the electronic resume and the print resume (respectively). The differences between these two resume types, especially the technical aspects of preparing them, are discussed in more detail later in the Delivery Methods section of this chapter.

Most resumes today are submitted to employers and recruiters electronically, either posted to employer Websites or third-party job boards, or sent as e-mail attachments. An electronically submitted resume does not need to have a sophisticated, eye-catching design. In fact, a complex design or layout can be a detriment in electronic submission. Columns, borders, tables, boxes, shading, rule lines, outline type, text blocks, headers and footers, and other graphic elements can make your resume difficult to place into the keyword-searchable database of the organization's Applicant Tracking System (ATS). Most employers, when they do view your resume, do so on a computer screen, where they are more concerned with content and keywords than with a fancy layout. In this electronic-submission world, a plain, simple design or a text-based resume is best. Though not sophisticated, these simple resumes should still be easy to follow and well organized. Hiring decision-makers don't like to see design overshadow meaningful content. "A targeted, well-constructed resume can benefit from an interesting or sophisticated layout, but the best layout in the world can't make up for a poorly thought out resume," notes a human resources official at a large Northeastern company. Some hiring decision-makers also point out that resumes can be creatively designed without being graphically heavy. Typographic variations and attractive layouts can make a resume look good but not overpowering.

The sleek, eye-catching print resume with a sophisticated design still has a place in executive job search. You should have an appealing print resume for these situations:

➤ Networking, where you are handing your resume to people you meet.

➤ Job interviews. The interviewer has already seen your resume at this point, but you should bring an attractively designed print resume to the interview as a leave-behind that will make a striking impression. You can also have it available to present to others you may meet at the interview who have not previously seen your resume.

➤ Sending your resume by postal mail or faxing it. Yes, some employers still ask for resumes in these seemingly old-fashioned ways. And even when they don't, you can often reinforce your electronic submission by sending a print resume and cover letter by postal mail.

An attractively designed print resume—recruiter Alice Hanson calls them "fancy eye-candy resumes"—can also be part of an overall branding effort in which all your printed pieces carry a consistent, memorable look, as discussed in Chapter 1.

Most of the resume samples in this book are design-intense print resumes to illustrate the possibilities in creating eye-catching documents. Simpler designs that would work well as electronic submissions appear on pages 147, 166, and 218.

Whether electronic or print, some guidelines apply universally:

➤ Fonts should be conservative and easy to read. Employing commonly used fonts not only befits an executive position, but also ensures that, when sent electronically, your resume will appear to the recipient the same way you sent it. If you use an exotic font, it's possible the recipient's computer doesn't have that font, and the document would open with a default font and look different from the way you intended. Use no more than two different fonts in your resume, and avoid colored type. Standard fonts include Times New Roman, Arial, Garamond, Georgia, and Century Schoolbook. Fonts that are a bit edgier but still acceptable include Verdana, Tahoma, and Century Gothic.

➤ Fonts should be large enough to be read. Generally, type smaller than 10.5 points is too small. Twelve-point type is quite readable but, other than for headings, will likely take up too much space in the average executive resume. Thus, 11-point type is ideal in most situations. Keep in mind that some fonts are smaller than others; 10-point type in Verdana, for example, is about the right size, whereas 10-point type in Garamond is too small to be easily read.

➤ You can give even a simple design visual appeal with typographic variety using boldface, italics, all-caps, and small caps. Use italics and all-caps sparingly, as these forms can be hard to read. Also avoid *too much* typographic variety in your resume.

➤ Be careful with paragraph alignment. Standard paragraph settings include flush left, flush right, centered, and justified. With justified type, both left and right edges of type are evenly aligned. Although this even look can be pleasing (and is routinely used in documents outside the United States), words often appear with extra spaces between them to achieve the justified look. Instead, most type on your resume should be flush left, with occasional centered elements. Avoid too much centering, as centered type can be hard to read.

➤ White space should surround the type on your resume. The default margin setting in Microsoft Word is 1.25 inches, which is usually more margin than you need. A 1-inch margin is pleasing, but executives may find it difficult to fit as much as they need to on a page with a margin that wide. A margin of .75 inches often works well, and margins should never be narrower than .5 inches. Endeavor also to place white space between items on the resume.

➤ Ensure that the reader can easily locate your headings and thus efficiently find information on your resume.

➤ Favor bullets over paragraphs. Most employers says they don't want to read paragraphs. "HR folks receive resumes, solicited or unsolicited, like snow flakes in a blizzard," says Doreen Perri-Gynn. "I won't read them." Instead, use small blocks of text, most of which is bulleted in a reader-friendly format. Strive for no more than two lines in a bullet point, and avoid lengthy lists of bullet points; no more than seven points is a good number to strive for.

➤ Eliminate clutter. Among elements that add clutter are underlining, parentheses, acronyms, and articles ("a," "the," "an"). Dates can sometimes add clutter when listed with professional affiliations or training; ask yourself if it's really necessary to include dates in those sections.

➤ Avoid splitting important elements over two pages. Ideally, for example, don't split the description of one of your past job so that it starts at the bottom of one page and continues on the top of the next page. Adjust your layout to contain that job on one page or the other.

➤ Number your pages, and include your name (first initial and last name will do) in case the pages of your print resume get separated.

Additional guidelines for print resumes include:

➤ Consider a layout/design that goes beyond ordinary yet is not so elaborate that employers find it distracting. Consult the samples in Chapter 7 for design ideas that appeal to you.

➤ Give special attention to the elements that lend focus to your resume. Usually placed on the first third of your first page, these elements may include a headline, branding statement, profile, summary, and keyword section. Be sure these are positioned to get attention, as well as big and bold enough to get noticed.

➤ Consider graphic elements that add interest, such as rule lines, boxes, shaded areas, columns, and tables, but don't get carried away.

➤ Avoid standard resume templates, such as those available in Microsoft Word. These templates, though not inherently detrimental, will produce a resume that is the antithesis of distinctive, as employers have seen thousands of resumes that use these templates.

Organizational Formats

One of the first decisions job-seekers must make when preparing their resumes is how to organize the resume's content. Today's resumes generally are:

➤ Chronological (actually reverse chronological, listing all your experience from most to least recent).

➤ Functional, which lists experience in skills clusters.

➤ A combination or hybrid of those two types, sometimes known as a chrono-functional format.

Chronological Resumes

The traditional, default format for resumes is the *chronological resume*. This type of resume is organized by your employment history in reverse chronological order, with job titles/names of employers/locations of employers/dates of employment/ accomplishments, working backwards 15 years or more.

A standard chronological resume is the ideal, especially if most/all of your experience has been in one field, you have no large employment gaps, and you plan to stay in that same field.

The chronological resume is preferred by the widest variety of employers, as well as by recruiters and most Internet job boards. Recruiters and hiring managers tend to like this resume format because it's easy to follow and clearly demonstrates your job history and career advancement/growth. This format is also recommended for all conservative career fields (such as accounting, banking, law, and so on) and international job-seeking.

Most of the samples in Chapter 7 are chronological resumes.

Functional Resumes

The resume format preferred by job-seekers with a limited job history, a checkered job history, or a job history in a different career field, is the *functional resume.*

Job-seekers who take a functional approach organize their resumes by skills and functions clusters. In a purely functional resume, company names, employment dates, and position titles are intentionally omitted. The functional resume can work for entrepreneurs returning to the workforce, for example, or others who wish to deemphasize dates.

This resume format is the least common, least preferred by employers, and detested by recruiters—and most Internet job boards do not accept this resume format.

Combination (Chrono-Functional, Hybrid) Resumes

Because the purely functional format has become the subject of employer backlash in recent years, some job-seekers have learned to structure their resumes in a mostly functional format but to also include a bare-bones work history in reverse chronological order, creating what is variously known as a *chrono-functional, hybrid,* or *combination format.*

The work-history section need include only job title, name and location of employer, and dates of employment. You don't need to list what you did in each job because that information already is listed in your functional sections.

The chrono-functional/hybrid/combination resume highlights outstanding skills and achievements that might otherwise be buried within the job-history section while simultaneously presenting, yet deemphasizing, the chronology of jobs. The focus is on clusters of accomplishments organized by functional area and the experiences that are most relevant to the position for which you are applying. If you are open to more than one type of job, you can reconfigure the functional clusters to emphasize the skills most relevant to the particular job you seek.

Chrono-functional/hybrid/combination resumes can suit a variety of job-seeker needs, such as a diverse job history that doesn't add up to a clear-cut career path and situations in which the job-seeker has work experience that is related but not an exact link to desired position. Job-seekers who have large employment gaps or many short employment stints prefer this format because it downplays employment history. This type of resume has been known to work for older workers, career changers, and job-seekers with academic deficiencies or limited experience.

Although the chrono-functional/hybrid/combination resume is more acceptable to employers than the purely functional format, some employers are unaccustomed to functional formats of any kind, finding them confusing, annoying, and a red flag that something is wrong in your background. At the very least, they will probably scrutinize a chrono-functional resume more closely to check for details and find the flaws that inspired the candidate to use this format. Some employers insist on knowing exactly what you did in each job.

Recruiters/headhunters particularly disdain functional formats, so this approach should never be used if you are primarily targeting recruiters with your job search. As noted, employers in conservative fields are not fans of functional formats, nor are international employers. Functional formats, even chrono-functional, also are not acceptable on many online job boards.

The chrono-functional resume has very limited uses but can be a viable marketing tool if executed well. HR professional Veronica Richmond notes that chrono-functional formats make sense only "if someone is attempting to move into something completely different but with some transferable skills. It'll certainly be harder for them, and it's a more difficult read, but may be necessary to highlight what they can do." The bare-bones employment history with dates is critical for Richmond, but she doesn't dismiss chrono-functional formats out of hand. "I might lose a gem," she observes. Another recruiter supports chrono-functional formats because she uses one on her own resume. "I know that some people don't like functional resume, but that is the type of resume I use," says the Washington, D.C.–based recruiter. "I have worked in different industries but the skills I have cross the different industries and they should not be discounted based on that. I have been successful with that format, but know it is not for everyone—or every industry. My bottom line is as long as the information is in the resume, in a clear and concise format, I can work with the resume."

See a chrono-functional sample on page 238.

More than one format?

Your resume is one of the most fundamental tools of job-seekers, so take the time and care to develop the best resume based on your previous work experience and job-search aspirations. For some job-seekers, this process may result in both a chronological resume and chrono-functional resume. For example, I once had a client with a strong background as a product manager in banking. Unfortunately, she had moved to an area where few banks had their corporate headquarters, so opportunities in her field were limited. She had to be open to other jobs that used her transferable project/product management, marketing, and customer-service skills. For those jobs, she used a chrono-functional format to emphasize transferable skills and position her for a possible career change. But she hadn't given up on approaching banks in her new locale, whether as a potential product manager or in a closely related position. Therefore, she still needed a traditional chronological resume, both because banking is a conservative industry and because a chronological format was still her best bet for obtaining a job similar to her previous positions.

Delivery Methods

When we talk about resume format, we're referring not only to how the content is organized, but also how the resume is prepared and delivered. Will you print your resume out for such uses as networking, mailing to employers, and presenting in interviews? Do you plan to deliver it via e-mail, post it on employer sites and job boards, send it to recruiters, or post on your own Website? Each of these uses calls for a specific method of preparation on your computer.

E-resume, or electronic resume, is a broadly used term that covers several types of resumes. The way a resume is intended to be delivered to its recipient determines the technological approach you should take to the resume's preparation. The following section describes the most common types of e-resumes and offers some general guidelines on how to create them.

The formatted, "print" resume, also known as a word-processed resume or traditional paper resume, is created in a word-processing program. Microsoft Word is the most widely used and is advisable to use for that reason. Some job-seekers use Corel WordPerfect, Microsoft Works, or other lesser-known programs. If you are sending your formatted, print resume as an attachment to an e-mail message, it is inadvisable to use a program other than Word unless you save the resume in Rich Text (.rtf; see Rich Text Format entry that follows). File extensions for formatted, print resumes include .doc, for MS Word; .wpd, for Corel WordPerfect; and .wps, for MS Works. Word 2007 saves documents with a .docx extension, and because many users have an older version of Word that cannot open .docx files, be sure to save your resume with a .doc extension. Common delivery methods for the formatted, print resume include regular postal mail, faxing, hand delivery, and e-mail attachment.

The formatted, print resume is among the best for its attractive visual presentation of the job-seeker. When sent as an e-mail attachment, however, its formatting may appear inconsistently from computer to computer, and it is highly vulnerable to viruses. Don't send a formatted, print resume as an attachment unless (a) you're sure it's the employer's preference or (b) you also provide another alternative, preferably your text-based resume pasted into the body of an e-mail message.

A text resume, also known as a text-based resume, plain-text resume, or ASCII text resume, is the preferred format for submitting resumes electronically. A text resume, which carries the .txt file extension, is stripped of virtually all its formatting and is not especially visually appealing, which is okay because its main purpose is to be placed into one of the keyword-searchable databases that the vast majority of today's large employers now use. The text resume is not vulnerable to viruses and is compatible across computer programs and platforms. It is highly versatile and can be used for:

➤ Posting in its entirety on many job boards.

➤ Pasting piece-by-piece into the profile forms of job boards, such as Monster.com.

➤ Pasting into the body of an e-mail and sending to employers.

➤ Converting to a Web-based HTML resume.

➤ Sending as an attachment to employers, although you may also want to send your formatted version.

➤ Conversion to a scannable resume.

Numerous resources are available to guide you through creating a text resume or converting your existing formatted resume to text, including this part of the Electronic Resume Workshop from Susan Ireland at *http://www.susanireland.com/eresumework.htm.*

You can see what a typical text resume looks like in the sample on page 181.

A Rich Text Format (RTF) resume can be created in most word-processing programs by saving the resume as Rich Text with a file extension of .rtf. Generally speaking, the formatting and attractive visual presentation created in the original document will hold up in the Rich Text resume, although more complex formatting (such as columns or tables) may not hold up. It's best to test the Rich Text resume by sending it to the computers of a few friends to see how the formatting looks on the other end. Rich Text can be an excellent choice as an e-resume attachment because it is compatible across all platforms and word-processing programs. It's also far less vulnerable to viruses than are Word documents. In terms of attachments, it's the best choice when you can't determine what file type the employer prefers, but it should be accompanied by the text version of your resume pasted into the body of the e-mail message to which the RTF resume is attached.

A Portable Document Format (PDF) resume offers the advantages of being completely invulnerable to viruses and totally compatible across computer systems (requires Adobe Acrobat Reader software, a free download, to be opened and read). Have you ever noticed that when you send a resume (or any document) as an attachment from your computer to someone else's computer, it sometimes doesn't look the same on the other person's computer as it did on yours? Maybe it has more pages on the other computer, or maybe Page 2 starts at the bottom of Page 1, or maybe the fonts are different. A resume converted to PDF, which carries a .pdf file extension, looks virtually identical to the original document from which it was created, thus preserving the resume's visual appeal, and it also appears consistently from computer to computer. A few employers specifically request PDF resume files.

The downsides include the fact that it can be more difficult to perform keyword searches on PDF resumes unless they are scanned first or the text is extracted from them. Many employers, such as recruiter Lisa De Benedittis, president of Elite Staffing Services in San Diego, say they do not want to receive PDF resumes. "I want MS Word only so I can remove your contact information, put my logo on the top, and send it to my client," De Benedittis says. "I can also correct any spelling errors." If a resume writer prepares a PDF document for you, you may not be able to manipulate or change it in any way (unlike, for example, a Word document, which you can easily change), so the PDF conversion should take place after you're totally satisfied with your resume and need no additional changes. Your PDF resume should be a companion piece, not a substitute, for a document that you can manipulate. The biggest downside is that you need special software to create a PDF document. The gold standard for creating PDF documents is Adobe Acrobat, which is rather expensive. Cheaper and even freeware or shareware programs are available. Mac OS X with comes a built-in program, Preview, that can convert any OS X file into PDF. Search for freeware and shareware using Planet PDF's "Find PDF Software" section (*http://www.planetpdf.com/find_software.asp*). Planet PDF is a rich resource on conversion of documents to PDF. You can also pay a print shop, such as Kinko's, or resume writer to convert your resume to PDF.

A resume published on the Web, which carries the file extension .html or .htm, and known as an HTML, Web-based, or Web-ready resume, is advantageous in a number of ways:

➤ They are stock-in-trade for the passive candidate so coveted by employers and recruiters. Hiring decision-makers prefer to hire candidates who aren't looking for a job—who are happily employed in their current jobs. The oversimplified view is that if you are looking for a job—and especially if you are unemployed and looking for a job—there must be something wrong with you. The comment of Kristina Creed, a senior manager at a for-profit education provider, illustrates this point: "Last I checked, good people don't look for jobs—companies seek them out." If you're happily employed and not looking—but you are open to being headhunted into a new job, a Web resume is a great way for employers and recruiters to find you using various search mechanisms.

➤ Employers can access your resume 24/7. If you're talking on the phone with an employer in another city who wants to see a copy of your resume, you can simply refer the employer to the Web address where your resume resides.

➤ A resume published on the Web can be expanded into a Web portfolio that includes links to work samples (case studies, spreadsheets, written work, photographs, reports, and so on) that can demonstrate and substantiate your skills and accomplishments to employers.

The only catch to having a Web-ready resume is that you need to have a place and a means to publish it. The most likely candidates for Web-based resumes are those who already have their own Web pages or access to Web space. But even if you don't have your own space, you can still use a Web-ready resume. Some Websites offer free Web-space hosting. Check also with your Internet service provider to see if Web hosting is included in available services.

Do not confuse a Web-ready resume with one that can be posted on job boards, such as *Monster.com*. Most job boards explicitly prohibit HTML resumes.

Scannable resumes, which were all the rage just a few years ago, are being used less and less frequently by employers today. Why? Because a scannable resume is basically a print resume that the employer turns into an electronic resume by using Optical Character Recognition (OCR) software and then placing it into a keyword-searchable database. With the growth of e-mail as a mode of communication, employers soon asked themselves, "Why are we going through the extra step of scanning hard-copy when we could have resumes e-mailed to us and place them directly into databases without having to scan them first?" A former student of mine who had entered the human-resources field once told me that resumes e-mailed to his company could enter the database immediately, whereas a resume that had to be scanned could take up to three weeks to be placed in the database because of the extra labor involved.

You still may encounter employers, however, who request scannable resumes. The rules for scannable resumes are virtually the same as they are for text resumes except that scannable resumes are generally printed out and sent by fax or postal mail. They can also be sent as e-mail attachments.

As you get ready to send your resume electronically, experiment with sending your electronic package to yourself to see how it looks when received. As with other resume formats, you may also want to send it to the computers of friends or family members to see if it appears as intended.

Many job-seekers use a service or feature offered by their e-mail provider that enables them to screen out junk mail by asking recipients of their e-mail to click on a link to verify themselves, or to type in a letter-number combination to prove they are humans and not automated spammers. Though the desire to cut down on junk mail is admirable, consider what this process puts a hiring decision-maker through. In the fast-moving world of hiring, many will consider the process "very irritating and time consuming," as Marya Calhoun, director, human asset management and development for a healthcare communication provider in Atlanta, Georgia, did. When sending out resumes, see if you can turn off this anti-spam feature.

Frequently Asked Resume Questions (FAQs)

➤ **Are there items I should not include on my resume, such as religious or political affiliations?**

Any disclosure on your resume that could get you screened out as a candidate is risky. You may take the stance that you don't want to work for an employer who would eliminate you because a hiring manager didn't like your political beliefs or religious affiliation. But given that, for most candidates, religion, politics, and any other controversial affiliations are not relevant to your next job, it's wise to leave them out.

➤ **How many pages should my resume be?**

Among the resume "rules" you may have heard is the one in which resumes should be limited to one page. It's true that most entry-level job-seekers should try to limit their resumes to a single page, but this length is rarely appropriate for those at senior and executive levels. Top-level job-seekers will find it virtually impossible to capture the breadth of their experience and accomplishments in a single page, and some employers expect longer resumes from those candidates, sometimes up to five pages. In a 2007 survey by Accountemps (*http://www.accountemps.com/*), a specialized staffing service, only 7 percent of senior executives from human resources, finance, and marketing departments favored one-page resumes for executives, and 61 percent favored two pages. Respondents were receptive to three-page resumes for executive roles, with nearly a third (31 percent) citing this as the ideal length.

One-page resumes can be useful for executives in certain situations, such as networking, in which the job-seeker wants to give potential network contacts a thumbnail glance at his or her career. See the sample networking resume on page 68.

➤ **Should I list education or experience first?**

For most executives, Education will be listed after Experience, unless a new degree is considered to be an especially compelling selling point. In academia, too, Education is generally listed before Experience.

➤ **How do I handle employment gaps?**

A chrono-functional resume is one way to deemphasize employment gaps, but, as we've seen earlier in this chapter, these formats are unpopular with employers and especially recruiters.

Another approach, if you can legitimately do so, is to frame periods of unemployment as stints of self-employment, consulting, or project work. Some job-seekers quit their jobs to pursue advanced education or training; you can account for a period of unemployment by listing yourself as a Graduate Student during that period. One survey respondent for this book called gaps "a huge red flag," so they should be explained in your resume if you can gracefully do so. Other options include explaining them in your cover letter or being prepared to do so in an interview. (However, gaps may preclude you from getting the interview.)

➤ **How can I avoid appearing to be a job-hopper?**

Job-hopping is far less a concern than it was just a few years ago. Mature job-seekers will remember a time when long-time company loyalty was expected. Those days are gone. Workers at all levels stay at their jobs for much shorter periods than they used to. That's not to say that job-hopping is no longer questioned. Very short, frequent job stints can certainly raise eyebrows. A chrono-functional resume will deemphasize job-hopping but comes with its own drawbacks. Another choice is to omit jobs of short duration. In these days of background checks, however, your omission can be risky. Most hiring decision-makers surveyed for this book emphasized that nothing should be left off because jobs you've omitted will be discovered eventually in the vetting process, and you'll be eliminated. It's best to list everything, but make a strong case for your qualifications in your cover letter and top third of your resume so that you get called for an interview. Then be prepared to explain and put a positive spin on problematic or short-duration jobs face to face.

➤ **How can I position myself for a career or industry change?**

A career change gives you the opportunity to sharpen the focus of your resume toward the new career or industry. Study ads and job postings in your desired new field, and frame your resume bullet points so that your skills and accomplishments in your current career can be seen as directly applicable to your new career. Use copious keywords that relate to your new career, and tailor your profile, headline, branding statement, or Objective Statement to your aspiration. See a sample career-change resume on page 166.

➤ **How do I handle multiple jobs with the same employer?**

I recommend listing each position separately, as if it were a separate job, even repeating the name of employer and employer location each time. This approach provides more consistency throughout the resume and clearly shows your progression from job to job. It can also illustrate rapid promotions when the prospective employer sees short time periods between positions.

➤ **How do I handle relocation?**

Although you can discuss relocation in your cover letter, it never hurts to also mention it in your resume. Express in your Objective Statement and profile your intention to relocate. Because some employers respond much more favorably to local candidates, consider using an address in your new city (PO box, a friend's address, mail-forwarding service) on your resume.

➤ **How far back should I go in my job history to avoid age discrimination?**

Hiring decision-makers are split on this point, another area affected by the growing practice of conducting background checks. Many, especially recruiters, are adamant about seeing every job listed from your college graduation to the present. They argue that background checks— or even just seeing you in person at an interview—will reveal your age anyway, so why hide it? Others recommend going back 15–20 years, with the idea that jobs beyond that point are likely not relevant to your next career move. If you have the opportunity to contact the decision-maker before sending your resume, you can always ask his or her preference. Another option is to include your jobs that are more than 15 years old, but list them in bare-bones fashion (title, employer, location) with or without dates of employment. You may want to title this section Previous Professional Experience. Even if you opt to leave off the dates, the recipient will at least know that you have provided full disclosure by listing all jobs. A similar option, as Melissa Holmes, senior technical recruiter, Levi, Ray & Shoup Consulting Services, Springfield, Illinois, suggests, is to insert a disclaimer statement to the effect that "additional employment history is available upon request."

➤ **What if my name is hard to pronounce or it fails to clarify my gender?**

This issue isn't as silly as it seems. Even if you're well qualified, an employer may hesitate to phone you for an interview if he or she can't pronounce your name or even doesn't know whether to expect a male or female. For the difficult-to-pronounce name, include a phonetic pronunciation of your name in small type in the "letterhead" portion of your resume. Example: "Sally Hsieh (pronounced 'Shay')." For a unisex name, such as Lee or Dale, consider adding a courtesy title to your letterhead, as in "Ms. Lee Anderson" or "Mr. Dale Burns." Especially consider adding a courtesy title if your name is almost always thought of as belonging to the opposite gender or if it is a non-English name, and English-speakers would not know whether to expect a man or a woman: "Ms. Michael Crane"; "Mr. Jocelyn Smith." You could also include a middle name that reveals your gender. Of course, you may consider your ambiguously gendered name an advantage and prefer not to reveal your gender (even though your gender will become obvious if you're called for an interview).

➤ **What if a former employer no longer exists or has changed its name?**

For the out-of-business employer, you can simply state "no longer in business," "ceased operations," or "defunct" after listing the employer's name. For an employer that had a different name when you worked there than it does now, list it this way:

> Andersen Consulting (now Accenture)

Or, if you work in a renamed company and fear its new name won't be recognized, list like this:

> Accenture (formerly Andersen Consulting)

➤ **As an entrepreneur transitioning back to the workplace, how can I make the most of my resume?**

Emphasize the entrepreneurial transferable skills that apply to the type of job you're targeting. Many employers, for example, seek executives who can handle startup and turnaround situations. They're also looking for senior-level professionals with experience in asset and liability management, budget development, building strategic alliances, business plan development, capital equipment budgets, competitive analysis, costing and budgeting, financial strategies, market strategy, profit and loss management/direction, new business development, operations management, research and development, return on investment, and strategic planning direction. Focus also on your entrepreneurial successes and accomplishments; avoid conveying any impression that you are leaving the entrepreneurial life because you didn't succeed at it.

➤ **How can I ensure my resume will be kept confidential?**

Request as much in your cover letter. It doesn't hurt to display the word "Confidential" boldly at the top of your resume. Some job-seekers who don't want current employer to know they're in the hunt go so far as to list that employer by describing the organization rather than actually giving its name.

➤ **Should I list hobbies and interests?**

Generally, no. These items are considered superfluous and trivial. Some job-seekers consider these items conversation-starters, and some employers feel the information humanizes the candidate and presents a fuller picture. Perri-Gynn wants to know about volunteer work. "That tells me a great deal about you," she says. Others feel hobby and interest information can expose the candidate to discrimination. A workaholic hiring manager "could perceive the candidate as frivolous with too many outside interests," observes Alison, a corporate recruiter for a specialized information provider. Inclusion of hobbies and interests is usually not a make-or-break issue. "It would never be a reason to interview or not interview a candidate," notes Andrea, a recruiter for a national retailer who asked to be identified only by her first name. As with most information on your resume, the option to list hobby and interest information is a personal choice, but it's usually more risky to list it than to leave it off. Ask yourself: Does this information add value to my resume? Space constraints may also guide your decision.

➤ **Should I list computer skills?**

At the executive level, computer skills are usually not necessary on a resume. As Diane Dutton, CEO of ESO Business Services, points out, "Any real executive-level person can adapt to any and all systems. It really doesn't matter what computer system the [executive's past employer] uses; our goals are the same and the systems are just tools." In the IT field, it may be advantageous to list computer skills or have available a summary of technical competencies (see Chapter 3). And certainly, if a job posting or ad lists required computer skills, those should be listed on the resume for keyword purposes.

➤ **Should I list past salaries?**

No. The resume is not a job application in which salary information is expected. If you are asked for a salary history, consider sending it as a separate document (described in Chapter 3), realizing that revealing salaries at an early stage of the screening process is usually a poor salary-negotiation strategy.

➤ **Should I list names of reporting relationships, supervisors?**

At the executive level, many employers like to see the titles of the people to whom you reported, but do not list their names.

➤ **Should I list references on my resume?**

Never list them directly on your resume. If they are requested, list them on a separate sheet (and do not volunteer this references sheet unless asked), as outlined in Chapter 3. Consider also leaving off the line "References: Available upon request." This statement is highly optional because it is a given that you will provide references upon request. The line can serve the purpose of signaling: "This is the end of my resume," but if you are trying to conserve space, leave it off.

➤ **Do I need more than one version of my resume?**

Probably. You likely need versions prepared for various delivery formats (print and electronic), as seen earlier in this chapter. As we've also seen on page 48, you may want to employ more than one organizational format to see which one works best. It's quite possible also that you will want versions of your resume targeted to several industries and/or types of job, as outlined in Chapter 1. To summarize, here is a fairly standard roster of resume needs:

➤ Formatted, print version for postal mailing and interviews (usually in Microsoft Word with .doc or .rtf file extension).

➤ One-page version of this print resume for networking (usually in Microsoft Word).

➤ Plain, simple version for submitting electronically as an attachment (usually in Microsoft Word with .doc or .rtf file extension).

➤ Text version for submitting to job boards, recruiter and employer Websites, pasting piecemeal into online profile forms, and sending electronically, either in the body of an e-mail or as an attachment (in text format with .txt file extension).

➤ HTML/Web version for publishing on a Web page (in HTML format with .html file extension or other Web programming language).

➤ Versions of any of these with content tweaked to specifically target individual jobs.

➤ Possibly both chronological and chrono-functional versions of anything listed here, if your situation calls for them.

➤ **What if I have no college degree or no four-year college degree, or did not attend college?**

If you have at least some college, list it. List an associate's degree or incomplete studies toward a bachelor's degree. For the incomplete degree, list the college, major, location, span of dates you attended, and, ideally, number of credit-hours completed. Your listing of an associate's degree, incomplete bachelor's degree, or no college at all should be beefed up with any training, professional-development, and certificate programs. In the unlikely event that you have absolutely none of these, leave off the Education section. Some employers (and most recruiters) will screen you out, but if you are aspiring to an executive-level job, you have probably been successful without educational credentials, and your professional accomplishments will likely be enough to propel you to an interview.

➤ **Should I hire a professional resume writer?**

In my career as a professional resume writer, the vast majority of resumes I have seen have been relatively weak. Recruiters and hiring managers tell me the same thing about the resumes that come across their desks.

That's why I see considerable value in the idea of hiring a professional resume writer. If you've followed the guidelines in this book and have decided you want to take the next step, a well-chosen resume-writing professional can truly make a significant difference in a job search. What you've learned in this book can serve as a strategic guide for getting the most out of collaborating with a professional resume writer.

One of the first signs that you may need a professional resume writer is that your resume simply does not seem to be working for you. If you are not getting called for interviews after sending out or posting your resume, it's possible that your resume could be improved. Of course, other factors also could be involved, such as whether you are following up after sending out your resume—but your resume itself is a good place to start troubleshooting.

Another fairly sure sign that you may need a professional is that people have told you your resume needs work—perhaps friends, coworkers, professors, recruiters, or others. Sometimes these folks are trying to tell you your resume needs *a lot* of work, but they are too kind to tell you that.

Remember in either of these situations—critical comments or poor results—you don't have to start right off the bat with getting your resume professionally revamped. Most resume-writing services offer low-cost or even no-cost critiques. By having a professional resume writer review and critique your resume, you can find out whether your resume needs just minor repairs—or major surgery.

If you are facing a change in your situation—from employed to unemployed, from one position to a switch to a different job or career, or from one city to another, from entrepreneur to employed—you may want to consider hiring a professional resume writer to help you effectively position yourself for the change you seek.

Similarly, the wise individual remains prepared for unexpected job changes. Ideally, your resume should be updated and ready to go at all times, even if you're not actively seeking a new position. If you were in a networking situation, and someone asked for a copy for your resume, would you have one ready? If not, consider hiring a professional resume writer to help you get your resume in shape.

You may have issues or problems in your job history that you don't know how to handle in your resume. For example, perhaps you have employment gaps in your background, or you have spent short periods of time in a number of jobs and worry about giving the impression of being a "job-hopper," or your job history is very diverse and doesn't point in any one direction, or you are returning to the workforce after parenting, running your own business, serving in the military, or other absence. Professional resume writers know strategies for dealing with all of these situations—and more—on a resume.

For the occasions when the appearance of your print resume is important—for networking, mailing, and interviews—a professional resume writer can apply layout and design techniques that enable your document to really grab attention.

If your resume cannot convey a sense of the value you can contribute to the organization extremely rapidly, consider hiring a professional to sharpen its focus.

Perhaps your resume was fine when you were at a lower job level, but now that you've climbed the ladder of advancement, your resume may lack the sophisticated look and message that indicates you are worthy of the salary and title you seek. A resume writer can help you bring it up to the appropriate level.

Resume writers are also familiar with all the formats needed for today's job search—formats such as text, PDF, and Web-ready resumes discussed earlier in this chapter. A professional resume writer can convert your resume to the appropriate formats, as well as advise you on which format is needed in which situation. Resume writers are also well-versed in the keywords job-seekers in every profession should use on their resumes so that their documents pop up in searches after being placed in the employer's keyword-searchable database.

Many job-seekers observe that they just don't have an objective grasp of what their most marketable skills are and how to highlight their best selling points on a resume. Or they have difficulty brainstorming their own accomplishments. A professional resume writer can help you identify these important points. Some resume writers use questionnaires, and others conduct interviews by phone or in person to help clients brainstorm this information.

Some job-seekers hire a professional resume writer because they do not have the time to create a truly effective resume. Although a resume writer can save you tremendous time, it's important to remember that you as the job-seeker do need to invest at least some time in the project. Whether the resume writer gathers your information by questionnaire or interview, time is needed to collect that data. Once that's accomplished, it's the resume writer who will be putting in time creating a dazzling product for you.

Remember above all that there is no shame in hiring a professional resume writer. You hire doctors, lawyers, financial advisers, and tax consultants when you lack the expertise in those areas, so why should resume-writing be different? Many employers and even more recruiters actually encourage the idea of professionally written resumes because hiring managers want to obtain your information in a reader-friendly form that clearly tells how you can benefit the organization.

You can find a listing of professional resume writers who prepare executive and senior-level resumes the Appendix on page 248.

Chapter Three

Branded Career-Marketing Communication Tools to Enhance Your Resume

Today's executive needs more than just a resume. To fully position you and sell employers on your unique value proposition, enhance your resume with a combination—also known as a suite, library, or portfolio—of career-marketing communication tools. This chapter explains the purpose of these documents and provides samples.

Tying together the various communication tools in this chapter is the concept of personal branding, an emerging trend in career-marketing communication, which, as touched on in Chapter 1, is variously defined as image, reputation, connection, a promise of the unique value of a product (you), and expertise. Randall Hansen writes on the career-development Website Quintessential Careers (*http://www.quintcareers.com/career_branding.html*) that "branding is the combination of tangible and intangible characteristics that make a brand unique. Branding is developing an image—with results to match." Those results should be conveyed in a way that enables the employer to mentally construct a compelling portrait of the return you can provide on the organization's investment in you.

Branding (often called personal branding or self-branding when applied to individuals) is essential to career advancement because branding helps define who you are, in what ways you are a great performer, and why you should be sought out. Branding is about building a name for yourself, showcasing what sets you apart from others, and describing the added value you bring to a situation. It's about establishing yourself as a leading specialist or authority in your area of expertise. Your brand describes your essence and the significance you bring to employers.

Most job-seekers are not proactive in establishing and building their career brand, hoping instead to let their actions speak for them when seeking promotions or new jobs. Others may have developed bits of branding through the years, but these pieces may have lost currency and fail to relate to each other. You can make yourself a much more attractive candidate by taking the time to master some basic tactics that can help build your career brand. If you don't brand yourself, others will for you—and possibly *not* in the way you'd like them to.

Father of personal branding Tom Peters wrote in his book, *The Brand You50 (Reinventing Work): Fifty Ways to Transform Yourself from an "Employee" into a Brand That Shouts Distinction, Commitment, and Passion!*: "Regardless of age, regardless of position, regardless of the business we happen to be in, all of us need to understand the importance of branding. We are the CEOs of our own companies: Me, Inc." He adds, "You're not defined by your job title and you're not confined by your job description."

Branding, especially personal branding, is primarily storytelling, and another advantage of branding yourself is that your story is unique. "When you learn to put words to your unique story, you can use it and the values you've developed to define you in a way that no one can copy," writes Chris Hiliki in *May I Have Your Attention, Please?*

Noting that most people are marketers to some extent, author of popular marketing books Seth Godin (*Purple Cow, The Big Moo, All Marketers Are Liars*) does not believe marketing without story is possible: "Either you're going to tell stories that move people, or you will become irrelevant," he writes in *All Marketers Are Liars* (Penguin, 2005). Organizational storytelling expert Steve Denning similarly notes in *The Leader's Guide to Storytelling* that "narrative is increasingly recognized as central in branding," and when he refers to a "storied product," he could just as easily be referencing a job-seeker as a non-human product.

Getting your brand story out there raises your visibility and builds your aura as an attractive candidate for hire. Symbiotically, elevating the world's awareness of you creates new opportunities for networking. Increasingly, in the Information Age, success can spring not just from whom you know, but also from who knows you and your story.

"Personal branding is about differentiation," writes William Arruda on the Website of the Reach Branding Club (*http://www.reachbrandingclub.com/whatis_personal_branding.html*). "Personal branding helps you stand head and shoulders above the competition by highlighting your unique promise of value."

A global suggestion for virtually all of the communication tools in this chapter is to create a cohesive, branded message and appearance. Ensure that each piece conveys the branding that you want to communicate. Match your resume's "letterhead" with the other letter-sized documents in your suite (such as cover letter, salary history, reference list, thank-you letter), and scale it down on smaller items such as networking cards. Use a consistent font or a set of fonts on all your materials. If you use color, make it consistent throughout. You may want to carry your headline and branding statement throughout your materials. The idea is that whenever a decision-maker sees one of your communication tools, he or she will think of you.

This chapter is arranged according to the phase of your job search in which each communication tool is most useful. Although some overlap exits, and some tools are useful throughout your search, most tools have an optimal place in the job-search sequence. At the end of the chapter, you'll find a full set of branded documents to illustrate how to carry your branding throughout your entire package. Here's how the sequence of communication tools breaks down:

Tool to build brand identity before the job search: Before you even launch a job search, know and be able to articulate clearly the value you bring to your next employer. Developing this message will provide a framework for your entire job search and serve as a major boon for crafting all other components of your career-marketing communication toolkit.

➤ Branding statement

Networking communication tools: These tools are useful throughout your job search, but especially before you have begun responding to ads and sending out resumes. And networking in more vital to executives than to any other group of job-seeker. For job-seekers in the aggregate, only about 1/5 of the job market is what we call "open" with only about 20 percent of job openings publicly known—and this number is only about 12 percent at the executive level based on a 2007 ExecuNet survey in which 88 percent of human-resources professionals said they don't advertise positions with total compensation above $200,000 (the figure was a somewhat lower 75 percent among recruiters). The higher level the job, the less likely it is to be advertised. Other statistics in the report that support the importance of networking among executives include:

➤ 66 percent of executives polled found their greatest job-hunting success through networking.

➤ Search firms find more candidates through networking than through any other source.

Clearly, communication tools that grease the networking wheels are of great value to executives.

➤ Elevator speech

➤ Brief networking resume

➤ Business/networking/branding cards

Communication tools for the active, pre-interview job-search phase: In addition to your resume, these are the documents that form the heart of your job search when you are actively attempting to secure interviews.

➤ Cover letter

➤ E-mail content

➤ Proposal to create job/position by describing how you can solve problems/ meet needs

Communication tools for the interview phase of the job search: The documents in this phase of your job search provide details about aspects of your background about which employers need additional information. They represent areas of your background that, if listed on your resume, would bog your resume down with excessive words, length, and details. As you approach and enter the interview stage, however, you may be asked to provide exactly these details.

In the initial screening phase of recruiting employees, decision-makers want to see the facts, says Deborah Wile Dib, who is known as the "CEO Coach for $200K to $1M+ CEOs and executives." At this point, the desired facts are limited to "chronology, companies, titles, education, skill sets, numbers," Dib says, adding that initial screeners also want "a hint of accomplishments and brand," and the candidate's resume provides a preview of things to come.

Beyond the screening phase and even the initial interview phase, decision-makers start to need more about the "passion, process, and problem solving" aspects of a potential hire, Dib says. Deeper digging marks this phase, Dib notes, and it's when various addenda can play an important role. "They deliver a deeper feel for the candidate, a wider scope, and show specifics of the bullet points on the resume," Dib says. "The addenda tell the stories that build chemistry and fit."

"Addenda have to mean something," Dib cautions. "They need to enhance the resume and create even more interest and excitement." That means they must show impact, usually in terms of generating profits, cutting costs, or improving processes. Dib notes that, though not all addenda can be "monetized" (publications, training, and technology summaries, for example, don't lend themselves), the "suite" of materials you provide at this phase should include at least one document that shows value.

You may also choose to send employers some of these documents *before* the interview phase—along with your resume and cover letter—and some may be requested as part of your application package (for example, a publications list is a standard enclosure for academic and scientific-research jobs). In the initial screening phase, however, the type of detail represented by these documents is generally seen as excessive. In fact, the hiring decision-makers surveyed for this book were nearly unanimous in stating that they do not want to see these types of documents included with your initial resume submission.

➤ 59

Examples of communication tools to consider having ready for the post-screening, interview phase of the job search include:

➤ Summary of leadership initiatives/ leadership profile

➤ Executive biography/experience narrative

➤ Project summary

➤ Technical skills summary

➤ Summary of training

➤ Publications summary

➤ Media mentions summary

➤ Presentations summary

➤ Reference list

➤ Salary history

Communication tools for use at the interview: These are the tools that you may want to take with you to an interview and be prepared to present.

➤ Resume for presentation (in PowerPoint)

➤ Print portfolio

Communication tool for after the interview: This is the one indispensable tool to be used immediately after an interview.

➤ Thank-you letter

Communication tools for passive candidates: These are the tools for candidates who are happily employed and not job-hunting—but receptive to being courted by recruiters and employers. Active candidates also can employ these tools but will need additional tools to search effectively.

➤ Portfolio (print and Web-based)

➤ Blog

The following are descriptions of each tool, along with guidelines for producing them, and samples.

Tool to Build Brand Identity Before the Job Search
Branding Statement

We've already seen a taste of branding statements in Chapter 1, especially as they are used on resumes.

An effective way to begin your personal-branding effort is to develop a branding statement—just a few sentences, a paragraph that sums up your value proposition. This element will guide your subsequent branding activities and can be used, not only on your resume, but also on your networking cards, Website, or blog. In *Career Distinction: Stand Out by Building Your Brand*, authors William Arruda and Kirsten Dixson suggest using a branding statement in an e-mail signature and a branded voicemail greeting.

In their book *Brand Yourself*, David Andrusia and Rick Haskins present a simple formula for a branding statement: Skills + Personality/Passion + Market needs = Branding Statement.

Chris Hilicki, author of *May I Have your Attention, Please? Build a Better Business by Telling your True Story* (John Wiley & Sons, 2005), makes a strong argument for basing your brand on your personal story. "When you build your brand identity on your true experiences, you will bring to the world the only thing that no one else can. Your true story conveys your unique value and is the "strongest foundation of your brand identity," Hilicki contends in *May I Have Your Attention Please?*

Arruda and Dixson, in *Career Distinction: Stand Out by Building Your Brand,* assert that a branding statement should have three characteristics: It consists of one sentence; it can be easily understood by a 12-year-old; and you could recite it from memory at gunpoint. They call the personal branding statement "a concise summary of how you intend to solve a problem, meet a need, or make a difference in the world."

Professional career coach Don Orlando offers these guidelines to help you develop a branding statement (which he calls a "value statement"):

➤ Focus on the value that employers will respond to at once. For example, when a potential client who is a senior manager asks me what I do, I tell them this: "I help you get paid what you are worth, win the job you've always deserved, and have fun in the process." Notice the focus on benefits ("…paid what you are worth…," "…the job you've always deserved…," and "… fun in the process."). I do not focus on the features (a great resume and cover letter, skill in finding the right references, and the like).

➤ Avoid listing traits. Being hardworking, or having strong communications skills, is admirable, but these traits are the minimum standards. They apply to every job. You soar so far above those minimum standards they literally go without saying.

➤ Keep it concise. Strip away any material that doesn't move your message forward.

➤ Draft your value statements. You may find two value statements useful—the short statement just a sentence or two long, just enough to make a memorable impression— and the longer statement of several sentences that more specifically tie to the employer's needs.

Here are some sample branding statements to add to those found on page 19 in Chapter 1. Note that branding statements can be written in the first- or third-person, although third-person is more common:

For me, bringing it in on time and on, or under, budget isn't good enough. I must balance two vital ideas. Every project is customer's project, but every project is our key to continued growth.

—contributed by Professional Career Coach Don Orlando of
The McLean Group

I do what it takes to please all my customers now and in the future. That includes contractors, sub-contractors, and craftspeople. I must stay close to them if the right things are to be in the right place at the right time. My most important value to all those customers is my skill in "banking" time. Having time to do the job right lowers our liability, helps us keep the best people, and makes a lasting impression on the guy who writes the check.

—contributed by Professional Career Coach Don Orlando of
The McLean Group

Organizational maverick who sets aggressive goals, takes decisive action, and confronts issues directly in providing effective leadership to an innovative, entrepreneurial-driven organization while building, achieving and sustaining ROI and profits through a team of talented professionals committed to its vision, values, and mission.

—contributed by Billie R. Sucher, Billie Sucher & Associates,
http://www.billiesucher.com

Here are two branding statements incorporated into the top sections of resumes:

MICHAEL DEWEY
1 Mission Circle ▪ Miami, Florida 33389 ▪ [484] 555-3334 ▪ jobseeker@aol.com

GENERAL MANAGER / COO / TURNAROUND GURU

Thrive on challenges and won't hesitate to make the necessary changes to revamp, rebuild, revitalize, and renew failing companies in the technology manufacturing industry to deliver top-tier products and services, overflowing revenues, and unparalleled profitability.

Technologically savvy General Manager/COO with entrepreneurial spirit and extensive experience in domestic and international manufacturing operations, including P&L responsibility, joint ventures, reorganizations, plant construction, and acquisitions. Successful executive with solid record of leadership achievement and profitable company turnarounds. Relationship-builder with strong people skills—assess their talents, motivate them and get buy-in. Visionary and inspirational leader, bottom-line focused, consistently provide successful results. Creative innovator, awarded U.S. patent for the design of a new electrical enclosure. Additional winning points include:

- ▶ Opportunity development
- ▶ Manufacturing cost reduction
- ▶ Revenue and income growth
- ▶ Company turnarounds
- ▶ Complex decision making
- ▶ Negotiating skills

—contributed by Makini Theresa Harvey, Principal, Career Abundance

---

LARRY R. STALWORTH

192 Bell Road West   jobseeker@msn.com   Home: [781] 555-5555
Sandstone, Massachusetts 02183   Cell: [781] 555-5555

THE RAINMAKER
EXCEPTIONAL LEADERSHIP IN
Strategic Growth / Operations & Facilities Management / Relationship Management / Technology

Creative, innovative **Chief Operations Officer** with a strong passion for delivering business process quality, accelerating profits, and navigating positive relationships.

Senior Operations Executive with a solid track record of building and managing a lucrative business, driving rapid revenue growth, and creating best-in-class operational structures to sustain growth and profitability. Persuasive, visionary, and inspirational leader adept at aligning team and individual effort toward corporate goals.

—contributed by Makini Theresa Harvey, Principal, Career Abundance

Networking Communication Tools

Elevator Speech

By now the elevator speech, also known as an elevator pitch, is a fairly well-known tool, not only for job-seekers but also for organizations and individuals with products and services to sell. Authors of numerous articles on the elevator speech offer speculations on the origin of the term—ranging from the notion that we often run into important people in elevators to the more common explanation that the elevator speech is a clear, concise bit of communication that can be delivered in the time it takes folks to ride from the top to the bottom of a building in an elevator.

Whatever the exact origin, the elevator speech is an exceptionally useful and versatile tool in numerous situations:

➤ Events designed specifically for networking.

➤ The casual networking opportunities we encounter nearly every day—the kids' soccer games, plane flights, waiting in line to buy tickets, and so on.

➤ Cold calls to employers.

➤ Cold calls to absent employers: Rita Fisher of Career Change Resumes suggests that leaving your elevator speech in the form of a voice-mail message virtually guarantees that the employer will call back. Hint: Assuming your speech is sufficiently compelling, call after hours when you know for sure you will get the employer's voice mail.

➤ Opportunities within your own company to talk with those whose positions to which you aspire, let them know you're doing a great job, and position you for promotion.

➤ Job interviews, where the elevator speech can provide the answer to at least two common interview queries: "Tell me about yourself" and "Why should we hire you?"

Wide variation exists among experts as to the ideal length of an elevator speech. Some authors say as few as 15 seconds; others say up to three minutes. There's no reason, however, that you can't employ both short and long versions. Different situations, after all, may well call for diverse approaches. The trick is to make your elevator speech so intriguing that people will want to spend more time talking with you.

At its most basic level, the elevator speech's structure is:

Hi, my name is _____ . I'm in the _____ field, and I'm looking to _____ .

The last blank would be filled in with your current career aspiration, whether it is to stay within your field and move up or move into a different career. You will probably want to embellish the speech with more details. Note also that you may want to incorporate elements of your branding statement into your speech. Test your speech on members of your inner circle. Then, based on the situation, append a request for action. Here are some action items that can be appended in various situations:

In a networking situation:	"What advice do you have for me? Can you suggest any employers I should be contacting?"
Cold-calling an employer:	"When can we set up a meeting to discuss how I can help your company?"
Telephone or e-mail situations:	"May I send you my resume?" (For in-person situations, you should always have resumes handy.)

Your speech should never sound memorized. But you are, after all, talking about yourself, so the material is not hard to remember. Write it out first—outline form is fine—then read it over a few times, and practice saying it without reading or memorizing it. Practice saying it in front of friends and members of your network, too. It's not a big deal if you forget a detail, as long as you remember the main points you want to get across.

Although many elevator speeches are written by sales reps to pitch products and services, the formulas from which the speeches derive can be easily adapted to situations in which the product is you, the job-seeker. This roundup of formulas suggested by experts should provide food for thought for the method that works best for you in planning and outlining your Elevator Speech.

For example, Certified Professional Virtual Assistant Jean Hanson, in an article at *www.ezinearticles.com* ("Your Elevator Speech—Have You Updated Yours Recently?"), suggests this formula:

1. Who am I? (introduce yourself)

2. What business am I in?

3. What group of people do I service? (be specific—do you have a niche?)

4. What is my USP (Unique Selling Proposition)? What makes me different from the competition?

5. What benefits do my customers derive from my services?

Here's how it could be adapted for a job-seeker:

1. Who am I? (introduce yourself)—No change.

2. What business am I in?—What field or industry am I in?

3. What group of people do I service? (be specific—do you have a niche?)—What position am I in? In what capacity do I serve?

4. What is my USP (Unique Selling Proposition)? What makes me different from the competition?—No change.

5. What benefits do my customers derive from my services?—What benefits can employers derive from skills, based on my proven accomplishments?

Hanson says that, in a selling situation, the listener's unspoken question is "Why should I do business with you?" Similarly, in a job-hunting situation, the listener's tacit question may be "Why should I (or any employer) hire you?"

The chart on page 65 shows a variation on Hanson's formula adapted from Randy W. Dipner of Meeting the Challenge, Inc. (left column), along with an illustration (right column) of how it can be adapted for a job-seeker.

Tony Jeary, author of *Life Is a Series of Presentations*, offers this elevator speech formula (*http://www.mrpresentation.com/newsletters.cfm?action=newsletters_details&newsletterID=794*):

1. Define your audience universe.

2. Define your content or subject matter.

3. Define your objective.

4. Define your desired image or style.

5. Define your key message.

Author, speaker, and consultant Marisa D'Vari suggests starting the elevator speech process by writing down three key points about your product (you, in this case) and discussing how these points will benefit the listener.

Finally, the business school at Pepperdine University (in an article at *bschool.pepperdine.edu/career/content/elevatorspeech.pdf*) suggests knowing your audience and knowing yourself, including

——— Dipner's Formula ———	——— Job-Seeker Variation ———
List target customers. Group them and ultimately define the customer.	List target employers. Group them and ultimately define the employer.
Define the need or opportunity. That is, what critical issue does the customer face? Define the need or opportunity. That is, what critical issue does the customer face?	What need or issue does the employer face?
Name the product or service or concept.	Introduce yourself.
Place the product, service, or concept into a generally understood category.	Identify yourself in terms of a job function or contribution. What do you do?
List the benefits—not the features—of the product, service, or concept provides to the customer. Group or prioritize the benefits to identify the single benefit that is the most compelling reason for the customer to buy the product, service, or concept. To the maximum extent possible, the benefit should be quantified.	List the benefits—not the features—that you provide to the employer. Group or prioritize the benefits to identify the single benefit that is the most compelling reason for the employer to hire you. To the maximum extent possible, the benefit should be quantified.
Develop a statement of the primary differentiation of the product, service, or concept. The differentiation is the single most important thing that sets your product, service, or concept apart from the competition.	Develop a statement of the primary differentiation of yourself. The differentiation is the single most important thing that sets you apart from the competition.

key strengths, adjectives that describe you, a description of what you are trying to let others know about you, and a statement of your interest in the company or industry the person represents. Armed with that knowledge, the job-seeker can then outline the elevator speech using these questions:

1. Who am I?
2. What do I offer?
3. What problem is solved?
4. What are the main contributions I can make?
5. What should the listener do as a result of hearing this?

Career coach Don Orlando, who doesn't like the term "elevator speech" (people neither want to give speeches nor conduct business in elevators), believes candidates should develop statements about the benefits they bring to employers, and how they will add to an employer's bank account.

You'll notice that one thing nearly all the experts have in common is their espousal of the importance of stressing your benefit to the listener and touching on how you're distinct from the competition. This principle encompasses many names—Unique Selling Proposition, value proposition, benefit statement, competitive advantage, deliverables, differentiation—but the bottom line is the same: What can you bring to the employer, and how can you do it better than anyone else?

Some sample elevator speeches are shown on the following pages.

Hi, I'm Joe Fredericks. I'm a versatile project/program management executive with 15-plus years of leadership and business management expertise gained from positions of increasing responsibility in both the U.S. Navy and the private sector. I recently reduced my employer's costs by 35 percent through leading a hardware and software redesign of the access control system, which also resulted in improved performance, increased reliability, and additional features.

■■■

I'm Valerie Obermarle, a creative outside-the-box thinker who approaches strategic development with innovative vision, high ethical standards, unsurpassed work ethic, and ability to communicate effectively across management levels and disciplines to build highly effective cross-functional teams.

■■■

I'm Janet Singleton. I like to think of myself as an accomplished organizational-development professional with more than a decade of experience in project leadership, needs assessment/definition, resource identification, and process/change facilitation. I took the initiative to improve medical benefits and develop systems for handling benefits-enrollment data after being recruited initially to set up an HR department for a company that has grown from eight to 25 employees.

■■■

Hello, I'm Cynthia Bee. I'm a licensed industrial engineering professional with eight years of experience in medical diagnostic manufacturing and personal products manufacturing and additional five years of experience in logistics.

■■■

Hi, Jack Burnham here. As a diligent, quantitatively skilled achiever, I'm equipped, through my master's-level training in taxation, to play a key role in your organization's tax research, analysis, and planning. I also have expertise in interpreting tax code, regulations, revenue rulings, and case law, as well as preparing tax returns for corporations, partnerships, individuals, estates, and trusts.

■■■

Hello, my name in Andy Fellows. I'm an entrepreneurial marketing professional with more than 15 years of uncompromising accomplishments in multiple facets of building, marketing, and operating highly successful academic product sales businesses. I attained a 170-percent increase in 12 months by expanding the academic market for software through direct sales to universities worldwide, channel partners, and publishers, as well as by implementing solid prospecting strategies to cultivate new business opportunities and broaden the customer base.

■■■

Hello, I am Ed Kendall. As an international marketing consultant, I realized more than a 50 percent increase in overall profitability and $500,000 in new revenue through directing Euro conversion in four countries while simultaneously improving client relationships and controlling project costs.

■■■

Hi, I'm Sandra Dinkleman. You might be interested in knowing that I recently stabilized a highly chaotic operational and customer-service situation by taking control and implementing new heightened customer-service standards and collaborating with staff members to improve the company image and boost staff morale.

■■■

I've been a driver of process improvement and a proponent of organizational change. Expertise in software and IT infrastructure has enabled me to build more effective technology teams and save costs for several organizations, including ASI and the University of Phoenix. My goal is to use my technical expertise and managerial talent in a broader operational leadership role.

—contributed by Karen P. Katz, M.Ed., Credentialed Career Manager,
www.CareerAcceleration.net

Brief Networking Resume

In networking situations, you need to have a resume ready to give your contacts, but it should be a pared-down, one-page networking resume (also called an Executive Summary) so your new contacts can quickly grasp your background.

The sample networking resume shown on page 68 can be supplemented at a later stage in the job search by the Leadership Profile on pages 89–90.

Networking/Branding/Resume Highlights Cards

Networking business cards, which have the look and feel of a traditional business card, give you the opportunity to provide critical career and contact information with people you meet in social and professional situations.

Networking cards are the same size and shape of business cards (3 1/2 inches wide and 2 inches high) and contain key contact information like business cards, but instead of listing a company and job title, a networking card focuses on a branding statement or unique selling proposition. Be sure to include all your pertinent contact information, including your name, phone number, e-mail address, and postal mail address; and Website address, cell phone, and fax numbers.

Consider taking your networking card a step further by turning your networking card into a resume highlights card listing your key qualifications (or accomplishments summary) on the card's reverse side—giving you a mini-resume to distribute when carrying your regular resume is not feasible. Integrate a branded appearance and content.

When designing your networking cards, remember to keep the design and layout clean and simple, use conventional fonts, font sizes of 10 to 11 points, and conservative ink and paper colors.

You can get your networking cards printed at a local print shop, at numerous sites on the Web, or even print them yourself using special business-card stock with 10 cards on an 8 1/2 × 11 inch sheet, using a template that most word-processing programs supply. The card stock comes in a wide variety of designs; consider buying a matching set of letterhead, envelopes, and business-card stock to maintain the branded consistency of your printed communications. Then, on your computer, in MS Word:

1. Go to the "Tools" menu from the top row.

2. Choose "Envelopes and Labels" from the "Tools" menu.

3. Under "Options," find the name of the paper manufacturer (for example, Avery) and then find the correct product number in the lower left corner.

4. Type in the information you want on your card in the text box and click on "New Document."

5. You can then format the cards exactly as you want them to print.

6. Print the final versions.

Once your cards are printed, be sure to purchase a business-card holder to protect your cards and keep them clean and crisp. Take them *everywhere* you go—to networking events, of course, as well as professional meetings, social gatherings, parties, weddings, and anywhere else you

MONICA B. SHAPIRO

ORGANIZATION DEVELOPMENT PROFESSIONAL | CERTIFIED EXECUTIVE COACH | ENTREPRENEUR

QUALIFICATIONS SUMMARY

- Strong, innovative leader with master's-level qualifications in Organizational Change and Leadership, along with 20+ years of experience and demonstrated expertise in building productive relationships with both executive team and support staff to increase organizational success.
- Co-author, *Coaching as a Postmodern Relationship, The Executive Coach*, Fall 1998.

CORE COMPETENCIES

Executive Coaching | Change Management | Leadership Development | Culture Change | Team Building
Strategic Initiatives

PROFESSIONAL EXPERIENCE

STAFF EDUCATOR, Summit County Health System, Hudson, OH, 2007 to present
- Develop and deliver educational programs to enhance leadership skills.
- Provide consultation to leaders regarding program design and content.
- Consult with executives to improve their facilitation skills.

PROGRAM DEVELOPER, Summit County Department of Human Services/Board of Vocational Education, Hudson, OH, 2004 to 2006
- Developed prominent County Committee to secure operational funding.
- Managed programs and develop leadership for literacy initiative.

LEADERSHIP COACH AND CONSULTANT, Life Leaders, Inc., Copley, OH, 2002 to 2004
- Facilitated controversial budget-commission conference.
- Provided innovative program development for training organization and leadership development for owners of start-up business.

MANAGER, CORPORATE EDUCATION AND DEVELOPMENT, Ohio State Automobile Association, AAA, Northfield, OH, 2000 to 2001
- Managed staff of 15 to provide functional and leadership training to 6,000-employee organization.
- Developed cross-functional teams charged with improving workplace effectiveness and customer service for major department. *(See also Leadership Profile.)*

LEADERSHIP COACH AND CONSULTANT, Bloomfield & Cannon, Northfield, OH, 1995 to 2000
- Developed dysfunctional senior team into dynamic leadership team. *(See also Leadership Profile.)*

CO-FOUNDER/OWNER, Alphonso Remodeling, Inc., Sagamore Hills, OH, 1981 to 1993
- Increased sales from $20,000 to $1.2 million in five years.
- Managed up to 20 remodeling projects annually to timely, successful completion.

EDUCATION, CERTIFICATION, AND PROFESSIONAL DEVELOPMENT

Master of Management/Organizational Change and Leadership
George Mason University, Fairfax, VA

Bachelor of Arts in Sociology
Bowling Green State University, Bowling Green, OH

Certified Executive Coach
Executive School of Psychology

Appreciative Inquiry Approach to Design
Experienced-Based Learning, National Training Labs

Integral Coaching Principles, Applied Innovations

PROFESSIONAL AFFILIATIONS

- National Organization Development Network, Ohio OD Learning Community,
- American Society for Training and Development, The Learning Community

- Member Editing Team, Ohio Organization Development Journal, *Best Practices in Internal OD*
- Chair, OD Special Interest Group for Ohio American Society for Training and Development

62 Bowling Green Drive, Hudson, OH 44236 ● Home: 330-555-9027 ● E-mail: jobseeker@snet.net

may run into potential contacts—everywhere. You should keep copies of your resume handy as well, but there are obviously numerous times where a resume would simply be too awkward to handle.

Following are examples of resume highlights cards:

Looking to bring creative marketing skills,
marketing education, and experience
and play key role on team that propels the
organization's success.

Fisher Stevens Johnson

1873 Appleyard Court	FSJohnson@yahoo.com
Winter Park, FL 32790	www.stetson.edu/~fsjohnso/
	(407) 555-2892

**Award-winning, buzz-producing publicist
with 5+ years PR experience wants to help
take your product to the next level.**

John S. Randall

3929 NE 119th St.	john@johnsrandall.com
Maitland, FL 32794	www.johnsrandall.com/
	Telephone: 407-555-1212

Michelle B. Armay

*Top-grossing salesperson five years running.
Give me your best or worst territory—and I'll produce
superior sales results.*

108 Hilltop Way	P: 415-555-2891
Redwood City, CA 9406	F: 415-555-1222
topgun@xmail.com	C: 415-555-1181

Qualifications Summary

- ➤ Dedicated professional with proven record
- ➤ Results-driven achiever and team-leader
- ➤ Effective and persuasive communicator
- ➤ Unsurpassed interpersonal skills
- ➤ Computer proficient in Word, Excel, Outlook, Access, PowerPoint

The Website of the vendor Thumbnail Resume also offers a good overview of how a networking or resume highlights card can look:

www.thumbnailresume.com/CardCreation/cardsamplesa.html

Communication Tools for the Active, Pre-interview Job-Search Phase
Cover Letter

If you were to claim that employers do not read cover letters, you would be 1/3 correct. Studies show that about 66 percent of hiring decision-makers read cover letters and consider them important in the process of selecting interview candidates. To some decision-makers, cover letters are extremely important, especially at executive levels, because they show how well you express yourself. Certainly employers expect a higher standard of writing and sophistication in executive cover letters than in those of candidates at lower levels.

Cover letters are important for other reasons, too. Though this book promotes the idea of sharply focused resumes that instantly tell the reader the candidate's job target, a cover letter is useful for expanding on the type of position you seek—and describing, in detail, exactly how you are qualified for that position.

In ways your resume may not, a cover letter highlights the aspects of your background that are most useful to the prospective employer. You will also win points for your due diligence in knowing exactly what those aspects are.

Your letter can explain things that your resume probably doesn't—such as gaps in your employment history, relocation, reentry into the job market after a period of entrepreneurship, or a career change. A cover letter can explain these circumstances in a positive way. You can emphasize, in a cover letter, your willingness to travel or relocate. Following are some passages illustrating some of these uses:

Planned relocation:

> I plan to return to North America upon finding the right job "fit" and am convinced that a firm such as yours represents a fit that is productive for both of us.

Employment gap:

> Following the abrupt closure of my former employer's business, I have taken a year to pursue some outside interests and am now eager to bring my talents to a firm like [name of firm] in the advertised position.

Career change:

> Though I've enjoyed progressive advancement in the risk-management field, I have realized that the investments area is where I can make the greatest impact.

Finally, a cover letter is a window into your personality. A good cover letter can suggest to an employer, "I'd like to interview this person; she sounds like someone I'd like to get to know better. This go-getter seems like just the kind of dynamic executive this organization needs."

Three kinds of cover letters are common, each corresponding to a different method of job-hunting. Most successful candidates will find that they do not employ any one method or use any one kind of cover letter, but rather a combination. To understand the three kinds of cover letters, let's look at these three types of job searches.

As we've seen earlier in this chapter, few vacancies are advertised, especially at the executive level. The main avenue for informing the public about these openings is through job postings on the Internet and want ads in newspapers, trade magazines, and other publications.

The first kind of cover letter is the *invited letter,* which is generally a response to an Internet job posting or want ad.

The invited cover letter enables you to speak to the requirements of the job posting. You can offer the employer the requirements sought because you *know* the requirements sought; they're all spelled out in the ad.

An example of an invited cover letter targetting the following job posting is shown on page 72.

With a reputation for innovation and creativity, this leading Australian charter airline, part of a major Australian Tour Group, has won numerous excellence awards and constantly challenges industry norms regarding product diversity and customer service. Having developed a ground-breaking customer proposition, they are seeking a dynamic, proactive and inspirational operations manager to bring a fresh perspective and revolutionise their approach to the delivery of all "below the wing" customer-facing operations. As Head of Ground Operations reporting to the Board, the brief is to challenge existing operational processes and procedures, drawing on the technical knowledge of your 100-strong team to harvest creative solutions and deliver improved, customer-centred operational performance. With carte blanche to review organisational structure and crucial 3rd-party supplier relationships, you will work with senior colleagues across Sales & Marketing, Procurement and Customer Service to deliver a "Great Experience—First and Always," high-quality customer experience.

Candidates must have at least 5 years of operational management experience, and a track record of successful organisational and cultural change delivery gained in a customer-focused industry, ideally involving significant outsourced supplier partnerships and exposure to a regulatory authority. A highly commercial and charismatic leader, able to enthuse and motivate large teams, you must display excellent relationship building skills at all levels, along with first class communication and influencing skills and a real appetite for change.

More examples of invited cover letters in response to Internet job postings can be found on pages 208, 221, 223, 226, and 234. Chapter 6 includes invited letters along with the job postings the letters responded to.

Because the vast majority of the market is "closed," you can't find out about vacancies unless you, network, dig deep, and mount a highly targeted campaign with "uninvited" letters and resumes.

The uninvited cover letter enables you to take a proactive approach to job-hunting instead of the reactive approach, in which you merely answer job postings. This cold-contacting can be an effective tool for uncovering hidden jobs where supposedly no openings exist. Your letter can make such an impression that you'll be remembered when a vacancy opens up. At the very least, you may obtain an interview in which the employer can refer you to others in the field who might be interested in you.

An example of an uninvited cover letter contributed by Professional Career Coach Don Orlando of The McLean Group is shown on page 73.

More examples of uninvited cover letters can be found on pages 199 and 211.

The third kind of cover letter is a very close cousin to the uninvited letter (but can also be used in invited situations). This letter, too, is usually uninvited but it has an edge. It prominently displays the name of a person your addressee knows. This letter, called a *referral* letter, is the product of networking, which is, as we've seen, critically important at the executive level.

Referral letters can come about from a variety of sources. You might talk with someone at a meeting of a professional association in your field who will tell you of an opening she knows of. An acquaintance at a party might tell you of someone he knows whose company could use an executive with your experience. A friend might tell you about a job she saw through her company's internal job-posting.

Jason Albright

162 Pine Tree Trail • Allentown, PA 18102

Daytime Phone: 610-555-0871 • E-mail: jobseeker@comcast.net

March 9, 2008

Alex Ridge
OZJET Airlines
15 Hewitt Way,
Tullamarine VIC 3043

Dear Mr. Ridge:

Your company's commitment to recruiting the "best" candidates for your clients is the reason for your first-rate reputation. I am convinced that I can help you in your search for the position of Head of Ground Operations. I am confident that my innovation, creativity, and fresh perspective are an excellent match for the client's need for someone who can revolutionize the airline's approach to delivering all "below the wing" customer-facing operations. Here's how I could contribute:

As a 12-year veteran of the travel industry, I offer the dynamic, operations-oriented leadership that ensures efficiency, planning-oriented project management that enhances profitability, and people-oriented guidance that yields productivity. I've done all that and much more in my previous positions, where I consistently scrutinized operations procedures with an eye toward greater quality and customer service.

My travel-industry operations experience has equipped me well to deliver customer-centered operational performance. I also offer the expertise to set up the systems that keep an operation running smoothly. I am a highly focused, proactive problem-solver who keeps operations moving forward like well-oiled machines.

I offer an excellent reputation for maximizing operational efficiency that speaks for itself. For example, in my most recent position, I designed and implemented a complete operational reorganization. My skills also include negotiating optimal, cost-effective contracts with third-party vendors. The exceptional relationship-building skills I cultivated in the investments industry bolsters my qualifications.

I have consistently proven my ability to mold a diverse team to form cohesive plans and successfully complete projects. I train team members so that that they barely flutter an eyelid when a crisis arises—and they love their jobs. I have frequently been called upon to apply my people skills to conceptualizing innovative solutions to problems. When a travel experience develops a hiccup, I excel at calling on external resources to help resolve the issue so that the team can then smooth the client's ruffled feathers. Given the inevitability of change for a dynamic airline with a ground-breaking customer proposition, my motto is, "Change is required; pain is optional." My job is to minimize the pain.

I would like to be considered for the Head of Ground Operations position. I am completely on board with your client's commitment to delivering a "Great Experience—First and Always," high-quality customer experience. I am an Australian citizen and very willing to relocate. I will contact you soon to arrange for an interview. Should you require any additional information, I can be reached using the contact information listed atop this letter.

Sincerely,

Jason Albright

Carla L. Johnson

4140 Carter Lane Kansas City, Missouri 64101 ✉jobseeker@knology.net ☎ 816.555.5555 – 816.555.6666

Tuesday, 07 March, 2006

Mr. John Markwell
President and CEO
ExpressJet Corporation
1200 Stateline Highway
Suite 100
Delray Beach, Florida 33000

Toward a mutually satisfying ROI

Dear Mr. John Markwell:

Let me put the bottom line right at the top: my search for companies who share my passion for success put ExpressJet at the top of my list. Here's why: as the CEO of an aggressively successful company, I took it as job number one to replicate my passion in every member of my team. And since nobody told me it couldn't be done, I made it happen.

Now that my company has been sold to a public entity, I want that dream to come true again, this time in a partnership with ExpressJet. But I would never make such a bold suggestion if I couldn't offer a strong return on investment for both of us.

For now, I want to concentrate on what years of experience have equipped me to offer you, your team, and your customers. What I do isn't magic; this professional code guides me:

- ❑ Being passionate about my business isn't good enough. I must instill systemic passion, helping every team member trace his or her daily efforts to our profitability. In short, I must align every team member's personal goals with our corporate aims.

- ❑ Being productive isn't good enough. I must have every employee, every vendor, every customer, see his or her personal growth tied to ExpressJet's corporate growth.

- ❑ Being compassionate isn't good enough. What I must deliver is courageous compassion. That irresistible force for good comes from my relentless search for excellence in others so I can reward them publicly.

- ❑ Being sales driven isn't good enough. I want our customers to see us as their success partner, believing using ExpressJet's per-seat, on-demand services as their *own* good idea.

Proof of that kind of performance is too important to be diluted by the usual résumé format. So I've included a leadership addendum on the next page. I chose those examples of my passion in action because I am confident they are transferable to your industry.

In the end, however, words on paper are no substitute for people speaking with people. Because your company has the culture in which I thrive, I would like to explore how I might serve the ExpressJet team. May I call in a few days to get on your calendar for that purpose?

Sincerely,

Carla L. Johnson

Encl.: Leadership addendum

The value of the referral letter is in its name-dropping. Grabbing the attention of the prospective employer by mentioning a name you both know in the first line of the letter can give you a significant advantage. Some variations on the referral letter include approaches like these:

"John Ross of Technology Unlimited suggested you might have openings for systems analysts."

■

"I met with Mary Jones last week, and she mentioned that you might have need for someone with a background in executive-level marketing."

The referral letter's advantage is not only in catching the reader's attention with a name but in driving the likelihood of an interview—out of courtesy to the referrer.

A sample referral cover letter is shown on page 75.

You'll see considerable variation among the cover-letter samples in this book, but the most basic structure for a cover letter is the following:

First Paragraph: Your first paragraph must spark the reader's interest, provide information about the value you will add to the employer's organization, and distinguish you from other candidates. Do not waste the opening paragraph of your cover letter by using such clichés as "Enclosed please find my resume," "Please accept the attached resume for your advertised opening," or "As you can see on my resume enclosed herewith...." Employers can see that your resume is enclosed or attached; they don't need you to tell them. Such trite phrases just waste precious space.

Focus on your Unique Selling Proposition (USP)—the one thing that distinguishes you from all the other candidates—and identify two or three benefits you can offer the employer.

Weak opening paragraph: I am writing to apply for the sales director position you have posted on your company Website.

Better opening paragraph: I have increased the size and sales levels of my client base in every position I have held, which in turn has increased my employers' revenues and profits. I want to bring this same success to the senior account position you have posted on your Website.

Second Paragraph: Your next paragraph should expand on your professional and/or academic qualifications. Provide examples that illustrate your ability to provide the benefits you mention in the first paragraph. Stress measurable accomplishments and achievements. Make clear connections between the job's requirements and your qualifications. If responding to a job posting or ad, be sure to tailor this paragraph to the needs described.

Third Paragraph: Describe your fit with the company and position. This is the paragraph in which your due diligence can pay off. You can portray yourself as an insider by demonstrating your knowledge of the organization. This is the ideal paragraph in which to relate yourself to the company's mission or mention a news item you've seen or trends you've noted involving the organization; for example: "Over the last two years I have followed the unfolding events at Guffman Enterprises with great interest as your firm moved into financial and broadband services."

Fourth Paragraph: The final paragraph of your cover letter must be proactive—and request action. This proactive approach is especially important at the executive level. You must ask for the job interview (or a meeting) in this paragraph. Express confidence that you are a perfect fit for the job. Put the employer on notice that you plan to follow up within a specified time. Don't depend on the employer to take action. It is imperative that you follow up. You will greatly increase your chances of getting interviews if you contact the employer after writing instead of sitting back and waiting for a call.

JAY REHAYEM-SMYRNOS

1004 Elm Hills Rd. • Boston, MA 02122-3507 • Phone: 617-555-7635 • E-mail: jobseeker@aol.com

March 15, 2008

Peter Maxwell
The Westin Copley Place, Boston
10 Huntington Avenue
Boston, Massachusetts 02116

Dear Mr. Maxwell:

Gene Deerfield suggested I contact you. My exceptionally strong education and background in hospitality management, along with my commitment to excellence and total customer satisfaction, align extremely well an Executive Director of Food and Beverage position at The Westin Copley Place. As Assistant Food and Beverage and Banqueting Director at a 953-room Boston hotel with 250 people in the Food and Beverage department, I am ready for the move into a director position. These key characteristics should be of particular interest to you:

- **Profit-Minded Leadership** in a highly unionized setting. I succeeded in reestablishing a positive working environment after a 15-day strike last year. I offer a comprehensive understanding of HR requirements, as well as skills in de-escalating and resolving conflicts.

- **Creativity** and strong aptitude for presentation and merchandising. I know how to achieve excellence and maintain competitiveness in a challenging marketplace.

- **Banqueting Experience**, given that I currently oversee the banqueting department of a hotel in one of Boston's largest in-hotel conference centers.

My operational skills range from reducing payroll costs to designing menus and identifying trends. I am known for my positive attitude and for providing service beyond expectations. Building a team environment and motivating the team to meet goals are also strengths.

As a great admirer of Westin Hotels, I would like to be considered for this position in which I know I can make a significant contribution. I will contact you soon to arrange for an interview. Should you require any additional information, you can contact me using the information at left.

Very truly yours,

Jay Rehayem-Smyrnos

Weak closing paragraph: I hope you will review my resume and consider me for the position. I look forward to hearing from you soon.

Better closing paragraph: I am eager to help advance [name of company]'s success, and I am convinced that we should arrange a time to meet. I will call your office in the next week to schedule an appointment.

Effective cover letters result from following a few guidelines:

➤ Don't send your resume without a cover letter. You don't know which 2/3 of recipients aren't reading cover letters, so it's always best to err on the side of including a cover letter rather than omitting it. Remember that, among 2/3 of employers, cover letters are expected and important.

➤ Address your letter to a named individual. Cover letters ideally should be addressed to a specific person, and with the uninvited letter this advice is especially true. If you want to get an interview and hence a job, you can forget about using such salutations as "Dear Sir or Madam," "Dear Human Resources Director," or "To Whom it May Concern." Those salutations tell the employer that you were not concerned enough to find out who it concerned. This personal touch is especially important at the executive level. Finding out the name of your intended recipient is just another part of the due diligence you should perform.

➤ Don't use a sexist salutation, such as "Dear Sir" or "Gentlemen." This piece of advice should go without saying, but mature executives probably remember a time when these salutations were standard. In fact, I still get them, especially from letter-writers from outside the United States—and I bristle when I receive them.

➤ Send an original letter to each employer. Given that a major function of the cover letter is to go beyond the resume in tailoring your qualifications to specific jobs, a boilerplate cover letter sent to multiple employers is pointless. That's not to say your letter can't have some boilerplate elements; just be sure to customize the bulk of the letter to its recipient.

➤ Don't send a cover letter that contains any typos, misspellings, incorrect grammar, or poor punctuation. As you'll see in Chapter 4, executives are far from immune to these unfortunate errors.

➤ Use simple language and uncomplicated sentence structure. Ruthlessly eliminate all unnecessary words. Follow the journalist's credo: Write tight!

➤ Speak to the requirements of the job, especially when responding to a job posting. The specifics of your cover letter should be tied as closely as possible to the actual wording of the job posting or ad to which you're responding. Using the employer's words is a plus rather than a minus. In his book, *Don't Send a Resume*, Jeffrey Fox calls the best letters written in response to want ads "Boomerang letters" because they "fly the ad words—the copy—back to the writer of the ad." In employing what Fox calls "a compelling sales technique," he advises letter writers to "flatter the person who wrote the ad with your response letter. Echo the author's words and intent. Your letter should be a mirror of the ad." Fox notes that when the recipient reads such a letter, the thought process is: "This person seems to fit the description. This person gets it."

A particularly effective way to deploy the specifics of a want ad to your advantage is to use a two-column format in which you quote in the left-hand column specific qualifications that come right from the employer's want ad and in the right-hand column, your attributes that meet those qualifications. The two-column format is extremely effective when you possess all the qualifications for a job, but it can even sell you when you lack one or more qualification. The format so clearly demonstrates that you are qualified in so many areas that the employer may be willing to overlook the areas in which you lack the exact qualifications. You can find a sample two-column letter on page 168.

➤ Consider special attention-getting formats. One of the challenges of getting an employer to pay attention to your cover letter is that letters tend to look uninviting, with large expanses of black type, broken up only by paragraphs. You can employ some reader-friendly formats (in addition to the two-column letter):

Bullets: Bullet points can break up the text of your cover letter and draw the reader's eye to your most compelling selling points. Be sure you don't re-hash your resume's bullet points. And unlike bullet points on a resume, those on a cover letter should either be in complete sentences (instead of clipped, "telegraphed" resume language) or should complete the sentence that leads into the bulleted list.

See an example of a bulleted cover-letter section on pages 75, 123, 199, and 226.

Word bullets: Word bullets (which can be used with regular bullets) also break up the text and are excellent for spotlighting words or phrases from the ad or job posting you're responding to. By pulling these words out of the ad, you can focus your letter sharply on how you meet the requirements that relate to those words.

See an example of a letter that uses word bullets on page 208.

Testimonial-format letter: A testimonial format for a cover letter provides a narrow left column in which you can place testimonials about your performance, especially those that support the content of your letter. This type of cover letter is designed to match a similarly formatted resume that also provides a space for testimonials.

Postscript: Adding a P.S.—especially one that's handwritten—to your cover letter is a technique that has been known to grab employers' attention. Ideally, your postscript should encapsulate your Unique Selling Proposition—the one quality that you feel will inspire employers to hire you above all other candidates.

➤ Keep your letter brief. Never, never exceed one page, and it's best to keep the letter well under a full page. Each paragraph should have no more than three sentences. In fact, in this time-starved age, hiring decision-makers are favoring shorter cover letters. You'll see exceptions to the brevity rule among this book's samples—executives sometimes need to be more detailed—but *when in doubt, leave it out.*

➤ Tell the employer how you can meet company needs. In his book, *No Parachute Required*, Jeffrey Gunhus writes, "The purpose of a cover letter is to explain how you (the candidate) will benefit me (the company)." Your letter should tell, very specifically, how you will meet the employer's needs, solve the employer's problems, or otherwise benefit the hiring company.

➤ Distinguish your cover letter from those of other job-seekers by quantifying and giving examples that amplify and prove the claims you make in your letter. Don't just offer unsubstantiated value judgments about yourself; use concrete examples to demonstrate your claims about yourself. Example:

> **I demonstrated my strategic ability when I successfully developed a direct corporate sales program and a corporate affinity program for ToyVillage.com, increasing sales 15 percent over the previous year.**

➤ Answer the question that the employer will be asking while reading your letter: "Why should I hire this person?" Answer with your Unique Selling Proposition.

➤ Don't rehash your resume. You can use your cover letter to highlight the aspects of your resume that are relevant to the position, but you're wasting precious space—and the prospective employer's time—if you simply repeat your resume.

➤ Avoid negativity. There's nothing to be gained by bringing up negative situations that have prompted you to leave your current job, pointing out shortcomings in your qualifications, or mentioning any other negatives that could get you screened out.

➤ Be sure the prospective employer can reach you. Leave no stone unturned in enabling the employer to contact you. Your resume contains your contact information, and, if you've followed this chapter's advice, your cover letter uses the same letterhead as your resume and thus also carries your contact information—in case the documents get separated. It also never hurts to repeat your contact information in the last paragraph of your letter, preferably a daytime phone number at which the employer can most easily reach you. And then be sure you can be reached there! Ensure your voice-mail or answering-machine greeting sounds professional—not, for example, your 3-year-old singing a cute song. Return calls from employers and recruiters promptly.

➤ If you are sending resumes and cover letters by postal mail, don't forget to personally sign your letters, preferably in blue ink.

E-mail Content/Cover Letter

An e-mail message that accompanies your resume is generally some version of your cover letter. It may be your full cover letter in the body of an e-mail message, but ideally it will be a shorter, more concise version—two to three paragraphs and no more than 150 words. The idea is that your cover letter should not be any longer than one screen in length (you may still wish to include the full version as an attachment). Here are some tips from Dr. Randall S. Hansen, in an article on Quintessential Careers (*www.quintcareers.com/email_cover_letters.html*), for making the most of an e-mailed cover letter:

➤ Don't waste your subject line. Don't ever leave the subject line of your e-mail blank (it will be more likely to go into the recipient's junk folder if you do), but don't waste it by just inserting the job number. Instead, use the subject line to entice the reader into your cover letter. For example, for a director of marketing position, your subject line could say: "Ready to Deliver ROI as Your Next Director of Marketing."

➤ Stick with plain styling (ASCII text). Write your cover letter on your favorite word processor, but strip away all formatting once you've completed editing it by saving the file as "plain text." Because some e-mail packages allow you to manipulate font style, color, and size, be sure your e-mail is also being sent in plain text—black font, normal size and typeface (10 point; Arial, Helvetica, Times Roman), on a white background.

➤ Check your line length. Make sure your lines are no more than 60 characters in length. Some e-mail packages automatically do word wrap for you (much like word-processing software), but you should check. You don't want your cover letter to arrive fragmented on multiple lines.

➤ Always use standard cover-letter protocol. Don't abandon standard business letter writing guidelines. Thus, make sure to include a salutation ("Dear Ms. Smith") and a standard closing (such as "Sincerely"). Leave blank lines between paragraphs. And avoid emoticons, abbreviations, wild colors, and other cool techniques and shortcuts used in everyday e-mails.

➤ Never hit "Send" without thoroughly spell checking and proofreading your e-mail letter. Don't just rely on your e-mail software's spellchecker. Take the time to really proofread it. A simple typo could be the downfall of a brilliant cover letter. Avoid all mistakes.

➤ Be sure to test your message before sending it to the company. Even if you're sure your letter is perfect, send it to a friend or another one of your e-mail accounts first and check for the content and style one more time.

Here's a sample e-mail cover letter:

Date: Tues, 15 May 2007 19:52:59 -0700 (EDT)
From: kevin lee smith [jobseeker@yahoo.com]
Subject: Seasoned Sales Rep Ideal for Regional Sales Manager (mtt-01/3439)
To: scott.hent@marriott.com
Content-Type: text/plain; charset=us-ascii

Dear Mr. Hent,

Having broken sales records and exceeded sales quotas in all my previous positions, I am the ideal candidate for the regional sales manager position at Marriott Vacation Club International.

As the leading sales representative for Disney Vacation Club, I developed key sales material, trained new sales reps, and reinvented the way club memberships are sold. My team's revenue was more than double the average for the entire operation.

The vacation club industry is a dynamic and growing industry, and I am convinced I can drive Marriott's growth and dominant position in the industry.

We should meet to discuss the position. I will contact you in the next 10 days to arrange an interview. Should you have any questions before that time, please feel free to call me at 904-555-2341 or e-mail me. Thank you for your time and consideration.

Cordially,

Kevin Lee Smith

Proposal to Create Job/Position by Describing How You Can Solve Problems/Meet Needs

A job proposal, usually in letter form, goes a step beyond an uninvited cover letter by proposing that an employer create a job that does not currently exist. Crafting such a proposal requires exceptional knowledge of an organization's problems and needs or of industry trends that may affect organizations across a sector. You may cultivate this kind of insider knowledge through research, through reading the business press and trade publications, or through strong awareness of and expertise in your field. It's also possible to attain the information you need through an interview with the employer. If you have been on an interview and sense that the employer has objections to hiring you—or has actually rejected you—you may be able to salvage your opportunity with that employer by using what you learned in the interview to explain how you can solve problems and meet needs. Employers often appreciate the outside-the-box thinking, time, effort, and research that go into such a proposal; certainly the passion demonstrated by researching a proposal letter is hard for employers to ignore. They are often willing to meet with you to hear more about your ideas.

Demonstrate in your proposal how you have applied your specific skills to solve a similar problem or meet a similar need in the past. Quantify your results and emphasize your value proposition. Be sure to tailor your resume to align with the thrust of your proposal's content.

Sample job-proposal letters are shown on pages 80 and 81.

Jason Albright

162 Pine Tree Trail • Allentown, PA 18102

Daytime Phone: 610-555-0871 • E-mail: jobseeker@comcast.net

Jan. 23, 2008

Dominick Devlin
World Access, Inc.
2805 North Parham Road
Richmond, VA 23294

Dear Mr. Devlin:

As a five-year veteran of the travel industry, I am well aware that constant change, global expansion, and rapid growth have become hallmarks of the travel field. The breakneck pace and need for a team member who can juggle multiple complex activities has inspired many firms to create project-manager positions. I would like to meet with you to discuss the contribution I can make as just such a value-added member of your team.

As you well know, our turbulent world and unexpected global events – 9/11, tsunamis, SARS and other highly feared diseases, cultural and political sensitivities, and sustainability – cause constant shifts in the international travel scene. In response, I offer the unique combination of planning-oriented project management that enhances profitability, operations-oriented leadership that ensures efficiency, and people-oriented guidance that yields productivity. I've done all that and much more in my previous positions, where I consistently scrutinized operations procedures with an eye toward greater quality and service.

My travel-industry project experience has equipped me well to deliver upscale travel/tour experiences to travelers with diverse interests and complex schedules while handling head-spinning logistical details and minimizing risk. The tools and techniques I have developed from this experience apply directly to the skills World Access needs – someone who can propose, develop, and execute ongoing project administration. I also offer the expertise to set up the systems to keep an operation running smoothly. I am highly focused and have kept projects moving forward like well-oiled machines.

My track record in maximizing operational efficiency and implementing projects includes negotiating optimal, cost-effective contracts with external vendors.

I am convinced that your firm could benefit enormously from creating a project-manager position. I will contact you soon to arrange for a meeting to discuss my ideas. Should you require any additional information, I can be reached using the contact information listed atop this letter.

Sincerely,

Jason Albright

ERICA JANSEN

11 BARRINGTON STREET • GILFORD, NH 03247
HOME: 603.555.9067 • MOBILE: 603.555.9840 • E-MAIL: EJANSEN@HOTMAIL.COM

March 3, 2008

Angela Serrano, CEO
FlavorBurst Soft Drinks
32500 116th Blvd. SW
Miami, FL 33172-4944

Dear Ms. Serrano:

I read with interest in the *Miami Business Journal* recently of the many startup fruit-juice companies that have entered the arena and have begun to slice into FlavorBurst's market share in the schools. I grew up drinking FlavorBurst juices with my lunch in the school cafeteria every day, and now as a marketing executive with a successful track record in gaining market share for consumer food products, I am writing to propose that you bring me on as Chief Marketing Officer to set a new strategic direction for FlavorBurst.

I have distinguished myself at Burlington Foods as an executive with the capability and judgment to take a business to the next level and remove the obstacles that prevent its growth and prosperity. I have been characterized as a strategic marketing expert credited with contributions to bottom-line performance success. Here's an outline of what I propose for FlavorBurst:

- Set the stage for a change in the corporate mind-set and harness the creativity of FlavorBurst's brightest thinkers. I'd like to introduce a concept similar to Google's "20 percent time" in which FlavorBurst's R&D people can spend up to 20 percent of their time on self-initiated innovative projects. I also have some ideas for engaging creative teams in field studies of FlavorBurst's products and the competition.

- Conduct a competitive analysis and identify FlavorBurst's vulnerabilities.

- Set up focus groups to test new flavors similar to what the competition has introduced.

- Launch an inexpensive social-media word-of-mouth campaign as I did successfully for the Grains of Goodness ™ brand at Burlington Foods.

- Explore ways to expand into the Gen X market. I'm sure many consumers in my generation have the same fond memories of FlavorBurst that I do. It's time to think beyond the school market and tap into those who grew up with your fruit juices.

- Develop a new strategic plan to regain market share and attain buy-in among the staff to meet strategic goals

Ms. Serrano, I am confident of my ability to deliver for FlavorBurst the same kind of results I've delivered to Burlington Foods. I can make an immediate and positive impact on sales, revenue stream, and profit margins. If you'd like to see—by this time next year—an article in the *Miami Business Journal* about FlavorBurst's turnaround, we should talk. I welcome the opportunity to expand on my initiatives and the results I anticipate FlavorBurst will gain from them, and I will contact you next week to set up a meeting. Thank you for considering my proposal.

Cordially,

Erica Jansen

Communication Tools for the Interview Phase of the Job Search

Summary of Leadership Initiatives/Leadership Profile

This document provides a more in-depth look than your resume at your career-defining accomplishments, usually in a Challenge—Action—Result format. (See samples on pages 83–93.) Each accomplishment illustrates key leadership strengths, performance indicators, and business savvy. The collection of success stories in this profile should illustrate such traits as how you handle crises and rise to challenges. The document may also contain testimonials about your performance. Executives use it effectively as a leave-behind in interviews and for networking. They also sometimes submit it with a regular resume, with a networking resume, or with a cover letter.

Note that the first two leadership profiles (pages 83–89) are different versions for the same candidate. Both contain resume-like elements but offer a fuller portrayal of achievements and results than do resumes.

Executive Biography/Experience Narrative

An employer may request your bio in this middle stage of the search, or you may choose to submit it to provide a fuller description of your career progression and accomplishments. It also may convey a more complete integration of your personal and professional life, touching on, for example, family and interests. A bio is typically requested if your candidacy will be presented for approval by a board of directors.

Your bio should convey a strong sense of who you are, where your expertise lies, and how you have solved business problems during your career. It may be an appropriate venue for illustrating your soft skills, which hiring decision-makers will start to take a greater interest in during this stage of the search. It is unquestionably an appropriate venue for projecting captivating elements of your personality, while striking a balance between confident and coming across as boastful, cocky, or arrogant. Your bio should be far more than a dry collection of facts, but rather a lively, compelling, memorable story of success and accomplishment. It should pique interest so the employer wants to learn more about you. (See samples on pages 94–98.)

Bios are usually written in third-person, in reverse chronological order, and in a one-page format.

Consider also using your bio in a print or Web-based portfolio.

Project Summary

Whether you are in project management or a different job function, providing a project summary can be an effective way to elaborate on details of your most successful projects and accomplishments in a narrative format.

Mathias Carroll's Project Summary, on page 99, is set up in a table format that describes each project deliverable in the far left column and then uses the other two columns to tell the story of the project in a Challenge-Action-Results sequence.

Howard Albertson's Project Summary (page 100) employs a more resume-like bullet scheme, and Elliot McPherson's Project Summary (pages 101–103) groups bullets into functional areas.

Technical Skills Summary

Because executives minimally perform hands-on technical functions, this type of summary is rarely required at the executive level. However, there may be occasions when you need to specify software, hardware, mainframe, programming, database, technical certifications, and other computer-related knowledge, or perhaps scientific or other technical expertise.

A sample of a technical skills summary is shown on page 104.

ZHANG LE

625 Park Ave., New York, NY 10021-6545 • 212.555.5735 • E-mail: jobseeker@sinonet.net

INTERNATIONAL SENIOR EXECUTIVE
US-ASIAN MARKETS • START-UPS and TURNAROUNDS • BUSINESS DEVELOPMENT

- High-profile senior executive extensively experienced in delivering bold marketing, communications and business-development programs for US and Asian interests.
- Savvy marketer who initiates and develops profitable B2B relationships for leading clients in the region.
- Profit-minded professional who drives aggressive revenue growth and market entry/expansion by using talent for connecting mission, product and service to untapped niches.
- Exceptional communicator who brings multicultural and trilingual (Mandarin-Cantonese-English) advantages in leveraging relationships with senior corporate and public leaders.
- Skilled negotiator who gains the edge in hammering out viable agreements by easily navigating diverse cultural environments.
- Motivated achiever who earned Excellence in Marketing Award and recognition by the Chinese government and private industry for outstanding contributions to promoting Chinese tourism worldwide.

EXECUTIVE SUMMARY

- Pioneered corporate barter in China, capturing up to a 50 percent yield on contracts 11 months after startup.
- Grew market reach of two Chinese start-ups, achieving combined sales of US$8.5M in little more than a year.
- Boosted tourism revenues 30 percent by creating a cohesive, cross-platform media and marketing program.
- Negotiated and won two contracts worth US$25M for leading global marketing-communications firm.

AREAS OF EXPERTISE

BUSINESS DEVELOPMENT STRATEGIES • P&L MANAGEMENT • INTEGRATED MARKETING PROGRAMS

Mission-Based Strategic Plans • Operations Management • Senior-Level Relationship Building • Entrepreneurship
New Market/Channel Development • Product Positioning • Joint Ventures/B2B Alliances • Client Acquisition
New Business Initiatives • Product/Program Rollouts • Creative Sales Plans • Advertising and PR Campaigns
Branding • Turnaround Management • Budget Management • Financial Performance • Regulatory Compliance
Cost Controls • Quick-Response Planning • Outsourcing • Negotiations • Contract Development • Team Building

EXECUTIVE PERFORMANCE HIGHLIGHTS

CONCEPTUALIZED AND LED WORLD-CLASS MARKETING CAMPAIGN FOR CHINA'S THIRD-LARGEST INDUSTRY

As a senior member of executive-management team for Chinese Ministry of Tourism, transformed corporate culture from a "good will" paradigm to a well-integrated, award-winning marketing model.

Value Added and Results Attained
- Turned around marketing efforts by refining business plan that boosted tourism sales by 25 percent.
- Designed and repackaged all collateral marketing communications, including advertising, public relations and promotional programs and materials.
- Skillfully structured integrated theme for worldwide implementation.
- Created multidimensional marketing concept to grow revenues by targeting special interest groups with allure of China's cultural tapestry.
- Established and chaired marketing committee, which included multi-disciplinary teams at multiple sites.
- Contained costs by linking corporate mission to unified operations, marketing, and communication efforts.
- Introduced first-time direct event and telemarketing programs into mix as new selling tools.

DROVE WINNING INITIATIVE AGAINST TOP COMPETITORS AND SECURED LUCRATIVE CONTRACTS

Retained by global giant in marketing communications to leverage expert negotiation and relationship-management skills and represent them at the table to broker and win domestic-agency bidding rights.

Value Added and Results Attained

- Lobbied at the most senior levels to gain two profitable contracts, competing against nine top-tier agencies.
- Conceptualized marketing theme for coveted China Ministry of Tourism contract.
- Optimized account management by structuring joint venture between international ad agencies.
- Supported local service delivery by deploying global resources.
- Designed and executed comprehensive business development and implementation plan.

DEMONSTRATED PROFOUND UNDERSTANDING OF INTERNATIONAL BUSINESS PROTOCOLS BY RECONCILING COMPLEX CONTRACTS

As principal of multi-channel international consulting company, represented Asia's largest, privately-held energy company to iron out complex contract issues among key players.

Value Added and Results Attained

- Mediated discussions that resolved rights for a promotional merchandising campaign tied to major film studio feature release.
- Applied troubleshooting expertise to renegotiating rights that united mutual interests.
- Created ground-up marketing strategy and landed US$40M in new sales within six months.

LED STRATEGIC MARKETING LAUNCH AND CORPORATE MANAGEMENT OF INTERNATIONAL TRADE STARTUP

As Managing Director of International Ace, Inc., launched and successfully accelerated its entry into local market.

Value Added and Results Attained

- Pioneered "corporate barter" concept as financial solution to Chinese companies, securing US$4M in new business at up to a 50 percent margin within 11 months of operational start-up in China.
- Played key role as principal architect of negotiations with media outlets, obtaining re-market of excess inventory in exchange for placing client's advertising costs at a 3:1 value ratio in air/space time.
- Personally brokered promotion with pharmaceutical firm, resolving client-imposed re-marketing limitations.
- Led sophisticated presentations to C-level executives that resulted in revenue-generating contracts with leading consumer-products companies.

WROTE AND IMPLEMENTED BUSINESS PLAN FOR STARTUP JOINT-VENTURE AND QUICKLY EXPANDED INTO US MARKET

Led startup joint venture to process and export Asian food products via wholesale/retail channels in the US.

Value Added and Results Attained

- Targeting key US wholesalers, grew Asian Treats from zero at inception to US$4.5M in annual revenues within 15 months.
- Developed innovative incentive and benefits programs that increased yield by 30 percent and reduced costs by 20 percent with minimum turnaround time and without layoffs.
- Attained annual production targets by negotiating favorable raw material and finished product prices.

EXECUTIVE ENDORSEMENTS

"Zhang Le's work in developing a marketing strategy supported the success of our product's growth into international markets ... His leadership, visionary planning and team-spirited approach were refreshing and quite effective ... He will be an asset to any marketing initiative ... I recommend him without reservation."

– Ronald Jeffreys, President/CEO, TeeVee.net

"Zhang Le provided the agency with an external perspective that was strategic and focused on the target group that we were trying to reach ... His candid approach and insights were instrumental in the planning process and closing the contract at hand ... He is a person who works well in a team environment."

– Henri Rose, President/CEO for Asia, Button, Button, and Rose

ZHANG LE

625 Park Ave. • New York, NY
10021-6545 • 212.555.5735
E-mail: jobseeker@sinonet.net

- *Mission, Vision and Strategy*
- *Executive leadership*
- *P&L Management*
- *Budget and Forecasting*
- *Strategic Business Planning*
- *Organization and Operations*
- *New Business Development and Roll Out*
- *Strategic Alliances and Partnering*
- *Strategic and Tactical Marketing*
- *Sales, Brand, and Channel*
- *Management*
- *Leadership Branding*
- *B2B Prospecting and Closing*
- *Advertising, PR, and Communications*
- *Cross-Functional Teaming*
- *Cross-Cultural Communications*

INTERNATIONAL SENIOR EXECUTIVE

US-ASIAN MARKETS • START-UPS and TURNAROUNDS BUSINESS DEVELOPMENT • BRANDING

VALUE PROPOSITION

High-profile executive helping US interests expand in Asia

- Energetic achiever who continuously succeeds in establishing and leading world-class business from inception to fruition and turning losing ventures into profitable enterprises.
- Savvy marketer vastly experienced in delivering strong marketing, sales, and business-development programs for US and Asian interests.

Bi-culturally insightful and profit-minded operations expert

- Strong leader who contributes multicultural and bilingual advantages to leveraging relationships with senior corporate and public leaders.
- Skilled negotiator who gains the edge in complex agreements by easily navigating through diverse cultural environments, winning initiatives against top competitors, and securing beneficial contracts.

Leading dealmaker with expertise in global business protocols

- Solid self-starter with track record for developing business strategies supporting growth into international markets.
- Astute contributor who reconciles complex contracts developed extensive understanding of international business protocols.

Diversely experienced visionary

- Motivated achiever who drives aggressive revenue growth and market expansion by utilizing talent for connecting mission, product, and service to untapped niches.
- Key player who leads strategic marketing launches and accelerates corporate management of international startups capturing local markets.

Business-development pro who consistently meets corporate goals

- Proficient problem-solver who created and implemented business plans for startup joint-venture for quick expansion into international markets.
- Facile decision-maker who designs innovative incentive and benefits programs that increase yields and reduce costs.

Consensus-builder who forges critical global alliances

- Creative thinker who initiates, structures, and negotiates profitable B2B relationships.
- Exceptional communicator who delivers sophisticated presentations to C-level executives to obtain profitable contracts.
- Innovative branding guru who developed brand campaign for US-led enterprise into Asian markets.

Entrepreneurial leader who performs well in team environments

- Respected manager with effective team-spirited approach.
- Accomplished motivator with solid reputation for leveraging company competencies, providing common vision, and creating energetic, productive organization.

CHALLENGES AND RESULTS

Challenges:

- Exploit market opportunities with speed and fundamentally sound read of potential revenue results.
- Represent US business interests for expansion into previously unexplored Latin and global markets.
- Beat realistic competition.

Actions:

- Formed business alliance and led organization from startup through growth and maturity stages.
- Presented well-formulated business, marketing, and financial plans to secure venture capital.
- Directed entire business lifecycle as a hands-on, tireless Chief Operating Officer, Managing Director, and Director of Marketing.
- Ignited sales and multiplied revenue stream without overreaching.
- Contained expenses while maintaining productivity and profit margins.

Results:

- Started two companies in China, one a US-based worldwide leader in barter and trading, and the other an Asian foods plant for product export to domestic US market.
- Deployed effective tactics for both companies to help meet all roll-out dates and budgetary objectives.
- Managed 250 production-line workers and 35 multi-function executives.
- While prospecting and closing sales, developing and winning contracts, and acquiring multiple-channel B2B clients, structured operational backbone of each company and managed all functions, including recruitment, human-resource management, legal compliance, accounting practices, and outsourcing.

Bottom line:

- ***Rapidly achieved combined sales of US$8.5M for enterprises.***

Challenge:

- Use cross-functional team approach and cross-cultural communications programs to turn around direction of outdated marketing plan for Chinese Ministry of Tourism.

Actions:

- Apply diplomacy and firm change-management skills while taking stock of political overtones.

Results:

- Refocused and energized marketing programs across multiple platforms.
- Managed innovative sales and marketing model that delivered 30 percent tourism revenue growth.
- Created multidimensional marketing concept that attracted special interest groups to extend their stay in China, significantly adding to growing revenue stream.
- Generated 35 percent of total revenues from Annual International Tourism Convention.
- Increased event's domestic and international exposure.
- Established business center as first-ever opportunity for buyers and sellers to meet individually.

Bottom line:

- ***Managed multicultural team of 150 at 15 offices worldwide that generated US$6.5B in revenue.***

EXECUTIVE ENDORSEMENTS

"Zhang Le's work in developing a marketing strategy supported the success of our product's growth into international markets ... His leadership, visionary planning and team-spirited approach were refreshing and quite effective ... He will be an asset to any marketing initiative ... I recommend him without reservation."

– Ronald Jeffreys, President/CEO, TeeVee.net

"Zhang Le provided the agency with an external perspective that was strategic and focused on the target group that we were trying to reach ... His candid approach and insights were instrumental in the planning process and closing the contract at hand ... He is a person who works well in a team environment."

– Henri Rose, President/CEO for Asia, Button, Button, and Rose

PROFESSIONAL HISTORY

Principal/Senior Consultant, ZLE INTERNATIONAL CONSULTANTS, New York, NY, 1996 to present

- Own and operate management consulting practice representing key Asian and US-based corporations in processed product energy, broadcast, advertising, PR, finance, tourism, and Internet industries.
- Provide strategic planning, international business development, marketing, corporate communications, sales and general-management services to companies globally.
- Plan and manage complete engagement cycle – from initial contact with C-level executives, project proposals, fee structuring and negotiations, to service and product deliveries.

Managing Director, INTERNATIONAL ACE, New York, NY, 1993 to 1996

- Managed market entry of international barter and trading company currently generating more than US$700M in annual revenues.
- Oversaw full executive functions, including strategic planning, operations, finance, P&L, marketing, HR, and administration.

Managing Director, International Marketing. CHINESE MINISTRY OF TOURISM, Beijing, China, and New York, NY, 1990 to 1993

- Promoted from senior regional management position to international marketing role, overseeing business planning, operations and communications efforts.
- Directed operations for Ministry's 15 locations worldwide, representing US$6.5B in annual revenues.
- Oversaw $45M marketing budget and managed 150-member multi-cultural team.
- Created and led specialized programs to advance China,s third-largest industry, international tourism.

EDUCATION

- **Bachelor of Science in Marketing**, Columbia University, New York, NY
- **Continuing Education**: Seminars on management, strategic marketing and international business at universities and private institutes in the US and China.

Leadership Profile

MONICA B. SHAPIRO

LEADERSHIP SUCCESSES AS ORGANIZATION DEVELOPMENT PROFESSIONAL, CERTIFIED EXECUTIVE COACH AND ENTREPRENEUR

STRATEGIC INITIATIVE, CULTURE CHANGE

Challenge   Four district offices at the Ohio State Automobile Association, AAA, were underperforming.

Action   As Manager of Corporate Education Department, negotiated corporate politics to gain buy-in from management and staff. Led development of Corporate Education Department of 21 staff members. Coached supervisors and staff individually and as a system.

Result   Developed productive, centralized department with new cohesive team providing services throughout 6,000-person organization.

LEADERSHIP DEVELOPMENT

Challenge   CEO's entrepreneurial leadership style inadvertently risked successful development of his organization, a biotech start-up selected for NASDAQ Biotechnology Index.

Action   As Executive Coach, System Coach, and Facilitator of restructuring process, guided leadership team as they restructured into three vital, CEO-led committees.

Result   Leadership team continues to succeed using this structure.

CULTURE CHANGE

Challenge   Director of prominent division of 6,000-person Ohio State Automobile Association challenged by severe customer-service failures.

Action   As Coach and Facilitator, partnered with staff to lead shift from a dysfunctional culture to a culture that valued collaboration and positive outcomes.

Result   Customer Service failures decreased by 45 percent.

LEADERSHIP DEVELOPMENT

Challenge   Executive Director's "lone ranger" leadership style rendered 10-person senior team ineffective and angry and put agency's funding at risk.

Action   Served as Executive Coach, System Coach, Facilitator with Executive Director and direct reports.

Result   Within 14 weeks, leadership team became effective. Members could now communicate (up and down) with positive results. Members resolved conflict to create productive relationships. The organization was awarded full funding of $1.2 million for the upcoming fiscal year.

ENTREPRENEURIAL LEADERSHIP

Challenge   Small business, Alphonso Remodeling, Copley, OH, was a startup in competitive market.

Action   As Partner, improved operations and developed productive relationships with clients, employees, suppliers and colleagues. Deployed strong conflict-prevention and resolution skills.

Result   Increased annual sales from $20,000 to $1.2 million in five years. Earned International Remodeling Contractor's Association Contractor of the Year Award 1989 and Remodeling Magazine's BIG 50 Award, 1988.

62 Bowling Green Drive, Hudson, OH 44236 ● Home: 330-555-9027 ● E-mail: jobseeker@snet.net

TEAM-BUILDING

Challenge   Senior team at Bloomfield & Cannon was ineffective, distrustful, reactive, fractured and at risk of losing IPO.

Action   Developed and restructured team.

Result   Developed senior team into collaborative leadership team. IPO was completed, and stock is doing well.

Leadership Profile contributed by Abby Locke, Premier Writing Solutions, LLC,
www.premierwriting.com

5014 Crimson Lane Drive
Fairfax, VA 22030

JOHN KENNEDY

Telephone: 202.555.0437
E-mail: jobseeker@aol.com

SENIOR ASSOCIATION MANAGEMENT EXECUTIVE

Offering 15-plus years' executive-level leadership and program development expertise in a member-driven, non-profit organization. Consistent record of success in delivering significant impact in financial management, member retention, educational programming and corporate sponsorship. Broad vision and perspective with focus on customer satisfaction and member relations. Excellent communicator who leads by example. Core competencies:

**Organizational Leadership & Planning – Board & Committee Liaison – Leadership Training – Policy Development
Regulatory & Legislative Affairs – Foundation Management – Member Services – Special Events Management
Program Development & Execution – Strategic Partnerships & Alliances – Conferences & Meetings
Staff Communication & Coaching – Sponsorships & Fundraising – Advocacy & Community Outreach
Political Action Committee – Research & Development – Public & Media Relations**

Member of American Society of Association Executives

Performance Milestones

<u>1989</u>: Assumed executive leadership of part-time association with 100 members and operating budget of $10K.

<u>1989 to 1997</u>: Successfully navigated organization's expansion in programs and services as secondary mortgage industry experienced huge growth.
- **Grew membership to all-time high with 400 members** and established headquarters in Washington DC with new government affairs department.

<u>1998</u>: Sustained organization's operations and services despite massive industry downturn and the loss of 100 corporate members which failed due to financial crisis.
- **Excess cash reserves built up during earlier growth years** helped uphold organization during industry depression.

<u>1998 to 2000</u>: Applied tactical financial management techniques that helped propel organization back to operating at a surplus.

<u>2001 to present</u>: Steered organization through continued industry transformations and membership declines as increased number of mortgage companies went through mergers.
- **Organization is recognized as industry leader regarding** its educational conferences, topical seminars and roundtable discussions.

Key Leadership & Program Management Successes

PRESIDENT – Local Mortgage Bankers Association, Washington DC (1989 to present)
Leading trade association representing the mortgage lending industry with 1,000 members)

Provide strategic planning and direction for association's programs, activities and services. Full scope of responsibilities include staff supervision, program development, board and committee liaison, budget development and member communications. Represent organization in agency hearings before the Federal Reserve Board, Department of Housing and Urban Development, Department of the Treasury and trade coalition meetings. **Systematically grew organization from part-time association to fully staffed operations with over 100% increase in membership and average annual budget exceeding $900K.**

Financial Management & Budget Expansion

Improved operational efficiency and financial stability by increasing member retention and sponsorship opportunities. Made pivotal decision to secure corporate sponsorships for annual conference and all other programs.
- **Drove cash reserves to peak level of $1.5 million during the 1990s.**

JOHN KENNEDY   **PAGE TWO**

<u>Financial Management & Budget Expansion</u> cont'd

- Stabilized organizational resources by capitalizing on sponsorships which now comprise 50% of annual income.
- Promoted annual conference as largest sponsorship program; sponsorships totaled $460K in 2005.

<u>Member Services & Member Retention:</u>

Instituted proactive measures for membership renewals and contacted members on continual basis to evaluate satisfaction levels and ongoing benefit needs.

- **Member retention ranked between 92 to 93% for the past 18 consecutive years.**

<u>Educational Programming & Conferences:</u>

Expanded educational programs and meetings from one annual conference, attorneys' roundtable and one regional meeting to wide cross-section of programs and services that adequately meet the changing needs of corporate leaders and executive members.

- **Complete suite of programs include annual conference, fraud prevention and detection conference, legislative day, compliance and servicing roundtable, attorneys roundtable and primetime for nonprime trade show.**

<u>Research & Development Studies:</u>

Originated research programs to gather industry specific data and hired university experts to analyze the data; the results were used in the development of several widely-published research studies in the nonprime industry.

- **Media, industry, regulators and legislators have benefited from these studies to gain a better understanding of critical aspects of the nonprime mortgage lending products.**

<u>Website Development & Online Database:</u>

Brought organization to the forefront of industry by designing and developing company's first comprehensive website. Increased member benefits and visitor traffic to the website by including online database which provides members with conference information, advocacy reports, industry news and views and statistical information.

- **The vast majority of members utilize the website capabilities to register for educational programs and stay abreast of current industry events.**
- **Maximized revenue-generating prospects by extending advertising space for members through the company's website and weekly electronic newsletters.**

<u>Advocacy, Regulatory & Legislative Affairs:</u>

Channeled association to take the lead and add powerful "voice" in legislative issues and regulatory affairs that monitor nonprime mortgage industry. Helped curtail excessive restrictions on member operations in the industry by advocating informed consumer choice, consumer education and ready access to fairly priced credit.

- **Testified before Federal Reserve Board on matters related to home mortgage disclosure act and predatory lending. Served on 2001 HUD predatory lending committee.**

Education

BA – University of San Diego

JD – Georgetown University

Leadership Profile contributed by Karen P. Katz, *www.CareerAcceleration.net*

Mark H. Roberts   Vice President, Retail Division   ZUUK®

jobseeker@xmail.com   234-555-9876

LEADERSHIP...EXPERTISE...and the ABILITY to...DELIVER

IMPLEMENT EFFICIENCIES to ACHIEVE EXPONENTIAL GROWTH and EARN CUSTOMER LOYALTY

Mark Roberts is Vice-President, Retail Division with ZUUK, a $430 million multinational provider of high quality building products. ZUUK is a principal supplier to US and Canadian box stores, as well as wholesale suppliers and showrooms. A member of the ZUUK executive committee, Mark has played a key role in directing all aspects of the organization, driving growth over 20 times during his tenure. His contribution is evident through:

□ **EXECUTION** of **STRATEGIC BUSINESS PLANS**

□ **LEADERSHIP** and **MANAGEMENT** of **HUMAN RESOURCES**

□ **IMPLEMENTATION** of **LEAN MANUFACTURING, LOGISTICS,** and **DISTRIBUTION STRATEGIES**

□ **DEVELOPMENT** of **EFFECTIVE CUSTOMER RELATIONSHIPS**

□ **MANAGEMENT** of **FINANCIAL** and **MARKETING PLANS**

- Mark began to prove himself as a "go-to leader" in 1987, when he started a construction company called M&S SPECIALTIES. The manufacturing side grew and was sold to EVERGREEN WINDOWS & DOORS in 1994, a company in business for more than 60 years. Mark spearheaded a four-year strategic plan that enabled the company to meet the needs of a $30 million customer, HOMEOWNER WAREHOUSE. Under his leadership, Evergreen incorporated CELLULAR MANUFACTURING, EMPLOYEE INCENTIVES, and CONTINUOUS IMPROVEMENT PROCESSES; Evergreen's revenue grew from $12 million to $38 million.

- Evergreen's LEAN MANAGEMENT and ability to handle debt (EBITDA) made it an attractive candidate for sale to ZUUK, based in Quebec, Canada (1998). Mark's role as General Manager of the North American retail division expanded from 1998-2002, with 5 manufacturing plants and $175 million in top line revenue.

- In 2002, he took on the additional role of Executive VP; during his three-year tenure, he consolidated the retail division and oversaw the implementation of an ENTERPRISE RESOURCE PLANNING SYSTEM, SAP.

- Beginning in 2005, Mark has assumed COMPLETE P&L RESPONSIBILITY for the NORTH AMERICAN RETAIL DIVISION of ZUUK. Since 2007, Mark has served as a mentor for new corporate leaders while continuing to spearhead growth initiatives.

In his role as a management executive, some of Mark's accomplishments include:

- Reduced costs by 16% over 2 years through consolidation of US manufacturing plants (from 21 to 15)
- Led introduction of enterprise dashboard; increased employee involvement within unionized environment
- Created manufacturing "key performance system;" common metric; rapid response to production variables
- Promoted division-wide performance objectives, employee review system, and succession planning
- Initiated 7-step gate system to clarify new product launches; resulted in 20% increase in new product sales
- Incorporated financial and environmental regulations into business plan; reduced P&L expenses by 19%

Mark and his wife have been partners in building their respective professional profiles while at the same time, building their family life in Chester County, PA. Feeling blessed by the success achieved over 20 years in the corporate world; Mark is eager to L-E-A-D in a new capacity. Mark is looking to match his abilities with a company looking to build customer loyalty and achieve exponential growth through operational efficiencies.

Biography contributed by Barbara Safani, Career Solvers, *www.careersolvers.com*

DANIEL R. HABER

15 Classon Avenue ▪ Brooklyn, NY 11215 ▪ Cell: 917-555-5555 ▪ jobseeker@gmail.com

Daniel Haber has a diversified background in finance and over 30 years of experience in strategic financial planning, capital sourcing, and treasury management in both domestic and international markets. With competencies that span both strategic and tactical planning, he's been instrumental in building and leading cohesive teams to raise capital, manage cash flow, build commercial and investment banking relationships, negotiate credit agreements and business contracts, orchestrate asset dispositions and divestitures, and mitigate financial risk. Over $6B in the public and bank markets internationally has been raised under his management and he has a proven track record as a change agent capable of turning around corporations with cash flow problems and earnings shortfalls in a short period of time.

As Vice President and Treasurer of Wohl Corporation, an international manufacturer of electronics parts, headquartered in Astoria, NY, Daniel transformed the financial health of the organization following a period of poor performance and a ratings downgrade. By enhancing capitalization and liquidity with a $250M equity issue, eliminating a $47M annual common dividend, and negotiating a $900M bank term/revolver credit agreement, the organization was able to regain its investment grade rating in just 15 months. Through subsequent refinancing efforts of long term debts, Daniel helped the organization to reduce interest expenses by 57% while doubling average maturity.

To consolidate liquidity and reduce financing costs, Daniel reorganized close to two dozen world-wide subsidiaries into a cash balance netting system that reduced debt levels and interest expense and leveraged offshore finance subsidiaries to improve tax efficiencies. Under his leadership, the firm realized $130M+ in savings following the implementation of cash flow at risk modeling techniques designed to mitigate aggregate risk. To augment financial security, he raised over $1B in project finance, government incentive grants, joint venture arrangements and start-up funding in Asia, Europe, and South America including a $125M government grant from the French government for a new project in the South Pacific.

Efficiencies were further improved through Daniel's campaign to reengineer the corporate treasury function by streamlining expenses and trimming overhead costs. As a result of his efforts, departmental operating expenses were reduced by 43% and headcount was cut in half at the same time the treasury department's role was expanding.

Daniel acquired much of the knowledge necessary to perform the VP and Treasurer role in his previous position with the firm. As Assistant Treasurer, he slashed after-tax cost of funds by 46% and reduced debt-to-capital ratio by creating a first of its kind $120M receivables securitization program encompassing North America, Europe, and Asia. In addition, Daniel negotiated over 40 bank credit agreements and he was instrumental in raising $250M for an Indonesian subsidiary with a ground breaking syndicated Japanese bank project loan market to finance expansion and repay inter-company debt.

Daniel joined Wohl Corporation as the Assistant Treasurer, and then Treasurer for its Beldor subsidiary, a leading producer of electronic parts located in Brooklyn, NY with sales of $375M. In this role, Daniel established the global treasury function, project financed new plants in Taiwan and Florida, and liquidated an underperforming joint venture operation in South Korea.

Daniel got his start in finance as an International Banking Officer for Bankers Trust in Manhattan and later for Deutsche Bank where he marketed export credit products, bank currency trading and euro-dollar deposit services, managed loan portfolios, and managed Asian correspondent bank relationships.

Daniel studied business administration in conjunction with the Executive M.B.A. program at Duke University's Fuqua School of Business in South Carolina after earning his B.A. in Finance at New York University.

Biography contributed by Jewel Bracy DeMaio, A Perfect Resume,
www.APerfectResume.com

JARED HORNER

1 Heaven Way
Ramsey, NJ 07446

jobseeker@optonline.net

201.555.1212
201.555.3434

EXECUTIVE BIOGRAPHY

"Envision and execute leading-edge financial practices that drive across-the-board organizational change and deliver positive bottom-line results."

Jared Horner, CPA, is a finance strategist and change agent with 20+ years' corporate leadership experience. Mr. Horner's core areas of expertise include Strategic Financial Planning, Financial Policy & Procedure, Revenue & Profit Enhancement, Budget Forecasting & Administration, Process Change & Improvement, and Performance Measurement & Auditing.

Mr. Horner's current title is Vice-President & Controller of Insurance Services Network in New York, NY. In that capacity, he strategically established a new financial infrastructure. He strengthened the finance sector's contribution to the company, and positioned the business to achieve Sarbanes-Oxley compliance.

Mr. Horner's perspective extends beyond finance, to how finance adds value to strategic business planning, new business development, and customer relationship management. With Insurance Services Network Mr. Horner directed an initiative to overhaul internal computer systems, a key change to drive improvements in customer relations. Under his leadership, Insurance Services Network launched a web-based tool for clients firms to provide Insurance Services Network with monthly reports.

Mr. Horner's prior professional roles were with Mason Breeman & Co., Inc. in New York as Financial Analyst, Merchant Banking, and Karter, Schlemmer in New York, as Audit Supervisor.

His professional designations include Certified Public Accountant, NY State Property & Casualty Broker Life & Health Agent, and NASD Registered Securities Representative.

Mr. Horner earned a Bachelor of Science Degree in Accounting from The Pennsylvania State University.

Biography contributed by Jewel Bracy DeMaio, A Perfect Resume,
www.APerfectResume.com

ERIC J. CHENAULT

3 Woodburn Lane
Danville, CA 94506
925.555.1212
jobseeker@gmail.com

EXECUTIVE BIOGRAPHY

*"Envision, design, and construct innovative buildings that capture buyers'
attention, provide competitive differentiation, and deliver consistently good
bottom-line results."*

Eric Chenault is a strategic executive specializing in development and construction. During the course of an 18-year leadership career, Mr. Chenault has conceptualized and directed a series of financially successful projects in high-end residential, resort, hospitality, and commercial industries.

Mr. Chenault specializes in innovative design and efficient construction to capture maximum revenue. He offers a breadth of knowledge: design, development, budgeting, marketing, and sales, and has leveraged these competencies to deliver financially-winning projects time and time again.

Currently Mr. Chenault is Vice-President of Vertical Development & Construction with Major Urban, a national residential homebuilder in San Francisco, CA. Mr. Chenault was brought into the organization as part of a team of key executives to launch the vertical urban division. His primary scope of responsibility was to direct an extensive pipeline of high-rise and mid-rise developments, totaling 16,000 homes within three master-planned communities.

Mr. Chenault envisioned a new design approach, defined fundamental development parameters and maximized utilization of advanced-technology and structural systems. His key projects include Tower Condominium, a 21-story boutique condominium constructed in December 2006. He also directed Humanity Ridge, Phase One, a 1,100-unit development projected to break ground in November 2008.

Previously Mr. Chenault was Vice-President of Construction with Cantor Construction, Inc. of Toronto, Ontario. At the request of the organization's President, Mr. Chenault started an in-house construction division, and drove a corporate culture change that defined and competitively differentiated Cantor as a premier developer, builder and provider of customer care and client service.

Key projects under his leadership at Cantor Construction include The Palestra, a 24-story high-end luxury condominium constructed in March 2000, The Lofts, a mid-range condominium conversion project constructed in May 2000, and Tristen Hill Condominium, a mid-range condominium conversion.

The core competencies Mr. Chenault possesses as an executive strategist in this field extend beyond high-end urban residential development. As Director of Construction with Ylink Corporation of King City, Ontario, Mr. Chenault oversaw the planning and construction of golf clubhouses, for residential golf course communities, new boutique villas and inns, and renovations of hospitality and conference facilities.

Mr. Chenault opened Chenault Fine HomeBuilding Co. of Mississauga, Ontario, and generated $6 million annually at peak acquiring building lots and developing and selling 10 custom homes. Mr. Chenault's academic credentials include a B.S. Equivalent in Architectural Design Technology from Munster College of Applied Arts & Technology.

Biography contributed by Terrie Osborn, Resumes, Etc.,
www.cnyresumes.com

ELIZABETH A. MICHAELS

PROFESSIONAL BIOGRAPHY

A leader in the Southern California Wholesale Mortgage Industry, Elizabeth A. Michaels recently combined her more than 15 years of industry experience to launch two new small businesses, EAM Lending Group Inc., and Mortgage Processing Support, in San Diego, California. EAM Lending Group develops successful collaborations between lenders and borrowers, competing against competitive broker business by obtaining maximum competitive financing for borrowers while charging minimal fees. Mortgage Processing Support provides services to mortgage brokers and mortgage correspondent lenders for a full range of mortgage loans including FHA, Conventional ALT-A, Subprime, Small Commercial, and Commercial.

Prior to establishing these two businesses, Elizabeth had been appointed as Area Credit Manager for Lincoln Mortgage Corporation in San Diego. At Lincoln, Ms. Michaels built and directed a team of fourteen credit and administrative professionals in managing client mortgage underwriting requirements. Her outstanding leadership and business acumen increased production from $8 million to more than $42 million per month. Within this position, Ms. Michaels was also selected to serve on the company's Training Review Team, offering input and recommendations in guiding strategic, company-wide decision making regarding a variety of staffing initiatives, with emphasis on standardizing training for underwriters, processors, and funders.

Before joining Lincoln, Elizabeth served as Account Manager at Sunburst Financial Corporation, in San Diego, assisting brokers and account executives by liaising with underwriters to clear underwriting conditions. This experience built on Ms. Michaels's previous role as an Underwriter for Del Ray Mortgage Corporation, where she utilized an in-depth knowledge of State-specific compliance in the underwriting of non-conforming loans for the secondary market.

Ms. Michaels's earlier industry positions included roles as a Loan Officer/Refinance Specialist for Gold Valley Mortgage Corporation and as a Mortgage Loan Processor for Diego Estates Savings and Loan Association, both in San Diego. With Gold Valley, she established herself as a top department producer, achieving more than $8.5 million each month in funding, as well as playing a key role in decreasing portfolio turnover.

Elizabeth A. Michaels is a forward-thinking, visionary executive able to successfully balance the risks of continual change and innovation through disciplined implementation. Her success in launching new operations and substantially increasing bottom-line contributions through an in-depth understanding of the home loan industry are further evidence of her dynamic, hands-on leadership style.

Ms. E.. Michaels is a Licensed Mortgage Broker, holds an associate of science in business administration from San Diego Community College, and has completed Finance coursework at University of California at San Diego, and underwriting coursework at the School of Mortgage Lending in Washington, D.C.

Biography contributed by Karen P. Katz, *www.CareerAcceleration.net*

Jane McLaughlin, Founder & President

555-555-5432 direct   jobseeker@LifeCycleSoftware.com   www. LifeCylceSoftware.com

WEB SERVICES...SYSTEMS INTEGRATION…BUSINESS INTELLIGENCE

Jane McLaughlin is the President of LIFECYCLE SOFTWARE, a company recognized for helping large and small organizations with PROJECT ANALYSIS, IMPLEMENTATION, CUSTOMIZATION and MANAGEMENT. Jane offers her customers the benefit of more than 25 years experience with corporate, academic, and governmental institutions, where she was instrumental in the development and implementation of numerous scientifically focused, enterprise-wide information, portal products and middleware. Customers appreciate her insight into their business needs and clear communication, which complements her technical background in Software Engineering. LifeCycle is SIX SIGMA CERTIFIED, and has worked with large global chemical, materials, and pharmaceutical companies, integrating solutions with partners such as ERP systems, SAP, and JD Edwards.

Jane gained technical expertise and business acumen as a **CONSULTANT** and **TEAM MEMBER / LEADER** with:
♦LIFECYCLE SOFTWARE ♦THOMSON SCIENTIFIC ♦HAZOX ♦INDEPENDENCE BLUE CROSS ♦UNISYS CORP
Customers and end-users gain value through her knowledge and skill in areas such as:

EXECUTIVE DASHBOARDS	COMPETITIVE & BUSINESS INTELLIGENCE	ENTERPRISE INFORMATION RETRIEVAL
CONTENT/KNOWLEDGE MANAGEMENT	BUSINESS PROCESS MANAGEMENT & HR	PORTAL & META SEARCH ENGINES
eCOMMERCE & WEB DEVELOPMENT	TECHNICAL PAPERS & PRODUCT DEMONSTRATION	OO SOFTWARE DESIGN & METHODOLOGY

In her role with LifeCycle Software, Jane has delivered value to customers through synthesis of disparate information and on-time delivery of applications. LifeCycle incorporates the resources of domestic and international technical partnerships and strategic alliances, e.g. Microsoft, Semantec, WSI, ITI Associates, etc.

- Business and regulatory risk is diminished
- End-users and client organizations experience increased access to information
- More stakeholders are empowered to make decisions and participate in analysis

LifeCycle has provided services to the Pharmaceutical, Manufacturing, Banking, & Legal fields. Highlighted accomplishments include:

- Building an HR dashboard product for Vienna HCA
- Management of Clinical Trials for Asubio Pharmaceutical
- Preparation for SAP executive dashboard & facilitation of data migration for a Washington, DC utility
- Pre-sales collaboration with APR Smartlogik to penetrate Pharmaceutical and Hedge Fund markets
- Designed Web Services & Knowledge seminars for Drexel U's College of Information Sciences
- Performed numerous analyses and business audits for small businesses in the Delaware Valley
- Collaborated with partners to serve regional banks through analysis of lending portfolios, debit card and ATM marketing strategies, and ProClarity reporting tools

Jane is an active member of her professional community through memberships and leadership roles, e.g.:
Enterprise Content Management Association (AIIM), Knowledge Management Group of Philadelphia, National Association of Women Owned Business, Society of Competitive Intelligence Professionals.
Jane earned a Bachelor of Science degree in Statistics & Computer Science from University of Delaware; she earned post-graduate credits in Electrical Engineering at Temple University.

Project Summary

MATHIAS CARROLL

91110 Forest Dr. Apt 126, Houston, TX 77096 ◆ Phone: 713-555-5555 ◆ E-mail: jobseeker@hotmail.com

PROJECT HIGHLIGHTS

Projects/Deliverables	Challenge	Action and Results
As Product Manager, Norwich Community Bank		
Tax Payments and Data Import Enhancements on Internet	Tax payment and import functionality on the Automated Clearing House (ACH) module of Internet.	Oversaw product delivery and all marketing. Achieved successful, first-in-market implementation.
Conversion of clients to new Internet system	Changes to Internet system warranted customer system changes.	Successful implementation with minimal customer issues.
Transmission System Enhancements	Antiquated transmission hardware system; $2+ million capital request had been consistently denied previous years.	Successfully collaborated with team to bridge past failings and placed product spin on a business case, which was approved.
Enhancements to External Communication to Clients	Customer correspondence was inconsistent with established brand image and noncompliance risk existed.	First to visualize and implement new use for established internal customer set-up system. Designed/implemented automated customer letter trigger to ensure consistent brand image and that important correspondence is sent to client while contributing to operational efficiency; became the standard for all departmental products.
Automated Pay/Draw mechanism via Internet	Product enhancement needed for Business Credit Line customers to initiate requests via Internet.	Developed System Specifications for product; first to establish cross-functional teams needed to implement properly and effectively.
Tax Payment Option on VRU Menu	Tax Payment via telephone was not part of long-established and marketed 800 number.	Oversaw idea and implementation, resulting in crossing business segments, which in turn reduced another customer channel and increased exposure of product to customers and sales.
Next-generation Internet product	Vendor selection of next-generation Internet solution.	Played key role on core team that oversaw acquisition of a new vendor, which exceeded $2 million purchase.
ACH Risk Initiative	Risk initiative designed to automate funding of ACH files and broaden credit policies to enable more customer penetration while managing risk.	First in market. Developed strategies to address gap in training and simplify a complicated process. Exceeded expectations and goals of project, garnering executive leadership praise on implementation success. Market studies showed lead in positioning and also exposed larger customer segment to product traditionally targeted for large corporate clients.

Project Summary

16 Chatterton Way • Bethany, LA 71007
Voice: 308-555-9053 • Fax: 308-555-9073
jobseeker@juno.net

Howard B. Albertson

Consulting Project Summaries

Halluse International, *Dixie, LA*, Jan. 2004 to May 2005
- Developed Sarbanes-Oxley (SOX) Section 404-compliance process documentation for Data Diagnosis division of this $2 billion publicly traded multinational transportation firm. Divisions represent approximately 60 percent of company's revenues. Halluse International has subsequently adopted documentation methodology and style as its standard for all its divisions.

Halluse Data Diagnosis, *Bethany, LA, CA*, Oct. to Dec. 2004
- As part of Halluse Data Diagnosis' SOX remediation efforts, designed, documented, and managed implementation of Data Diagnosis' IT systems access security processes and policies. Tests of controls by Halluse International's external auditors revealed no material or significant deficiencies.

Import Management, *Dixie, LA*, June 2003 to Nov. 2003
- Developed process documentation and economic operating model for proposed weapons of mass destruction and contraband container inspection facility for Ports of New Orleans and Baton Rouge.

Halluse Data Diagnosis, *Keithville, LA*, Feb. 2001 to Dec. 2002
- Analyzed and documented Data Diagnosis's financial processes and interfaces to its operational systems. Developed systems requirements and managed Request for Proposal process to replace accounts-payable, accounts-receivable, and general-ledger systems.
- Developed total cost of ownership (TCO) analysis of alternative decision support systems and used it to support management's successful request to corporation's executive committee to purchase decision-support system.
- Developed IT staffing white paper and staffing recommendations for management approval.
- Developed system requirements to automate Data Diagnosis' container and chassis repair authorization and accounts-payable process.
- Developed system requirements for Data Diagnosis' internet-based equipment reservation and booking system.
- Audited $18 million intermodal equipment repair invoice file containing 160K invoices with 650K detail line items. Identified $3.3 million in overcharges and questionable billings, resulting in full refund to Halluse Data Diagnosis.

Brighthouse Long Distance, *Keithville, LA*, May 2000 to April 2001
- Developed and oversaw execution of integrated test plans for Brighthouse Long Distance alternately billed services (e.g., operator and directory assistance; calling card services).

Project Summary

219 East Avenue
Christopher, IL 62822
Office: 618.555.8291 • Cell: 618.555.9073
jobseeker@gmail.net

Elliot McPherson

Projects

BRANDING INITIATIVES

Fighting for Youth
- Branded the multi-service military as Freedom Fight, and expressed the brand in a new Website, www.freedom-fight.com.
- Served as site team leader, chief information architect, content/copy developer, and general manager.

Coca-Cola USA
- Persuaded six Coca-Cola bottlers who were a distant second to Pepsi to test Coca-Cola Challenge program; average test market share increased 30 percent.

Del Monte Corporation
- Repositioned Meow Mix Cat Chow ($70 million in sales) as a food cats love to eat using memorable, taste-focused advertising.

ORGANIZATIONAL INITIATIVES

Allen Michaels Marketing Services
- Established new US international marketing services function to produce support materials in five languages.
- Established country direct-marketing, advertising, and PR capabilities within Canada, the UK, Switzerland, Australia, and New Zealand by developing trust-based relationships with senior Emery local managers and competing vendors.

Allen Michaels Marketing Services
- Built motivated six-person marketing communications services team that initiated and managed corporate advertising, direct mail, and sales-support materials launching Allen Michaels' new FedEx air-express operation.

Coca-Cola USA
- Improved performance of Coca-Cola bottlers nationwide by awarding incentives based on mutual local planning process requiring bottlers to focus on limited number of core retail objectives.

BUILDING TEAMS AND TRUST

Fighting for Youth
- Led 11-member drug-prevention task force that created new Parent Drug Resource Center—a content area for America Online—resulting in thousands of better informed parents of teens.
- Played leading role as member of complex, multi-vendor network to launch, maintain, and refresh Office of National Drug Control Policy's online campaign.

A. Jacobs & Co.
- Improved Microsoft client satisfaction by coaching members of eight-person staff on how to establish better relationships with their client counterparts, Microsoft Program Administrators.

MARKETING AND COMMUNICATIONS STRATEGY

Fighting for Youth
- Directed $1 million Web-based, youth-targeted media and creative drug prevention campaign for White House's Office of National Drug Control Policy (ONDCP).
- Measured detailed campaign impact by ad theme, ad format, and site/site network.

Fighting for Youth
- Led five-year lead-generation direct-mail youth-recruiting campaign for Department of Defense integrated with telemarketing and fulfillment back end.
- Campaign generated more than 150,000 qualified, low-cost inquiries who enlisted in military at an 11 percent rate.

A. Jacobs & Co.
- Supervised and approved 60+ mail-event strategies, each with a relevant offer, for nine business clients within Microsoft (e.g., IMGB System 2000 workstations, GB-400 computers) producing primary response rates as high as 9.8 percent.

Galant & Geoffrey Advertising
- Developed television and print advertising strategies and media plans for Burts Bees Products, General Mills Cereals, Pro Printing Monograms, Sonoma Valley Wine Club, National City private banking, and Publix Supermarkets.

Fighting for Youth
- Directed integrated, three-agency $10 million communications campaign to launch new Fighting for Youth A.M. and Fighting for Youth P.M. Services.
- Campaign included advertising, lead-generation direct mail, sales collateral, and publicity behind new National Football League Fighting for Youth Award.

BUSINESS GROWTH AND PROFIT

Del Monte Corporation
- Increased market share 10 percent in FY73-FY74 (from 41.4 percent to 45.4 percent) strengthening Meow Mix Cat Chow's No. 1 cat food position.
- Exceeded brand profit targets by 7 percent during same period.

Fighting for Youth
- Developed 200,000+ sales inquiries and more than $6 million in incremental revenue with $1 million national direct-mail campaign; developed new relational customer database used to segment mailings.

Mailers Direct
- Tested three direct-mail events targeting customers of International Delight Instant Coffee that increased brand purchase rates from moderate users, resulting in clear one-year payback of all mail costs.

WEBSITES

Fighting for Youth
- Developed site plans, information structures, and content for three websites sponsored by the Pentagon for parent audience, teen audience, and adults 18-30; used site metrics to determine marketing impact and to suggest content changes.

Fighting for Youth
- Planned and managed $200,000 online advertising test for military site measuring online ad format, keyword placement, and message test variables.

TEACHING AND MENTORING

Michigan State School of Business
- Achieved excellent student ratings while teaching Strategic Marketing Management as Adjunct Professor of Marketing.

J. Cleese Advertising
- Developed and taught acclaimed two-day direct marketing seminar for N Brown: Building Global Competitive Advantage in the Order-by-Mail Industry.

Fighting for Youth
- Mentored and trained five interns/junior account executives.

Technical Skills Summary

LANE CLARKSON

416 BEARING LANE, HADLEY, MA 01035
PHONE: 413-555-7163 • E-MAIL: jobseeker@gmail.com

TECHNOLOGY PROFICIENCIES

Selected areas of technology competency:

Operating Systems
- Windows Vista
- Windows XP
- Windows 2000
- MS-DOS
- Novell
- AIX Unix

Networking
- LAN
- WAN
- TCP/IP
- WINS
- DHCP
- DNS
- SAMBA
- VPN
- Active Directory
- ISDN
- DSL
- T1, T3, Frame Relay
- Fax Server

Security
- Proxy
- Webtrends
- Security Manager

Integrated Development Environments
- Delphi
- Gupta
- PowerBuilder
- Visual Basic
- Cold Fusion
- Paradox
- MS Access
- Borland J Builder

Network Application Software
- Archserve
- Ghost
- Webtrends and Security Manager
- SAP
- TrackIT

Hardware
- IBM
- HP
- TI
- Compaq
- Dell
- Cisco
- AIX
- RS600
- Switches
- Wiring

Programming Languages
- C
- C++
- Basic
- Professional Basic
- Rbasic
- Visual Basic
- Java
- Pascal
- Turbo PascalDelphi
- Python

Script
- Java Script
- SQL
- HTML
- CSS
- VBA
- VB Script
- Unix Shell
- Perl

DBMS, Databases, Database Connectivity
- MS SQL Server
- DTS
- MS OLAP
- Data Mining
- Rexx
- DB2
- MS Access
- Paradox
- VSAM
- ODBC
- ADO

Office Suites
- Microsoft Office:
  - Word
  - Access
  - Excel
  - PowerPoint
  - Publisher
- Adobe Acrobat Reader
- Crystal Report
- Lotus cc:Mail
- Lotus Notes
- Outlook

Web
- IIS
- ASP
- FrontPage
- Macromedia Dreamweaver
- .net

Desktop Application Software
- ErWin
- Visio
- Paint Shop Pro
- ACDS
- Wsftp
- AutoCAD
- MS Project
- VI
- Adobe:
  - PageMaker
  - Photoshop
  - Premiere

Phone Systems
- Lucent AUDIX messaging

Summary of Training

A summary of training is useful if you have participated in so many training programs that listing them on your resume would be prohibitive. It could also be used to boost your credibility—especially if your educational background is deficient. Use the same protocol to list training as you do to list education on your resume: outcome of the training (such as diploma or certification), if applicable, name of the training, sponsoring institution, location (city and state) at which it took place, and date completed or span of dates of the training. Your training summary can be organized by date, as is the sample included here, or by type/topic of training.

See page 106 for a sample of a summary of training.

Publications Summary

Publications summaries are generally required in academic fields, as well in science, medicine, and other types of research. If you fall outside of these fields but have authored at least several publications, you may still find a publications summary valuable for showing prospective authors your visibility and thought leadership.

A sample publications summary is on page 107.

Media Mentions Summary

Some employers seek media stars, valuing would-be executives who can generate press coverage for themselves and their companies. If your due diligence reveals media-worthiness as an important criterion for a prospective employer, showing your proven ability to garner the media spotlight is the way to go.

On page 108 you will see a sample summary of media mentions.

Presentations Summary

In professions, such as training, consulting, and sales, experience in delivering presentations is critical. A presentations summary provides evidence of sufficient experience in presenting. These summaries usually provide the name or topic of each presentation, the venue in which it was delivered, location (city and state), and date.

A sample presentations summary is shown on page 109.

Reference List

You will likely need a reference-list document because you should never list names of references on your resume. (See a sample on page 110.) References belong on a separate sheet of paper that matches the branded look of your resume, but is simply titled "References." Never submit references to employers until they request them, but do be sure and keep a list of references with you when interviewing so that you can be prepared to present them when the employer asks. Your references should be those who know your strengths and abilities in detail. They should also have a good handle on your soft skills—leadership, teamwork, communication, problem-solving—as this is the point at which the employer will want to explore those skills, and, beyond talking directly with you, checking with references is the best way for prospective employers to get a feel for these skills. Obviously, you need to ask whether each person is comfortable serving as a reference for you.

Each reference listing on your document should contain complete information from each reference: full name, current title, company name, business address, and contact information (daytime phone, e-mail, cell phone). Each listing should also describe how, and in what capacity, the reference knows you, as well as how long the person has known you. Deb Dib notes that reference lists require meticulous proofing, as typos often lurk in contact information.

Summary of Training

ROSE SEQUOIA

2 115th St. ♦ White Springs, FL 32096 ♦ Cell: 904/555-9740 ♦ jobseeker@gmail.com

SUMMARY OF COMPLETED TRAINING

2007
- Traditional to Brain Based, Child Guidance Center, Inc., Alachua, FL, January
- Mental Health Collaboration Teleconference, Florida Community Mental Health Services, Tallahassee, FL, January
- Child Development and the Creative Curriculum, Child Guidance Center, Inc., Alachua, FL, January
- Traditional to Brain Based Part 2, Child Guidance Center, Inc., Alachua, FL, February
- Distance Learning Training to be an adult education Teacher/Consultant, University of North Florida, Jacksonville, FL, February

2006
- Conversation on Curriculum, Child Guidance Center, Inc., Alachua, FL, January
- Child Development Cluster (Outcomes), Child Guidance Center, Inc., Alachua, FL, January
- Obesity Teleconference, Community Health Scholars Program, FL, January
- Early Literacy Teleconference, North Florida Institute, Orange Park, FL, January
- Infant & Brain Development, Child Guidance Center, Inc., Alachua, FL
- PRISM Training (Series 1-3), University of Florida, Gainesville, FL, February
- DSQIC Representative On-site Training, University of North Florida, Jacksonville, FL, February
- Fatherhood/Male Involvement Institute, Child Guidance Center, Inc., Alachua, FL, February
- Mother Goose Family Literacy Training, Community Health Scholars Program, FL, March
- MMSR Training & Work Sampling, Louis de la Parte Florida Mental Health Institute, Tampa, FL, March, April, May, June
- Teleconference: Speech & Language Disorders: Beyond Simple Sounds, Community Health Scholars Program, FL, March
- Teleconference: Speech & Language Disorders: Behavior Management, Community Health Scholars Program, FL, March
- Creative Curriculum, Child Guidance Center, Inc., Alachua, FL, April
- What is autism?, Louis de la Parte Florida Mental Health Institute, Tampa, FL, May
- Family Service Coordinators Training, University of North Florida, Jacksonville, FL, June
- Florida Model for School Readiness & Work Sampling Assessment System, Florida Community Mental Health Services, Tallahassee, FL, July
- OSHA, University of Florida, Gainesville, FL, September
- Child Abuse and Neglect- September

2005
- Teleconference: PT/OT Services for young children with disabilities, Child Guidance Center, Inc., Alachua, FL, January
- Early Childhood Profession Training, Child Guidance Center, Inc., Alachua, FL, February
- Teleconference-What's new in ADD, Florida Community Mental Health Services, Tallahassee, FL, February
- CPR/First Aid, North Florida Institute, Orange Park, FL, March
- Teleconference: Enhancing Child Outcome, Child Guidance Center, Inc., Alachua, FL, March
- Child & Sexual Abuse, Child Guidance Center, Inc., Alachua, FL, April
- Fun with Feelings, Child Guidance Center, Inc., Alachua, FL, April
- Creating a Community where young people thrive, Child Guidance Center, Inc., Alachua, FL, May
- Peace of Mind: Spread the Awareness, North Florida Institute, Orange Park, FL, May
- Achieving School Readiness Florida Business Round Table, Tallahassee, FL, Spring
- DSQUIC Training/Family Service Workers-On-site training University of North Florida, Jacksonville, FL, May
- Dealing with Difficult people, University of Florida, Gainesville, FL June
- Understanding Learning Disabilities, Child Guidance Center, Inc., Alachua, FL, June
- Family Literacy Design & Development (PODS), North Florida Institute, Orange Park, FL, July
- Early Intervention/Early Childhood Summer Institute, Tallahassee, FL, July/August
- Creativity in the Classroom, University of North Florida, Jacksonville, FL, August
- Taking Care of Myself in the Workplace, Florida Community Mental Health Services, Tallahassee, FL August
- Time Management, North Florida Institute, Orange Park, FL, September
- Head Start Professional Development Seminar, University of Florida, Gainesville, FL, October
- Head Start Dental Training, North Florida Institute, Orange Park, FL, November
- Witness Protection Training, Louis de la Parte Florida Mental Health Institute, Tampa, FL, November
- Teleconference: Coping with Grief, North Florida Institute, Orange Park, FL December
- School Readiness Symposium- December

Publications Summary

PETER M. STORK, PH.D.

4837 Steeler Blvd., Pittsburgh, PA 15213
Home: 412/555-4567 • Office: 412/555-2982
E-mail: jobseeker@pitt.edu

PUBLICATIONS

Fluid Flow/Heat Transfer

- Stork, P.M., Greene, D., and Foo, X.: Modeling Heat Transfer Oil Line Cooldown, *Journal of Petroleum Technology*. In Press.
- Stork, P.M., and Klein, C.S.: A Simplified Model for Oil-Water Flow, *Chemical Engineering Science*. Feb. 2006.
- Stork, P.M., Klein, C.S., and Foo, X.: Modeling Wellbore Oil Flow and Heat Transfer, *Journal of Flow Dynamics*. June 2005.
- Greene, D. and Stork, P.M.: Gauge Placement Matter in Transient Data Acquisition, *Chemical Engineering Journal*. Feb. 2005.
- Stork, P.M., Klein, C.S., and Foo, X.: Application of a Simulator for Testing Oil Well Capacity, *Journal of Petroleum Technology*. Sept. 2004.
- Stork, P.M., and Klein, C.S.: Predicting Fluid Temperature Profiles Oil Wells, *Journal of Petroleum Technology*. Aug. 2003.
- Greene, D., Stork, P.M., and Jordan, A.K.: A Transient Gradiated Model for Testing Gas Wells, *Journal of Petroleum Technology*. June 2003.
- Stork, P.M., Klein, C.S., Amene, A., and Foo, X.: A Model for Circulating Fluid Temperature, *Journal of Flow Dynamics*. June 2003.
- Greene, D. and Stork, P.M.: Controlling Circulating Fluid Temperature in Well Operations, *Journal of Petroleum Technology*. June 2003.
- Stork, P.M.: Bubbly and Slug Flow in Vertical and Inclined Wells, *Journal of Flow Dynamics*. Aug. 2002.
- Stork, P.M., and Klein, C.S.: Aspects of Heat Transfer During Two-Phase Flow in Wells, *Journal of Flow Dynamics*. Aug. 2001: 211–16.
- Stork, P.M. and Greene, D.: Estimation in Countercurrent Vertical Two-phase Flow, *Chemical Engineering Journal*. 79, No. 16 (2001): 2567–74.
- Stork, P.M. and Greene, D.: Modeling Transient Data Following Mud Circulation, *Journal of Petroleum Technology*. March 2001: 17–24.

Pressure Transient Analysis

- Stork, P.M., and Klein, C.S.: Modeling Wellbore Phase Redistribution, *Journal of Flow Dynamics*. 2002.
- Stork, P.M., and Klein, C.S.: Understanding Changing Wellbore Storage, *Journal of Energy Resources Science & Technology*. Dec. 2001.
- Klein, C.S. and Stork, P.M.: Two-phase Flow Correlations in Pumping Oil Wells, *Journal of Flow Dynamics*. June 2001: 121–28.

Media Mentions Summary.

JORDAN WHITE

610 DUSTY TRAIL • SONOMA, CA 95476-4174 • PHONE: 415-555-0850
E-MAIL: JOBSEEKER@AOL.COM

SUMMARY OF MEDIA MENTIONS

The following publications have included my quotes in editorial referencing the impact of the Internet on the travel industry:

Date	Publication	Headline
July 08, 2007	WebTravel News	Stipe Network promises travel agent support
June 22, 2007	Interactive Travel Report	Stipe Network has ancillary services
June 19, 2007	Leisure Travel News	Agents Offered New Paths to GDS Access
June 01, 2007	Travel Distribution Report	Stipe Network adds tour-booking component
May 22, 2007	Travel Weekly	An Alternative for Agents
May 04, 2007	Travel Distribution Report	STIPE offers two years' free CruiseExpert as booking incentive
May 04, 2007	Travel Weekly Crossroads	STIPE launches CruiseExpert, offers free Connectivity
April 29, 2007	Travel Agent Magazine	STIPE offers free CruiseExpert
December 27, 2001	Interactive Travel Report	STIPE offers free CruiseExpert
December 09, 2001	Positive Space	TellU International offers travel retailers Web-Based-reservation system
November 2001	Travel Weekly Crossroads	CRS and Internet Alternatives

The aforementioned articles were the primarily the result of one-on-one interviews with media and included my own quotes or commentary. I have also facilitated Stipe Network mention and quotes from other Stipe Network executives in numerous other articles in both electronic and print media.

Presentations Summary

ANDREA COLBURN
132 BLUEBIRD LANE ▪ MONETTA, SC 29105
jobseeker@aol.com ▪ 803/555-3976 ▪ FAX: 803/555-9780

PRESENTATIONS SUMMARY

- Colburn, A. (May 5, 2007). Tell Me About Yourself: Storytelling that Propels Careers. Golden Fleece Group, Chevy Chase, MD. http://www.goldenfleececon.org/

- Colburn, A. (2007). The Student Experience in Speed Teaming: A New Approach to Team Formation, 2007 College Teaching & Learning Conference/Applied Business Research Conference, Waikiki, HI.

- Colburn, A. (March 2006). Employment Interview Preparation: Assessing the Writing-to-Learn Approach. Association for Business Simulation and Experiential Learning (ABSEL), San Francisco, CA.

- Colburn, A. (2006). Using an Asynchronous Discussion Board for Online Focus Groups: A Protocol and Lessons Learned. 2006 Applied Business Research Conference, Orlando, FL.

- Colburn, A. (March 2005). Application of Traditional and Online Journaling as Pedagogy and Means for Assessing Learning in an Entrepreneurial Seminar. Developments in Business Simulation and Experiential Learning. Association for Business Simulation and Experiential Learning (ABSEL). Orlando, FL.

- Colburn, A. (Jan. 2005). Employment Interview Preparation: A Writing-to-Learn Approach. 2005 Applied Business Research Conference and The 2005 College Teaching and Learning Conference, Orlando, FL.

Reference List

PHILLIP AVERY

10 WHEATGRAIN WAY, ANOKA, MN 55303

763.555.9109   jobseeker@msn.com

REFERENCES

Ms. Mariah Fisch
President
National Steel Corporation
4100 Edison Lakes Pkwy.
Mishawaka, IN 46545-3440
812-555-3200
mfisch@nsc.com

Ms. Frisch was a client when I was a consultant at Accel Worldwide and has known me for more than 10 years.

Mr. C. Benjamin Riley
Senior Project Manager
Sprint Corporation
2330 Shawnee Mission Pkwy.
Westwood, KS 66205
620-555-2903

Mr. Riley was a co-worker at Delta Airlines who has known me for 18 years.

Mr. Kevin O'Horn
Vice President, Marketing
The Quaker Oats Company
Quaker Tower
321 N. Clark Street
Chicago, IL 60610-4714
312-555-3930

Mr. O'Horn was a client of Consolidated Health Group and has known me for almost 10 years.

Ms. Stephanie Thomas
Quality Systems Director
Sara Lee Corporation
3 First National Plaza
Chicago, IL 60602-4260
312-555-2990

Ms. Thomas was a client when I was a consultant at Accel Worldwide and has known me for more than 10 years.

Salary History

A salary history is often standard operating equipment in the job search—but it's the one item you hope *not* to use, or at least not until you can use it strategically late in the hiring process.

At executive levels, employers are less likely to ask for salary information early in the process. If you were at a lower level, employers use salary as an easy screening device to help weed out applicants.

If you are asked for a salary history early in the process, particularly even before an interview, decide whether you want to work for an employer who would screen you out of the hiring process based on salary. Information is power in job-hunting, and your goal should always be to hold on to your power as long as possible by delaying discussions about salary—ideally until you've obtained an offer. That's when the employer has made the statement "we want you on board," and that's when you have the power to negotiate.

If you decide to supply a requested salary history, note that employers want to see frequency and size of raises and promotions, so include beginning and ending salaries, as well as salary bumps that accompanied promotions. Also include any additional monetary aspects of the compensation package, such as bonuses. As with all printed documents in this chapter, maintain your consistent branding by matching your salary history's paper, style, letterhead, and font to your resume and cover letter.

A sample salary history is shown on page 112.

Communication Tools for Use at the Interview

Resume for Presentation (in PowerPoint)

Some employers are asking executive candidates to present their qualifications using presentation software, usually Microsoft's PowerPoint, as a way to lend greater structure to interviews. "The presentation consists of a work-history overview, major accomplishments and recognition received at each job, and a summary of strengths and developmental needs," writes recruiting expert Lou Adler, suggesting a presentation of six to eight slides. Adler notes that "this structured interview approach forces both the candidate and interviewer to stay on point and prevents misunderstandings." A PowerPoint resume might include testimonial quotes, a Branding Statement, a bare-bones history of career highlights, and bullet points showcasing top accomplishments.

Standard rules of good PowerPoint presentations apply to the PowerPoint resume:

➤ Keep the words on each slide to a minimum.

➤ Use type that is large enough to read.

➤ Keep the design simple; avoid hard-to-read fonts, too many fonts, and overuse of colors and effects.

A sample PowerPoint resume appears in the complete branded package at the end of this chapter.

Print Portfolio

A print portfolio is a visual tool that you can present in interviews to vividly provide proof of your performance. It's one thing to talk about your performance—or list it on your resume—but another to show visuals that irrefutably demonstrate your success.

A portfolio should be filled with artifacts and information that clearly show your accomplishments and tell a story of how you are the ideal candidate for the position sought. The portfolio is ideally introduced in response to an interview question that begins, "What kind of experience do you have with _____?" You can then respond, "I can show you all about my experience in this area in my portfolio."

John Oakley

7 Shawnee Road • Short Hills, NJ 07078 • Phone: 201-555-0303
E-mail: jobseeker@nnj.rr.com

SALARY HISTORY

Branch Manager, Dawson Company
Ending Salary: $188,000 annually, with bonus and full benefits package
Starting Salary: $170,000 annually, with bonus and full benefits package

Sales Manager, Laboratory Products, Spectra Gases
Ending Salary: $150,000 annually, with bonus and full benefits package
Starting Salary: $125,000 annually, with bonus and full benefits package

Project Development Consultant, Pantaleon Enterprises
Ending Salary: $105,000 annually, with bonus and full benefits package
Starting Salary: $90,000 annually, with bonus and full benefits package

Among the items that a candidate might include in a print portfolio are:

- Index/table of contents
- Resume
- Career goals/objectives/summary
- Branding statement
- Professional philosophy/mission statement
- List of accomplishments
- Success stories/narratives
- Case studies
- Photos depicting the candidate working on projects
- Media coverage
- Project summary report
- Project samples
- Charts, graphs, illustrations of results
- White papers
- Business plans
- Samples of work and reports
- Articles written for publication
- Performance reviews
- Leadership experience, leadership profile
- Transcripts, degrees, licenses, and certifications
- Awards and honors
- Volunteering/community service, including photos of the candidate in action
- Professional-development activities
- Professional memberships
- Letters of recommendation, commendation, kudos
- Reference list
- Testimonials
- Answers to common job interview questions
- Research the job-seeker has conducted on the company

Avoid personal items related to family, friends, pets, parties, hobbies, health, and marital status, as well as religious, political, or social affiliations.

Package your portfolio items in a high-end, three-ring leather binder. You may want to place each item in a high-quality plastic sheet protector. Use dividers to separate sections.

Although you likely will not present your portfolio until you are in the interview, it's not a bad idea to alert employers to your portfolio's availability on your resume, cover letter, or networking card.

Communication Tool for After the Interview

Thank-You Letter

In addition to the simple common courtesy of sending, without fail, a thank-you letter after each interview, a post-interview thank-you letter can play a number of other roles after the interview. With a well-crafted thank-you letter, you can:

➤ Emphasize how well you fit in well with the company culture, especially now that you know more about it having experienced the interview.

➤ Build on the strengths of the interview and highlight the match between you and the job.

➤ Bring up anything you thought of after the interview that is pertinent to the employer's concerns. The letter is also an opportunity to expand on responses you gave. If, for example, the interviewer told you exactly what the company was looking for in a candidate, you probably explained how you meet that description. But with further reflection after the interview, you can describe more fully how you fit the profile.

➤ Execute damage control to address (carefully) anything that went wrong in the interview or to speak to any objections you sense the employer may have to hiring you.

➤ Indicate that you are providing additional materials (such as references) that the interviewer has requested or that you feel might positively affect the hiring decision.

➤ Suggest what your immediate contributions would be if you are selected for the position.

➤ Restate your understanding of the next step in the process. At the executive level, you will likely experience a lengthy series of interviews. Asking, in each interview, about the next step and mentioning it in your thank-you letter will provide a small psychological prompt for the reader.

➤ Use the letter to restate your enthusiasm for the job.

Thank-you letters at the executive level will usually be typed business letters, though you could hand-write a letter if the culture of your targeted employer and the relationship you established with the interviewer suggest this personal touch. Studies show that taking the action to thank the interviewer is far more important than the form that action takes. For that reason, and because e-mail has become the dominant form of business communication, e-mailed thank-you letters are increasingly acceptable. It's a good idea, however, to follow up your e-mailed thank you with a hard-copy version.

At the executive level, you are likely to interview with multitudes of people, and, yes, you should send a thank you to each one. You can use a boilerplate letter as a template, but vary at least a sentence or two to individualize the letters in case your recipients compare notes.

Send a thank you within 24 hours of the interview.

Thank-you letters are generally quite brief—about three paragraphs. The thank-you letter sample from Candace Lindemann that follows illustrates a lengthier, more detailed letter that typifies an aspiring executive's need to show that she grasps the challenges of the position and is ready to meet that challenge. Following that sample is a more concise letter that will suffice in many situations.

CANDACE LINDEMANN

346 Jackson Street • Oakville, CA 94562 • 707-555-3028 • jobseeker@pacbell.net

Aug. 29, 2007

Hayley Sanders
Chair, Board of Directors
Institute for Human Advancement
1115 Van Ness St.
San Francisco, CA 94102-6033

Dear Ms. Sanders:

I'd like to thank you and the interview panel for talking with me on August 28 about the Executive Director position at IHA. I very much enjoyed our meeting and truly appreciate all the time and care you took in telling me about the job and learning more about my qualifications. I valued not only the relaxed atmosphere of the interview but that fact that the panel's questions and the topics discussed were both energizing and challenging. Our meeting made it clear to me that the IHA staff is committed to the revitalization of the institute and its mission, and I would welcome the opportunity to be part of the team at this point in the institute's development.

I was delighted to acknowledge that my background provides me with excellent qualifications for this position. In fact, our conversation convinced me that I am exactly what the institute needs. As you no doubt discerned, I am extremely excited by the idea of helping the team design a formal evaluation of the institute. In particular, I note that modern insights on evaluation of an organization do not focus on the pathology of the institution but instead reveal "what's working and what's not." Once the team has made that determination, I would like to participate in using this information to strategize implementation of a new vision. I affirmed through our interview my enthusiasm for marketing the institute. The fact that the current crisis in this field is worldwide provides the institute with an opportunity to think in terms of the bigger picture.

I hope I clearly demonstrated to you that my background compares favorably with your needs. It is also reassuring to know that I could turn to the institute's board should I need guidance in a particular issue. I would add that, increasingly, resilience in the face of change is the foundation of the human-advancement movement. In particular, most leading organizational theorists recognize what they call the "resiliency of organizations," and the need to provide space for the conflicting energies therein. I am convinced that my background of successfully applying organizational theory would enrich the ongoing dialogue in IHA.

Again, I very much appreciated the opportunity to meet with you and present my qualifications. Please feel free to contact me if you need more information about my background. Thank you again for the enjoyable and thought-provoking interview.

Sincerely,

Candace Lindemann

VERA BALDWIN

2838 Lakeshore Dr., Chicago, IL 60601 • 773-555-9725 • Cell: 516-555-4560 • E-mail: jobseeker@mindspring.com

Dec. 18, 2007

Ms. Stephanie Thomas
Chief of Quality Systems
Sara Lee Corporation
3 First National Plaza
Chicago, IL 60602-4260

Dear Ms. Thomas:

Thank you so much for talking with me on Dec. 17 about the Operations Director position at Sara Lee. I very much enjoyed our meeting and truly appreciate all the time and care you took to learn more about my qualifications.

I felt a rapport with you—and indeed with everyone with whom I met—that I know would contribute to a productive and collaborative relationship.

As you no doubt discerned, the scope of responsibility for this position closely parallels my background. My experience at BJD Trading in partnering with business units to identify IT priorities is especially relevant. My extensive experience as managing director of information technology has prepared me well for this position.

It has been especially encouraging to me during the interview process at Sara Lee that those I've met with have recognized how well my background aligns with the Operations Director position and have expressed confidence that I am an excellent fit with the position. Recapping my strengths and fit with the position:

- I can provide out-of-the-box thinking and visionary leadership strengths that would enable me to lead revitalization of the IT department while taking the department up to next level and providing optimal support to the technical infrastructure.
- I bring the adaptability and customer-focused mindset that enables me to raise the level of IT service to the organization.

I have no illusions; I am well aware that the position will be quite demanding and that it is a critical position within the company. But I am totally confident of my ability to develop and mentor managers to enable them to develop their teams, my skills in managing budgets exceedingly well, and my knack for interacting effectively with various levels within the organization.

Again, Ms. Thomas, thank you so much for such an enjoyable meeting. Please feel free to contact me if you need more information about my background.

Sincerely,

Vera Baldwin

Communication Tools for Passive Candidates

Web Portfolio

As noted in the Chapter 2 discussion of Web resumes, an online presence enables employers to find you anytime. A sophisticated Web-based portfolio with easy navigation to many of the same kinds of artifacts as in a print portfolio provides an impressive online presence for passive candidates.

A Web portfolio will typically have an opening page, and then four to five additional pages and a user-friendly navigation system to link to those pages. One page should be a contact page with information about how to contact the candidate. In place of an e-mail address—to avoid spam e-mails—the contact page can offer a form that interested parties can complete and submit to reach the candidate. Other pages might contain:

➤ Philosophy

➤ Branding statement

➤ Q&A: Responses to interview questions

➤ Resume, including links to versions in various file formats, such as Word (.doc), PDF (.pdf), and text (.txt)

➤ Accomplishments/Results/Career Highlights

➤ About me/Bio

➤ Credentials

➤ Strengths

➤ Case studies

➤ Press coverage

➤ Blog

These main pages can link to many of the same items that might be included in a print portfolio.

An advantage of a Web-based portfolio is that it can also contain audio and video components, such as a video profile of yourself, slide show, or a clip of a presentation you've done.

Unless you have top-drawer Web-design skills, consider purchasing Web portfolio services from a reputable professional. Conduct a search on the Web for portfolio vendors, and choose one with designs that appeal to you. Consider gathering references from clients to determine how the vendor is to work with. Interview vendors to get a feel for their style and their process in working with you.

See the full portfolio at *www.quintcareers.com/portfolios/executive/*.

Blog

More and more executives, especially within corporations, are starting blogs (short for Web log). A blog, if professional and regularly maintained, can be an excellent way to extend your brand, show your expertise and thought leadership, and enhance your online presence.

Bloggers post regular—sometimes daily—commentary and invite responses from and interactions with their readers. Busy executives will likely find daily postings too daunting and shoot for weekly or a few times a month.

In their *Career Distinction: Stand Out by Building Your Brand*, authors William Arruda and Kirsten Dixson suggest using most blog postings "to establish your thought leadership on a particular topic or group of related topics. The key to a stand-out blog is to own a niche and find your authentic voice for commenting on the niche. You might focus your posts on your specialized competencies, the concerns of your target audience, or your unique way of delivering value to your audience."

Bloggers generally use commercial publishing platforms that range in cost from free to several hundred dollars for a license. Common blogging software platforms include Typepad, Blogger, Wordpress, and Movable Type.

A blog can be linked to a personal Website or portfolio or can be a stand-alone element for building your personal brand and online presence.

Many executive blogs are sanctioned by the organizations that they lead. The blogs serve to promote the organization and connect executives with their customers. Do you doubt, however, that recruiters find these executives based on their blogs and attempt to lure them away? Some examples of corporate executive blogs include:

- Oracle Executive Blogs: *www.oracle.com/corporate/executive/blog/index.html*
- Randy's Journal, a blog hosted by Randy Tinseth, vice president, marketing for Boeing Commercial Airplanes: *http://boeingblogs.com/randy/*
- GM's FastLane blog, a forum for GM executives to talk about GM's current and future products and services: *http://fastlane.gmblogs.com/*
- cnewmark, the blog of Craig Newmark, founder of Craigslist: *www.cnewmark.com/*
- Agile Executive Blog, the blog of Pete Behrens, founder and principal consultant of Trail Ridge Consulting, LLC: *www.trailridgeconsulting.com/blog/*
- The Ventana Research Blog by Mark Smith, CEO and EVP: *www.ventanaresearch.com/blog/*
- Blog of Broadgate Business Financial company founder Michael Anders: *www.broadgatebusinessfinancial.com/ExecutiveBlog/ExecutiveBlog.html*
- Entellium Executive Blog by Paul Johnston, Entellium CEO: *http://pauljohnston.typepad.com/*
- Blog by Bryan Inch, general manager of financial service, RaboPlus: *www.raboplus.com.au/blog/*

Executives or aspiring executives also maintain blogs outside the purview of employment, positioning themselves as passive but receptive free agents who would welcome overtures from the right employers.

Complete Branded Package

The set of samples that follows ties together many of the pieces discussed in this chapter and shows how the candidate's branding is executed consistently through the package. The package, contributed by Sharon Graham, principal consultant, Graham Management Group, consists of:

- Resume
- Uninvited cover letter
- Invited cover letter
- Bio
- Leadership profile
- References
- Cover for print portfolio
- PowerPoint resume
- Thank-you letter

Dr. Randall S. Hansen contributed to this chapter.

Gordon H. Drake, MBA

123 Booth Crescent •• Oldbridge, New Jersey •• 12345
555.123.1234 (H) •• 555.123.4567 (C) •• ghdrake@gmail.com

INTERNATIONAL BUSINESS DEVELOPMENT EXECUTIVE

Building Teams •• Inspiring Excellence •• Generating Results

An award-winning global business development, sales, and marketing executive who brings more than 15 years' expertise increasing corporate market share and profitability. Engages and empowers high-performing teams that consistently exceed all expectations and quotas. Builds channel and direct sales pipelines to maximize existing business and capture new revenue. Overhauls organizational culture and positions teams for unprecedented growth and success.

CORE COMPETENCIES

- Leadership & Team Building
- Strategic Planning & Execution
- Profit & Loss (P&L) Management
- Market Penetration & Expansion

EXECUTIVE HIGHLIGHTS

- President's Club Award
- Sales Leader Award
- Top Sales 2001 – 2007
- Top Profit 2003 – 2007

BUILDING TEAMS

- Established a top-performing business development division from the ground up, successfully taking it from $14 million to $55 million in fourteen months.
- Built and led successful sales and marketing teams of up to 50 people, always delivering revenue growth and profitability.
- Expanded international distribution with sales exploding from $55 million to more than $90 million in just three years by developing cohesive management and sales teams.

INSPIRING EXCELLENCE

- Achieved unprecedented employee retention of 92% through employee engagement and incentive programs.
- Leveraged knowledge in other areas to promote cross-selling. Introduced team selling across divisions and achieved award-winning cross-sell results in year one.
- Implemented budget accountability with channel managers, reducing travel, and entertainment expenses by 15% annually.

GENERATING RESULTS

- Consistently produced millions in revenue and cost savings in the first year of hire for organizations ranging in size from $14 million to $1.4 billion.
- Built the fastest growing national brand in the history of the North American wireless peripheral industry, with a market explosion resulting in an average of two new stores opening weekly.
- Drove 400% increase in year-over-year sales and positioned company strategically in preparation of upcoming IPO; exceeded corporate value and growth expectations.

Continued...

Gordon H. Drake, MBA

Page 2 of 3 ▪▪ 555.123.4567 (C) ▪▪ ghdrake@gmail.com

CAREER CHRONOLOGY

InterActive xTech – New York, NY   **2003 – present**

$90 million provider of integrated technology solutions for small businesses and home offices.

VICE PRESIDENT, GLOBAL SALES & MARKETING

Recruited to oversee and grow sales and marketing operations. Led and managed 4 international teams consisting of 50 direct and VAR channel sales staff focused on solution sales.

- Optimized operational efficiencies through internal restructure, role centralization, and introduction of formal communication processes.

- Designed and implemented a new sales compensation and incentive program to attract, motivate, and retain top quality sales professionals; hired 3 additional regional managers as a result.

- Implemented innovative *Buy and Sell* sales incentive programs, driving a $12 million growth in revenue in one quarter alone.

Year	$ Revenue Attained	% Profit
2006	$90 million	23%
2005	$67 million	12%
2004	$55 million	12%
2003	$14 million	8%

Tek Au Courant – Markham, ON   **1995 – 2003**

$1.4 billion technology peripherals provider to the wireless industry.

DIRECTOR OF SALES & MARKETING, Canadian Operations (1999 – 2003)

Promoted to oversee the retail sales, marketing, and promotion for 104 stores with $100M in sales volume and take responsibility for same-store growth and new store development in Canada.

- Developed the brand in limited distribution centres, leading to an incredible growth period, doubling revenues, and taking the brand from a rank of 4th to 1st ; won President's Club Award.

- Conceived and instituted kiosk reseller concept and secured contract with multi-billion dollar North American retailer; won largest initial contract in the history of the organization.

- Devised and launched vertical marketing campaigns and employee purchase plans. Enhancements contributed to growth and month-over-month sales increases.

SENIOR MANAGER, RETAIL OPERATIONS, Canada (1995 – 1999)

Retained to develop the fastest growing region, encompassing 54 stores in 17 States, and direct the implementation of marketing programs, sales teams, and training programs.

- Managed all in-store sales performance and marketing programs, leading to an increase in consistent comparable store growth of over 14%; recipient of Outstanding Sales Leader Award.

- Spearheaded sales from $64 million to $81 million in a large network of department stores, specialty stores, and boutiques.

Continued…

Gordon H. Drake, MBA

Page 3 of 3 ** 555.123.4567 (C) ** ghdrake@gmail.com

FORMAL EDUCATION

MASTER OF BUSINESS ADMINISTRATION (MBA)	University of Toronto
MARKETING DIPLOMA	George Brown College

PROFESSIONAL DEVELOPMENT

Sales Advantage	Dale Carnegie Training
The 7 Habits Of Highly Effective People	Franklin Covey Canada
Dealing with Difficult People	Stitt Feld Handy Group
Strategic Negotiating	The Niagara Institute
The Power of Full Engagement	LGE Performance Group
SPINN: Professional Sales Training Program	LGE Performance Group

SPEAKING ENGAGEMENTS

International Reseller Conference, New York, NY – Keynote Speaker, *Channels Not Silos*	2006
Technology Council, Ottawa, ON – Invited Guest Speaker, *Building and Leading a Strong Team*	2005
Canadian Technology Week, Toronto, ON – Moderator, Marketing Panel	1996 – 2004

COMMUNITY COMMITMENT

Award Adjudicator, Recall North America Cross-Sell Award	2007
Board Member, Technology Council Of North America	2006
Mentor, Canadian Youth Business Foundation	2002 – 2003
Fundraiser, Canadian Breast Cancer Foundation	1999 – 2003

Building Teams ** Inspiring Excellence ** Generating Results

Gordon H. Drake, MBA
123 Booth Crescent ▪▪ Oldbridge, New Jersey ▪▪ 12345
555.123.1234 (H) ▪▪ 555.123.4567 (C) ▪▪ ghdrake@gmail.com

February 1, 2008
Mr. Reginald Graham
Chief Executive Officer
GlobeTech Retail Solutions
123 Main Avenue
New York, NY, 12345

Dear Mr. Graham:

In researching organizations where my success in business development, sales, and marketing are well matched, GlobeTech Retail Solutions stood apart from the rest. The purpose of this letter is to introduce myself and explore the possibility for us to share valuable information and uncover opportunities to benefit from our new relationship.

Based on Globetech's reputation and effectiveness in creating brand recognition, I am interested in learning more about your role in the dynamic technology solutions environment. I would also like to relate to you how my success with two market leaders can benefit your organization.

In recent years, my accountabilities have included business development initiatives that generated outstanding revenue and new market growth. My experience and expertise appear to be well aligned with GlobeTech in the following areas:

▪ **Building Teams:** Created highly effective global sales and marketing teams that drive revenue.

▪ **Inspiring Excellence:** Improved brand ranking from #4 to #1 position within four years.

▪ **Generating Results:** Produced $90 million annually and improved profits by 15% in four years.

With a balanced style that is both people and task-oriented, I have a proven ability to design new ways to improve productivity, efficiency, and bottom-line results. Therefore, I believe there is mutual benefit in connecting with you to learn more about your business needs and to define ways in which my experience can translate into an asset for your organization.

Mr. Graham, I have taken the liberty of enclosing a short PowerPoint presentation that tells a bit more about me. In the next few days, I will give you a call to see whether we can set up an appointment. If you would like a copy of my résumé and professional profile before we meet, please let me know by e-mailing ghdrake@gmail.com or calling 555.123.4567.

Sincerely,

Gordon H. Drake

Building Teams ▪▪ Inspiring Excellence ▪▪ Generating Results

Gordon H. Drake, MBA

123 Booth Crescent ▪▪ Oldbridge, New Jersey ▪▪ 12345
555.123.1234 (H) ▪▪ 555.123.4567 (C) ▪▪ ghdrake@gmail.com

January 1, 2008
Mr. Reginald Graham
Chief Executive Officer
GlobeTech Retail Solutions
123 Main Avenue
New York, NY, 12345

Re: Vice President, International Business Development

Dear Mr. Graham:

GlobeTech Retail Solutions is an industry leader with a reputation for excellence and I am a sales and marketing leader with proven success in producing multi-million dollar increases. This – and much more – is what I offer to the position of Vice President, International Business Development. The attached résumé provides the details of my career and demonstrates the merit in meeting, to pursue our mutual interests.

Known for more than a decade of leading successful business development, sales, and marketing initiatives, I have also developed expertise in:

- **Building Teams:** Launched new initiatives and mentored sales team members producing $90 million annual revenue in four short years.
- **Inspiring Excellence:** Delivered innovative programs and operational improvements to improve employee retention to 92% while reducing travel and entertainment expenses by 15%.
- **Generating Results:** Utilized relationship-building talents and business acumen to enhance bottom-line results and create year-over-year increases in profitability.

Results-driven, resilient, and highly approachable, I build and mentor effective teams through a range of initiatives. Experience has taught me the value of cultivating team morale and leading individuals to peak performance through education and effective communication. I have a talent for keeping teams focused on sales objectives and motivated toward successful outcomes.

I am stimulated by challenging problems and have been the pacesetter in operations improvement and event management, as well as sales and marketing. Whether putting a new product to market or growing the business in general, I always raise the bar for myself and inspire similar goals for my team. This ensures consistent, timely results that are well above target.

GlobeTech has a reputation for a *people-first* approach to corporate development. The fact that you have established your business on this foundation has enticed me to pursue this opportunity to utilize my expertise in business and team development at GlobeTech Retail Solutions. I look forward to arranging a meeting that is conducive to your agenda where we can further discuss the dynamic leadership that I bring to this role.

Sincerely,

Gordon H. Drake

Enclosure: Résumé

Building Teams ▪▪ Inspiring Excellence ▪▪ Generating Results

Gordon H. Drake, MBA

123 Booth Crescent ▪▪ Oldbridge, New Jersey ▪▪ 12345
555.123.1234 (H) ▪▪ 555.123.4567 (C) ▪▪ ghdrake@gmail.com

Gordon H. Drake is an inspirational leader with over 15 years of business development experience in the technology industry. What he brings to any organization is highlighted in his personal tagline: *Building Teams, Inspiring Excellence, and Generating Results*. He is a relationship-driven sales and marketing professional who nurtures and empowers his teams to deliver unprecedented bottom-line results.

Established at the forefront of the North American retail technology industry, Gordon is a progressive business driver whose results are measured not only in the impressive numbers he delivers but also in the dedication and commitment his teams offer. His mission is to develop top-performing teams and empower them to become integral members focused on the organization's growth. The organizational culture he creates results in higher rates of retention, and accountable teams who strive for excellence and take pride in delivering superior results.

Gordon's most recent role with InterActive xTech in New York, as Vice President of Global Sales and Marketing, has added further testimony to his strength as a leader who drives growth while building high performance teams who delight in creating profitability. In four short years, he has taken the organization from $14 million in annual revenue to $90 million, while improving profitability by 15%.

Throughout his career, Gordon has consistently attained new business growth beyond all expectations. In his earlier roles, he earned numerous prestigious awards including the President's Club Award and the Sales Leader Award. Leading Canadian sales and marketing initiatives at Tek Au Courant, he brought the organization from fourth ranking to number one position.

Gordon is a powerful presenter and communicator, capturing the attention and interest of various North American leaders. His professional speaking engagements include the Technology Council where he was an invited guest speaker. Additionally, the International Reseller Conference retained Gordon as their 2006 keynote speaker. A long-standing supporter of Canadian Technology Week, he was asked to moderate the Marketing Panel for eight concurrent years.

Gordon possesses a Masters of Business Administration from the University of Toronto, with a concentration in Marketing. He is an ongoing learner who engages in professional development to fine-tune his skills and knowledge. Gordon stays current with industry and business trends, and parlays this knowledge into incredible bottom-line results for the divisions he leads.

While Gordon is career-focused, he is also very active in his personal life. He spends quality time with his wife, Mary and his two Labrador Retrievers, Marley and Maverick. His hobbies range from golfing to cross country skiing.

With his expertise in *Building Teams, Inspiring Excellence*, and *Generating Results*, **Gordon H. Drake** is an asset who pays huge returns on investment. If you would like to discuss all that he can do for your company, please call 555.123.1234 or e-mail ghdrake@gmail.com any time.

Building Teams ▪▪ Inspiring Excellence ▪▪ Generating Results

Gordon H. Drake, MBA

123 Booth Crescent ▪▪ Oldbridge, New Jersey ▪▪ 12345
555.123.1234 (H) ▪▪ 555.123.4567 (C) ▪▪ ghdrake@gmail.com

LEADERSHIP INITIATIVES

BUILDING TEAMS

CHALLENGE: Two leadership changes in one year created extensive management and employee anxiety levels, which negatively affected organizational culture.

STRATEGY: Methodically and tactfully downsized underperforming departments. Retained four top-level producers to train and lead the international teams. Drove organizational values and targets.

RESULTS: Credited for maintaining continuity of operations and providing leadership stability. Increased revenue from $14 million to $90 million in four years.

INSPIRING EXCELLENCE

CHALLENGE: Inherited a demoralized sales team with tenure and challenged with the task of turning morale around while implementing restructured policies and procedures.

STRATEGY: Spent face time with employees to allay fears; emphasized positives and provided professional prospective. Implemented budget accountability with managers.

RESULTS: Significantly enhanced employee morale and loyalty; produced a 15% improvement in retention and a 15% reduction in travel and entertainment expenses, and $12 million revenue growth directly attributed to employee incentives.

GENERATING RESULTS

CHALLENGE: Sales were stagnant at approximately $14 million for three consecutive years, while profit margins were decreasing substantially.

STRATEGY: Implemented a variety of innovative programs including *Buy and Sell* and expanded international distribution channels.

RESULTS: Drove up to 400% increase in year-over-year sales in the first year alone, with an overall 15% increase in profit margins over a four year period.

Year	$Revenue Attained	% Profit
2006	$90 million	23%
2005	$67 million	12%
2004	$55 million	12%
2003	$14 million	8%

Building Teams ▪▪ Inspiring Excellence ▪▪ Generating Results

Gordon H. Drake, MBA

123 Booth Crescent ▪▪ Oldbridge, New Jersey ▪▪ 12345
555.123.1234 (H) ▪▪ 555.123.4567 (C) ▪▪ ghdrake@gmail.com

INTERNATIONAL BUSINESS DEVELOPMENT EXECUTIVE

PROFESSIONAL REFERENCES

Ruth Armstrong
President and Chief Executive Officer
Tek Au Courant
555.476.1343 extension 123
ruth.armstrong@tekaucourant.com
Direct supervisor for 7 years

Sam Goldring
Senior Vice President- Global Business Development
Tek Au Courant
555.476.1343 extension 124
sam.goldring@tekaucourant.com
Direct supervisor for 5 years

Jason Palmer
Partner
Hyslop, Palmer & Brown
555.976.4222
palmerj@hpb.com
Fellow Board member at the Technology Council of North America

Building Teams ▪▪ Inspiring Excellence ▪▪ Generating Results

Gordon H. Drake, MBA

INTERNATIONAL BUSINESS DEVELOPMENT EXECUTIVE

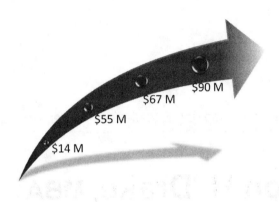

$14 M

$55 M

$67 M

$90 M

Building Teams ▪▪ Inspiring Excellence ▪▪ Generating Results

123 Booth Crescent ▪▪ Oldbridge, New Jersey ▪▪ 12345
555.123.1234 (H) ▪▪ 555.123.4567 (C) ▪▪ ghdrake@gmail.com

Gordon H. Drake, MBA

INTERNATIONAL BUSINESS DEVELOPMENT EXECUTIVE

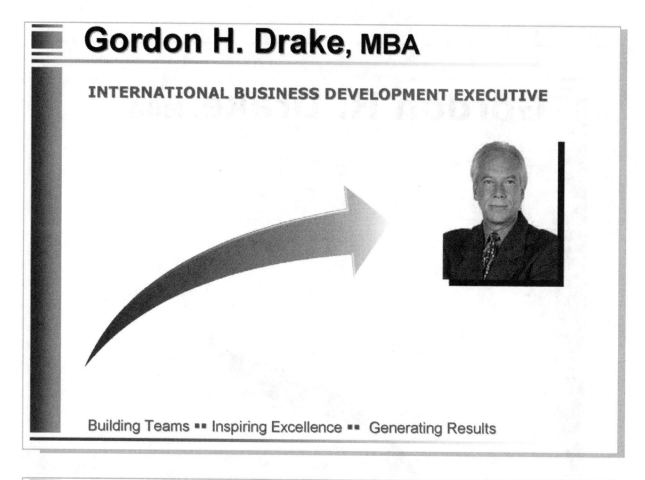

Building Teams ▪▪ Inspiring Excellence ▪▪ Generating Results

Gordon H. Drake, MBA

PROFESSIONAL PROFILE

Global business development, sales, and marketing executive...

- Brings 15 years' expertise increasing market share and profitability.

- Overhauls organizational culture for unprecedented success.

- Engages and empowers high-performing teams that exceed quotas.

- Builds pipelines to maximize business and capture new revenue.

Building Teams ▪▪ Inspiring Excellence ▪▪ Generating Results

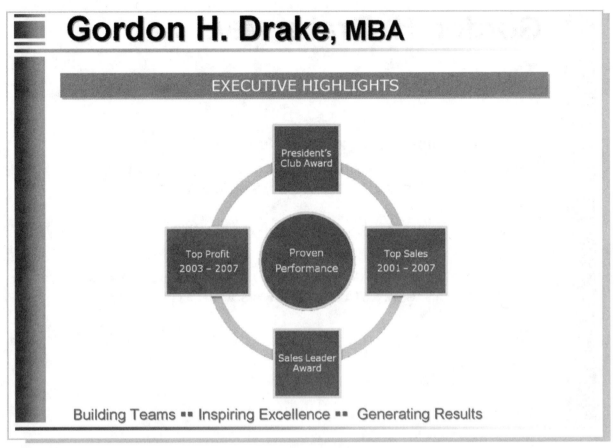

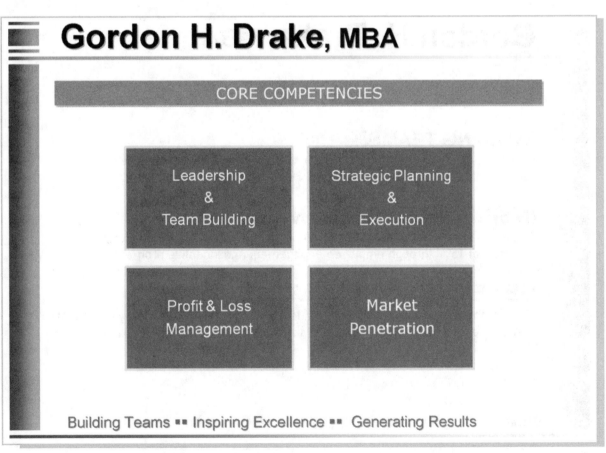

Gordon H. Drake, MBA

CAREER CHRONOLOGY

InterActive xTech – New York, NY
2003 – present
VICE PRESIDENT, GLOBAL SALES & MARKETING

Tek Au Courant – Markham, ON
1995 – 2003
DIRECTOR OF SALES & MARKETING, Canadian Operations (1999 – 2003)
SENIOR MANAGER, RETAIL OPERATIONS, Canada (1995 – 1999)

Building Teams ▪▪ Inspiring Excellence ▪▪ Generating Results

Gordon H. Drake, MBA

CAREER HIGHLIGHTS

BUILDING TEAMS...
▪Established an top-performing business development division from the ground up, successfully taking it from $14 million to $90 million in four years.

INSPIRING EXCELLENCE...
▪Achieved unprecedented employee retention of 92% and employee expense reduction of 15% through employee engagement and incentive programs.

GENERATING RESULTS...
▪Consistently produced millions in revenue and increases in profitability in the first year of hire for organizations ranging in size from $14 million to $1.4 billion.

Building Teams ▪▪ Inspiring Excellence ▪▪ Generating Results

Gordon H. Drake, MBA

LEADING SALES TEAMS TO CONSISTENTLY EXCEED QUOTA

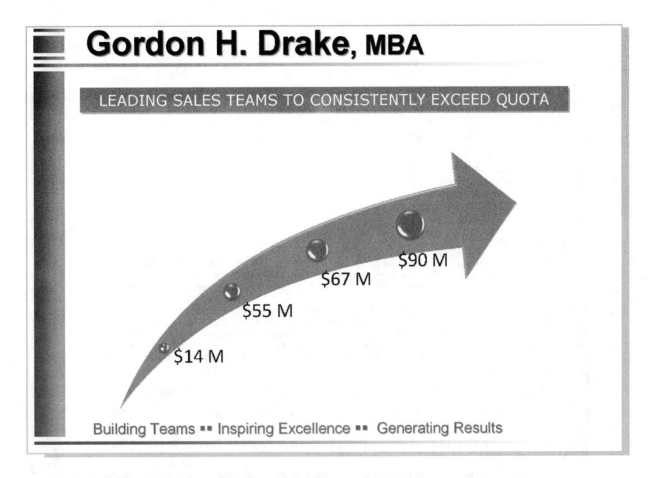

$90 M

$67 M

$55 M

$14 M

Building Teams ▪▪ Inspiring Excellence ▪▪ Generating Results

Gordon H. Drake, MBA

FOR MORE INFORMATION, PLEASE CONTACT:

Gordon H. Drake, MBA

555.123.1234 (H)
555.123.4567 (C)
ghdrake@gmail.com

123 Booth Crescent, Oldbridge, New Jersey, 12345

THANK YOU FOR YOUR INTEREST

Building Teams ▪▪ Inspiring Excellence ▪▪ Generating Results

Gordon H. Drake, MBA

123 Booth Crescent ▪▪ Oldbridge, New Jersey ▪▪ 12345
555.123.1234 (H) ▪▪ 555.123.4567 (C) ▪▪ ghdrake@gmail.com

March 1, 2008
Mr. Reginald Graham
Chief Executive Officer
GlobeTech Retail Solutions
123 Main Avenue
New York, NY, 12345

Dear Mr. Graham:

It was a privilege to meet with you and discuss the vision of GlobeTech Retail Solutions and how I can contribute as your Vice President, International Business Development. It would be an honor to put my talents in building teams, inspiring excellence, and generating results to work for you.

As we discussed, the standards that GlobeTech displays are closely aligned with my own values and principles. Industry associates and peers have remarked at my ability to provide direction with credibility, which translates into retention, results, and corporate integrity. I excel at working in cross-functional teams and spearheading projects to establish new markets and boost market share. In addition, I have a highly developed sense of discernment in identifying strategic locations and directing traffic to those points of sale.

Allow me to reinforce the points from our discussion with the following highlights:

▪ Successfully took a global business development operation from $14 million to over $90 million in four short years.

▪ Gained the trust and commitment from a geographically dispersed team, producing top-performing employees and a 92% retention rate.

▪ Built the fastest growing national brand in the history of the Canadian wireless peripheral sector.

The added value that I bring to this role comes from my professional origins as an award-winning retail sales and marketing executive where I learnt the benefits of work ethic and relationship building. Having experienced the retail business from professional roles to executive class positions has broadened my perspective. I know what it takes to get the job done and am typically the *go to* person when things need to be resolved.

The innovative and forward thinking philosophy of GlobeTech demonstrates a commitment to future business growth. Certainly, a leader in sales force development will only complement your progressive ranking in this industry, and I see myself in that role as part of your team. I look forward to the next step in developing our relationship and will follow up with you in the week ahead.

Sincerely,

Gordon H. Drake

Building Teams ▪▪ Inspiring Excellence ▪▪ Generating Results

Chapter Four

The Opinions That Count: Resume Preferences and Peeves From Hiring Decision-Makers

In the subjective world of career-marketing communications, where opinions vary widely and consensus is hard to find, the pet peeves and preferences of those with the power to hire offer enlightenment for crafting your executive resume—especially what to avoid.

Through a list of the Top 30 Executive Resume Pet Peeves, hiring decision-makers reveal the landmines aspiring executives can avoid while positioning their career-marketing documents to meet decision-maker needs. Fifty-nine hiring decision-makers were surveyed for this book about their peeves and preferences. One of them, Melissa Holmes, senior technical recruiter, at Levi, Ray & Shoup Consulting Services (Springfield, Illinois) speculated that while executive and senior-level candidates make the same resume mistakes as all other job-seekers perhaps hiring decision-makers are less forgiving.

Top 30 Executive Resume Pet Peeves of Hiring Decision-Makers

1. **Resume has spelling errors, typos, and grammatical flaws.** Hiring decision-makers cited this peeve more than any other. It may surprise some that misspellings and typos pervade even executive-level resumes, but they do. A job-seeker–submitted sample I considered for this book, for example, contained the common error of spelling "manager" as "manger." You'll note that this misspelling won't be picked up by spell-check functions because "manger" is a correctly spelled word. So is "posses," the plural of posse, which I often see on resumes when the job-seeker intends "possess."

   "I once received a resume where the applicant misspelled the name of the university from which he received his MBA," said Jeff Weaver, regional manager for a global information services company.

   "Poor spelling and grammar...is particularly worrying," said Pete Follows, senior consultant, for SaccoMann, Leeds, UK. "If a candidate is not giving due care and attention to a document to improve their own personal circumstances, what care would they take with documents with less personal significance?"

A few tips on avoiding typos, misspellings, and grammatical errors:

➤ Use spell-check functions but remember that they aren't enough.

➤ Proofread. Then put the resume down overnight and proof it again in the morning with fresh eyes.

➤ Try proofing from the bottom up. Reading your resume in a different order will enable you to catch errors that you may have glossed over before because your brain was accustomed to reading your verbiage in the expected order.

➤ Ask a friend or family member to proof, preferably one who is a meticulous speller and grammarian.

➤ Be careful about company and software names, which are frequently misspelled and can damage your credibility.

➤ Consider hiring a professional resume writer.

2. **Resume is too long.** Although there is no consensus among employers and recruiters about resume length, most feel one page is too short. Maureen Crawford Hentz, manager of talent acquisition, development and compliance at Osram Sylvania (Boston, Massachusetts), particularly disdains "abbreviated" or "teaser" resumes that urge the recruiter, "for more information, call me." Many recruiters believe that two pages is about the right length; for some, three pages is the outside limit that they will read. "If the resume is longer than two pages, it needs to be well worth it," noted Hentz's colleague at Osram Sylvania, Harlynn Goolsby. Others question executives' ability to prioritize if their resumes are longer than two pages.

Because recruiters pass candidate resumes on to client employers, they must also consider employer preferences. "Most of my clients profess that they are too busy to read anything lengthier—thus, I deliver what they require," said Chris Dutton, director at Intelligent Recruitment Services and Owner, Intelligent IT Recruitment (Manchester, United Kingdom). Recruiter opinions about resume length have been colored in recent years by the growing practice of reading resumes on a computer screen rather than printing them. Resumes that might seem too long in print are acceptable on screen.

For many decision-makers, page length is less important than providing sufficient details is. "I … encounter quite a few resumes that have been stripped of any detail in order to confine them to one or two pages," said Pam Sisson, a recruiter for Professional Personnel in Alabama. "My immediate response is to ask for a more detailed resume. A resume that's three or four pages but actually shows the qualifications and experience necessary for a position is *much* preferred, in my opinion, to one that has cut out all the substance to meet some passé idea of a one-page resume." Senior IT recruiter John Kennedy agreed: "Resume length is of very little importance so long as the information is accurate, verifiable, and pertinent to the position. If a candidate has 20 years of experience directly relating to the position being applied for and that experience is verifiable, it should be listed even if the resume goes four-plus pages."

3. **Resume is too wordy—contains too much information.** Strike a balance between a meaty, content-rich resume and a concise, readable document. Employers want both. Limit bullet points while still telling your full story. As mentioned previously, cut out unnecessary words. If you've sliced out as much as you can and the resume still looks text-dense, look for ways to break up blocks of content. "Long sentences with deep paragraphs put me to sleep, and I have a good chance of missing something important because I don't have time to read a novel," said Brian Howell, CSAM of The QWorks Group.

4. **Resume is written in third-person.** Survey respondents were surprisingly vocal in their irritation over this resume affectation. Although the pronoun "I" is generally not used in resume, it is the understood—but unwritten—subject of a resume's bullet points. Note that "I" is the unwritten subject of this bullet point:

   ■ [I] Facilitate restriction-removal processes on restricted/private placement securities.

   When the bullet point, however, is written with a third-person verb, as in the following, the subject becomes "he" or "she:"

   ■ [He] or [She] Facilitates restriction-removal processes on restricted/ private placement securities.

   Some senior-level job-seekers are even more blatant in their use of third person, annoying employers with summary statements such as:

   George Jones is a globally experienced broker and trader with significant, progressive brokerage experience and expertise.

   ■

   As an Information Resources Management manager (IRM) at both the corporate and project level, Bob Smith has consistently demonstrated his ability to understand customer needs and develop and implement effective IRM solutions for both commercial and government contracts.

5. **Resume does not list phone number, only an e-mail address, or has inappropriate e-mail address.** In the age of electronic submission, many candidates seem to think decision-makers will want to communicate by e-mail only, but a phone number on your resume is an absolute must. Be sure to include a daytime phone number, as that's when recruiters are most likely to call you. The recruiting process often moves too rapidly for e-mail; recruiters prefer to call—and expect you either to answer or call back without delay. Without a phone number, "I can't call you," said Seattle-based recruiter Alice Hanson, "and most jobs I have on my desk need to be filled in 24 to 48 hours. I find a good candidate and can't connect—it drives me wild." If employers can't reach you very quickly, they'll move on to the next person. They still want to see e-mail addresses listed as an alternate contact method, however, and recruiters note a surprising number of candidates who fail to provide sufficient contact information.

   Your e-mail address must be professional. "I don't want to know if you are 'sokkerguy' or 'kittylover,' says Joe Briand, partner at The Clarion Group (Placerville, California). "Use Yahoo or Gmail and get a professional-sounding address for your job search."

6. **Resume contains the personal pronoun "I."** It might seem like a silly protocol to omit "I" when the understood subject of resume bullet points is, in fact, "I." But eliminating personal pronouns (I, me, my) is simply an accepted style, and not following that style, Hanson noted, makes the candidate seem "amateurish."

7. **Resume contains a weak Objective Statement.** Most people in hiring positions do not read Objective Statements. "Omit objective statements [because] the applicant, as a matter of principal, has no objective; the *company* has the objective," advised Kennedy. "Whatever you write, your objective is to get a job," said Alison, a corporate recruiter for a specialized information provider, who asked to be identified only by her first name.

"I can never figure out why people think employers are breathlessly waiting to provide them with opportunities. I am especially puzzled when it is in an executive resume," noted Joy Montgomery, owner of Structural Integrity in California, citing a typically poor objective statement."

Objective: A challenging position where I am able to use my considerable something or other skills in a fulfilling opportunity....

Similarly, Weaver offered this self-serving and slightly exaggerated Objective Statement as a typically weak example.

Objective: Seeking to obtain a position within a growing company where my existing skills will benefit my employer, and be part of an environment where I will be challenged so that I may gain even more experience.

8. **Resume content lacks results.** Hiring decision-makers want to see the results you attained for past employers, what you accomplished, the value you added, and how you made a difference in your past jobs. They want to gain a sense of the complexity and significance of what you've done. Some recruiters recommend a bulleted list of key projects indicating accomplishments and results.

As many achievements as possible should be measurable, especially quantifiable. Scott advises metrics or results for at least 40 percent of your bullet points for each job. "Anytime you can quantify your accomplishments, you give them more credibility," said Howell. Among measurable items that employers want to see are sales volume (and ranking in comparison with peer and compared to previous periods, percent of quota), number (and titles) of direct reports, number of people you've hired, size of teams you've led, your position within the team, amount of money you've saved, success in completing projects, and initiatives that result in revenue-generation, process-improvement, and cost-containment.

9. **Resume is so full of quantitative data that it's hard to read.** Your resume must tell stories of your successes and results. Numbers are great, but well-chosen words and well-crafted phrases will also get your message across. Excessive use of numbers can hurt your resume's readability, so don't go overboard.

10. **Resume is too general.** To keep from limiting themselves, candidates sometimes create a very broad resume that lacks specific information. A peeve for Holmes is "failure to include enough information for a recruiter to determine fit. Executives more so than less-senior level candidates should be aware of the importance of effective communication, and yet they seem less motivated to tailor their resume to the specific job in which they are seeking."

11. **Resume is not tailored to the targeted vacancy.** Shawn Slevin, HR and human capital solutions provider for Chair Swim Strong Foundation (New York City area), called resumes that are the same for every position "cookie cutter." Instead, your resume should closely match the requirements of the job you are targeting. While hiring decision-makers don't pay much attention to Objective Statements, the headline technique can be effective in telling the recipient immediately what job or type of job you're targeting. When targeting a job advertised by a corporate recruiter in a specific company, demonstrate in your resume that you've researched that organization and can tie your accomplishments to the employer's needs.

As recruiter Lisa De Benedittis, president of Elite Staffing Services (San Diego area), noted: "Resumes are auditions without the benefit of *you* being around. I will decide if you are a match for my job/client within 20 seconds. Your resume will speak volumes about your communication skills. Do you use words to demonstrate your value or is it boilerplate? Did you put thought and effort into this audition?"

12. Resume contains inexplicable acronyms and industry-specific jargon.

Here's an example of a head-spinning array of acronyms and jargon from one resume reviewed for this book. The reader can figure out many of them, but it would be so much easier if they were spelled out:

- Manage the Asia Pacific WCS IT Outsourcing Transition & Transformation Programme Waves 1& 2. This is part of the Global Transition & Transformation Programme, a cluster of 82 major projects over a period of 3 years for an APAC budget of 8.7M Euros, executed by EDS but controlled and monitored by ABN.

- Transitioned to EDS ~300 Technology staff in Singapore, H Kong , Sydney, Tokyo, Shanghai including the ABN Regional Processing Centre on time and within budget.

- Negotiated Wave 2 T&T budget cost avoidance of 0.5m Euros.

- Provide direct management support to the A/P Technology CIO & Management Team, encompassing Financial Control Process Co-ordination, Resource Management, Portfolio & Project Control Project (A/P 320 projects with a budget expenditure of ~34M Euros). Responsible for the functional & organizational development of the Global Retained Technology Organization (NTO) and the development of the Global Governance Framework schedule (part of the Global Service Agreement contract).

- Established & Implemented the Value Management Plan to achieve best practices within WCS Technology.

- Developed the Global Retained Organization & Functional model on time & within budget.

- Managed the TOI - WCS (Investment & Commercial Banking) Global IT Operations and Global Change Control Teams.

- Provided Global Infrastructure Operational Services, defined/set Global Standards and Global IT Processing Services Strategy. This encompassed managing the Global IT Ops/Change Control Teams of > 300 staff and relevant expenditure budgets of >100M Euros.

- Restructured Global Lotus Notes Ops Team - FTE Savings by 70 % and London Change Control Team-FTE Savings by 35%.

- Implemented Automation and AS/400 LPAR technologies to reduce RPC Singapore & Amsterdam Operational Costs by 25%.

- Negotiated a new TCO with IBM in Singapore with a cost savings of over 2.3M Sing. Dollars.

- Expanded Singapore RPC Processing Services Capabilities to establish a Centre of excellence.

- Established ISAP Global Change Control TAT Acceptance Criteria Policy & Standards.

- Established Global IT Processing Services Strategy / Business Model.

- Developed the WCS Global SLOs and Major Contributor of the first TOI Service Catalogue

"Acronyms that are company-specific need to be reworked into a generic description of the same type that is easily understandable to those outside of that environment," advised senior technical recruiter Holmes.

13. **Resume language is replete with "fluff," flowery words, and "resume-speak" instead of specifics.** Your resume "needs to have good factual information and be clear as to what it is that you actually do; it doesn't need to be fluffy and overwrought," said survey respondent Thomas Burrell. Meg Steele, director of recruitment and employment mobility at Swedish Medical Center (Seattle area), decried the lack of specifics in resume language: "The most irritating characteristic on senior-level resumes is an overuse of flowery language without substantiation," she said. "I want to see actual accomplishments, not summary statements that imply an understanding of functional areas that reported up to the individual. A good leader knows enough about what his or her people are doing to speak intelligently about the problem that was being solved by this or that initiative. So, if [candidates] say 'oversaw development of strategic solutions,' they should have some more specific examples of said 'strategic solutions' and what the impact was to the business [and] the employees." Agreed Alison, corporate recruiter for a specialized information provider: "Weed out the garbage and tell me what you made, saved, achieved and make it quantifiable.

Characterized as "resume-speak" by survey respondents were words including "visionary," "thought leader," "evangelist," "innovative," "motivating," "engaging."

14. **Resume language is egotistical and self-congratulatory.** Harlynn Goolsby of the Human Resources Department at OSRAM Sylvania compares this type of resume verbiage to a "bio or the introduction for a guest speaker."

Some examples of puffed-up phrases include "inspirational leader," "as quoted in …," and "winner of countless awards."

15. **Content focuses on soft skills and neglects hard data.** Seeing soft skills listed on a resume is a rock-bottom priority for hiring decision-makers, who prefer to explore soft skills in the interview stage (and by talking to your references), because it is difficult to substantiate them on paper. "If you have to tell me you have these skills, you probably don't have them," said Kristina Creed, a senior manager at a for-profit education provider. Limit use of soft skills—such as communication, teamwork, and leadership—to those that are germane to the position you're targeting. Portrayal of soft skills will be more credible if you substantiate them with solid examples of how you've demonstrated them. If hard skills are required, be sure to include them, too, and be very specific about them (types of projects, technical skills, and expertise).

Soft skills are also helpful if you are in a profession in which hard skills predominate, and soft skills are unexpected but desirable. "If you're a software engineering manager who has a real talent with people and is technically excellent—highlight it," Richmond suggested. "You're a rarity, so have *great* stories ready to back it up."

16. **Span of work experience in a given job is listed with years only, instead of with months and years, or is listed inconsistently from job to job.** Decision-makers want to see specific dates of employment—months and years (not days). "A job that ran December, 2004 to January, 2005, if months are not listed, looks precisely the same as a job that ran January, 2004, to December, 2005—a significant difference," noted senior IT recruiter John Kennedy. Similarly, De Benedittis noted, "if your resume says 2004–2005 that could be a 30-day job or a 12-month job. I don't want to guess and neither does my client. Put a month and a year on your resume, even if it is short term; we won't be fooled because we will ask you the exact dates and we will verify the information."

17. **Not enough description of the scope of a given job is provided beyond the job's title.** Some candidates assume their title will tell the full story, but titles often have different meanings from organization to organization. You must convey a sense of what the scope of each position encompassed.

18. **Candidate leaves jobs off the resume.** Though this peeve is not universal, many decision-makers want to see the candidate's entire job history from college graduation on. They suggest a bare-bones (position/title, employer, city/state, dates) listing of older jobs under a heading such as "Prior Experience" or "Previous Professional Experience."

    Decision-makers expect you to account for all gaps between jobs. "Give it to me as straight as possible," Hanson said. "If you have been out of work for a year, put a bullet in that explains why. If you have multiple jobs that ended after three months, tell me you completed three three-month contract positions successfully." Most in hiring positions want to see when you graduated college and discount the age-discrimination argument because your graduation date will be discovered anyway when the recruiting firm is verifying information. "If a company is going to discriminate, truncating the resume may get you in a door, but won't get the person the job if they are going to discriminate," Kennedy said.

19. **Disproportionate space is devoted to older jobs.** Decision-makers expect to see the greatest proportion of content dedicated to your most recent and most relevant positions. They find it odd if you've devoted much more attention to an older job than one that was more recent. "Unless it was an amazing accomplishment, I'm not concerned that you grew sales by 20 percent back in 1987," Howell said.

20. **The exact same verbiage is used to describe functions in different jobs.** You may very well have had the same functions in multiple jobs, but you don't add to the value of your resume if you express these functions the same way for each job. It's not even necessary to list them for each job; once you've listed that function, the reader knows you have the experience. One job-seeker repeated the bullet point below for every job—changing only the number of staff supervised in each position:

    ■ Managed 32 subordinate staff from different Asian ethnic groups on recruitment, personnel, training issues.

21. **Resume fails to list educational credentials.** Chapter 2 mentions leaving off an Education section if you have absolutely nothing to list there, but that situation is extremely rare at the highest corporate levels. Virtually everyone has at least some training under his or her belt. But some candidates might not realize that an Education section is expected, or they leave it off because they feel theirs is deficient. Education needs to be listed because employers want to see it.

22. **Resume contains personal information.** Mature job-seekers may remember a time when including personal information on a resume was standard practice. This information often included height, weight, birth date, social security number, marital status, children, and health status (as if anyone would admit on a resume to health that was anything less than excellent). Today's hiring managers do not want to see this information because it raises discrimination issues. Doreen Perri-Gynn, associate vice president of human resources at Yang Ming (America) Corp., doesn't want to know "if you have three children and your wife is a happy homemaker or your husband an accountant. This is extraneous information that may prevent a manager from hiring you because he/she wants to keep his benefits budget down." Because this type of information is still often included on resumes and CVs outside the United States, Perri-Gynn advises Europeans when applying in the United Sates to "kindly leave off the

picture, and family information. We do not require your children's names, ages, schools, wife's maiden name and who her parents are. The United States bases hiring criteria on skills and accomplishments."

23. **Resume contains long lists of awards, trainings, and similar items.** These are the items that often add unnecessary length and wordiness to a resume. Here's an opportunity to ask yourself the "so what?" question. For every item you are considering listing, ask if it really adds any value to the resume. It's not incumbent upon you to include everything you've ever accomplished, earned, or learned. Prioritize. Choose the items that will best make your case as the best qualified candidate for the job you seek. Consider also creating supplemental documents with awards, trainings, publications, presentations, media mentions, and similar items (as detailed in Chapter 3). That way, you'll have them available if they're requested, and you might also have an opportunity to discuss them in the interview stage.

24. **Resume is in a functional format or otherwise lacks dates.** As we saw in Chapter 2, employers do not like functional formats or even chrono-functional because they want to see dates and get a clear picture of how your career has progressed. "I ignore resumes that do not include dates," said Miriam Torres, president of HRStaff Consulting, an executive-search firm (Miami Beach, Florida). In fact, decision-makers will often read your resume from the bottom up to see how your career has developed.

"I need to tell hiring managers where you worked, when you worked there and what you did under each job," recruiter Hanson said. "If you are old or haven't worked in a year, a resume isn't going to hide that. I'll figure it out, be sure of that, or I'm not worth my salt. Functional resumes undersell. I assume there is something wrong when I see them." At Hanson's recruiting firm, resumes are reformatted into a standard company style before candidates are presented to employers. "When I go to format the candidate's resume into our chronological company resume template, functional resumes are pure hell," she said. "Creating a chronological resume from a functional resume takes time, and time is not what recruiters have much of."

While some job-seekers have successfully used functional formats to de-emphasize problematic elements of their careers, recruiters tend to discount this "de-emphasis" as an attempt to hide something. A functional resume might not completely exclude you, but, given a choice, recruiters will always gravitate to chronological resumes. "I haven't found a time when a chronological resume doesn't make sense," said Creed.

25. **Resume has poor or inconsistent formatting, unclear layout.** "A resume should be clear, concise and provide enough relevant information to encourage the phone call it's meant to generate," said Human Resources Professional Veronica Richmond of Oakville, Ontario, Canada. My preference is for easy reading, because I see just too many resumes per position to fight a layout that is not clear. I want to find the relevant information easily."

An example of poor formatting that Curtis Pollen doesn't like to see is "everything lined up on the left margin including name, address, heading information." Pollen, who is senior director of talent recruitment for the American Heart Association (Wallingford, Connecticut), rails when the "content layout doesn't flow smoothly, for example, [the candidate] will list all accomplishments up front then just provide jobs and dates down below. I like to see what accomplishments were achieved in a particular job to ensure there is a match for the position I am recruiting for."

Pollen also noted that candidates don't pay enough attention to how the resume looks when loaded to a job board or his organization's career site, sometimes resulting in "resumes where everything runs together and is hard to read." Pollen advises job-seekers to check the format to ensure it looks appropriate before submitting it.

Candidates who don't bother to check the way their resumes print out annoy Weaver, such as when a two-page resume spills over—by just a few lines—onto an unintended third page. Granted, computer incompatibilities often are the culprits for a format that is inconsistent between sender and recipient, but candidates can experiment with sending their resumes to friends' computers to ensure they print out as intended and, as Weaver advises, tweak the margins or remove unnecessary page breaks to eliminate an unintended straggler page.

26. **Too many fonts appear in the resume.** As noted in Chapter 2, use no more than two fonts in your resume.

27. **Resume file name is "Resume.doc" or "Resume.pdf."** I know from my experience as a resume-writer that an astonishing number of job-seekers give their resumes the file name "Resume.doc." Can you imagine how many of these identically named files a hiring decision-maker receives? They don't distinguish the candidate, and the recipient must always rename the files to keep them organized. Add your name to the file name and perhaps the month and year you are submitting it: KHansenResumeDec07.doc, for example.

Also, be sure that your resume is in a file format that the recipient can open. The only file format that is virtually foolproof is one with a .doc extension (not .docx as produced by Word 2007), but, if you have any doubt, do a test run of your attachment by sending it to a friend to ensure the recipient can open it. You can also ask the employer if your file format can be opened on the company's computers.

28. **Resume is not accompanied by a cover letter, or cover letter is not targeted to the open position.** As we've seen in Chapter 3, not all employers read cover letters, but, to some of the decision-makers who do read them, cover letters are very important. Your resume should always be accompanied by a cover letter. And given that one of the main functions of a cover letter is to describe how your qualifications match a specific job vacancy, it is pointless to send a boilerplate cover letter that is not tailored to the targeted position. Benjamin Smith, corporate recruiter at HR services-provider Mercer, especially eschews "cover letters that are clearly form-written and the job title is inserted into the first line."

29. **Resume contains lies or misleading statements or misrepresentations.** Despite high-profile individuals whose resume lies have been publicly reported, and despite the increasing use of background checks, lying remains rampant on resumes. A recent study conducted by J.J. Keller & Associates, Inc., a provider of risk and regulatory management solutions (*www.jjkeller.com*), revealed resumes lies about past employment (the largest category), education, professional licensure and certifications, and military service.

It's just too risky to lie because you will probably get caught. Hiring decision-makers are far more attuned to falsehoods than ever before, and many employers are doing background checks. It doesn't even take an official background check to uncover lies; ExecuNet's 15th Annual Executive Job Market Intelligence Report (*www.execunet.com*) pointed to more than 1/3 of executives who have found problems, such as misstated academic qualifications and falsified company or title information, through simple online searches.

Don't be tempted to lie, stretch the truth, or misrepresent the facts. That weekend certificate program you completed at Harvard isn't the same as a Harvard MBA.

30. **Facts stated in one part of the resume are not supported elsewhere.** It's not unusual to see a candidate make a statement in the sales-oriented top portion of the first page of a resume that is not backed up anywhere else in the resume, perhaps claiming a skill or experience that is never mentioned again. The candidate may also state a certain number of years of experience in a field, but when the decision-maker reviews the experience section, the years don't add up to the number claimed.

Sometimes stated years of experience don't provide a true picture of the candidate's background. "Some people can state they have a lot of experience in a particular field, but if you look at length of time, they are jumping around every few months," said a Human Resources generalist from Fairfax County, Virginia, who asked not to be identified. "They are not really gaining much experience in only a few months at a job."

Chapter Five

Your Resume and Executive Recruiters

Recruiters play a far greater role in the job search for executives than for any other level of job-seeker. Because they and their clients spend lavishly to recruit the right senior executives, recruiters seek more detail in resumes. This chapter reveals the nuances of resumes targeted to recruiters.

How Recruiters Operate and How They Work With Resumes

Agency recruiters are hired by client employers to fill specific positions. The two major categories of recruiters—contingency and retained—refer to how they are hired and paid by client employers. Of course, professional recruitment firms today are paid by the employer, not the applicant/candidate. Contingency recruiters are paid when a position is successfully filled. In a retained recruiter situation, client employers retain recruiters by compensating them (fully or partially) before initiating a search assignment. Candidates generally do not seek out retained recruiters; instead, these recruiters (who tend to recruit executives at the highest salary levels) seek out a small pool representing the cream of the crop. You can usually tell that retained recruiters don't want you to submit a resume to them because their Websites offer no option for candidate resume submission. Corporate recruiters are internal employees of companies who recruit candidates for their own employer.

At any given time, most agency recruiters are working on very specific searches that their client employers have hired them to fill. They may advertise these searches, but frequently they don't, because candidates who are looking for a job are not favored. Instead, recruiters often prefer to find the passive candidate, the top performer who is happy in his or her job but could be lured away by a better offer. This thirst for passive candidates, as mentioned in Chapters 2 and 3, is why it's a good idea to have your resume and a portfolio online. Even if you are not in the hunt, your credentials are readily available just in case an employer wants to make you an offer you can't refuse.

Because of the specificity of searches, cold-contacting recruiters with your resume is often not effective unless you happen to be a fit with a search the recruiter is working on at that moment.

Still, your resume will probably be entered into the recruiting firm's database and may be found in future keyword searches. And establishing relationships with recruiters will keep you in their minds when they have a search that you fit. Recruiters rely on their contacts to find candidates. Referring good prospects to the recruiters you're working with will earn a recruiter's appreciation. From a relationship-management standpoint, it's a good idea not to work with more than about two or three recruiters at a time and to disclose to each that you are working with other recruiters. And do remember that it's employers who hire and pay recruiters. You as the candidate are clearly important because you are the commodity that enables them to meet employers' needs. Even more important is providing the client with a candidate who is the exact right fit. At the outset of your relationship with a recruiter, ask how and how often the recruiter will welcome contact from you. You want to maintain the connection but not become annoying.

Despite the desirability of the passive candidate, many recruiters do advertise the positions they've been hired to fill, and you will often find ads and job postings in which the recruiting firm is acting on behalf of the employer. You'll often see phrases in these job postings such as "Our client seeks..." or "Our client is...." You are likely to have much greater success in specifically targeting these advertised positions than in cold-contacting recruiters who may or may not be conducting a search that fits your qualifications—but your resume should be sharply tailored to the advertised position.

Most recruiters specialize in a particular industry niche and get annoyed when approached by candidates whose qualifications don't match their niche. It's never a good idea to blast your resume to every recruiting form on the Web. Carefully research those whose niches fit your qualifications. Sites such as Oya's (*http://i-recruit.com/*) and Online Recruiters Directory (*www.onlinerecruitersdirectory.com*) provide comprehensive listings of recruiter Websites, categorized by niche and location.

Recruiters are continuing to progress toward a paperless environment and receive resumes almost exclusively electronically. Like the majority of larger employers, recruiters use Applicant Tracking Software (ATS), some with artificial intelligence called resume parsing that electronically reads and process the information found in the resume and feeds the information into a keyword-searchable database. Software-makers claim this intelligence reads, understands, and classifies a resume as a human would.

Many recruiters read resumes on their computers screens and deal with paper resumes only, for example, when they print them out to write notes on them or when a job-seeker sends a hard-copy resume by postal mail.

Some recruiters are gravitating away from resumes and using software that asks job-seekers to create a profile. Others offer on their Websites job-board-like online forms in which to paste resumes.

If you begin to visit the Websites of the recruiters in directories like Oya's and Online Recruiters Directory, you will notice little consensus about resume preferences. In fact, you may be struck by the bewildering maze of conflicting and often outdated advice. (Some sites, for example, offer advice on scannable resumes even though very few firms scan resumes anymore.) If you are in doubt, most recruiter Websites offer a contact e-mail address or form that you can use to ask the recruiting firm's resume preferences. Some key questions to ask:

➤ How many pages do you like to see in executive resumes?

➤ Do you want to see a Profile/Summary section? Keyword section?

➤ Other than employer names, dates, and accomplishments/results, what information do you want to see about my past positions? Employer location? Reporting relationships? Scope of responsibility? Description of employing organization/company?

➤ Do you want a cover letter?

➤ How do you want the resume computer file to be prepared (text? Word? PDF?) and sent (e-mailed as an attachment, pasted into the body of the e-mail, pasted into a form, or a combination of these possibilities)?

A word of caution, though, from Darlene and Dennis Nason, whose contingency recruiting firm specializes in the financial industry: "Try not to call recruiters directly. E-mail is more effective, because recruiters need phone time for their searches." For simple questions about preferred resume and cover letter submission formats, consider calling and ask the recruiting firm's receptionist. If you cannot determine how a given recruiter wants to receive resumes, send a text version (see pages 79 and 181) in the body of an e-mail message with a Word version attached. This Word version should be fairly plain and simple—not overly designed; you can bring a more design-intense version to the interview. Use a descriptive subject line in the e-mail in which you send your resume. If responding to an ad or job posting, use the title of the targeted position in the subject line. If cold-contacting the recruiter, use a subject line that describes the type of position you see, similar to the headline on your resume. For example: "VICE PRESIDENT, ENGINEERING."

How to Optimize Your Resume to Succeed in This Process

To navigate the often contradictory or outdated resume-submission advice on the Websites of many executive-recruiting firms, I asked recruiters what they want to see—and don't want to see—in executive and senior-level resumes. Here are the key points they offered:

Content and keywords are king: Even more than for any other audience, executive recruiters look for keywords on resumes. Keywords are vital for use with Applicant Tracking Software, but they are equally important when they are scanned by the human eyes of recruiters. Jennifer Scott, principal with HireEffect (Stamford, Connecticut), advises 15 to 20 different words or variations on the top 30 percent of a resume's first page. At one time, candidates were advised to use well-known acronyms in their fields (TQM, for example) or to use both the acronym and the spelled-out version (Total Quality Management, TQM), but because acronyms may have different meanings or nuances in different fields, the current advice is to prefer words over acronyms—or use both. Keywords must match words in job postings as closely as possible. It's worth repeating Chapter 2's advice that 50 percent of the keywords from an ad or job posting should appear in your resume if you expect an interview. Use conventional headings so the recruiter knows what to look for. Some job-seekers use exotic headings, such as Academic Background for Education or Career Highlights for Professional Experience, just to be different.

Keywords can also be future-oriented, advises Darrell W. Gurney in his insider's look at the world of recruiters, *Headhunters Revealed.* A financial analyst whose past experience has not included work in Securities and Exchange Commission (SEC) or 10K reporting, but who wants to move into this area, can state these skills as areas of interest (for example, in an Objective Statement):

> OBJECTIVE: To secure a growth-oriented position as a Senior Financial Analyst
> with a focus on SEC and 10K reporting

Be sure the recruiter can contact you quickly: Include all ways of contacting you on your resume, but especially your daytime phone number. Recruiting moves quickly, and recruiters need to be able to reach you right away. Be sure you have voice mail or an answering machine to take messages, and return recruiter calls promptly. If your contact information changes, inform the recruiter.

Reader-friendliness and organization trumps design: Most recruiters will tell you that they are not interested in seeing intricately "designed" resumes. They find elaborate design distracting. Before presenting candidate resumes to their client employers, many recruiters reformat the resumes into a standard layout used by their recruiting firm, so the design of the resume as the candidate originally submitted it becomes moot. (And design elements, such as tables and columns, that make it difficult for a recruiter to reformat your resume will not score points.) Technology also creates a demand for simple, text-based designs that can be easily displayed on devices such as PDAs.

Recruiters prefer clean, simple designs that are easy to read and in which information is well organized and easy to follow. "Distinct section headers, clearly outlined dates of employment, and easy-to-read text are musts," says a recruiter for a national retailer who asked not to be identified. Professional resume writers generally assert that recruiters are more interested in design than they usually admit. Resume writers believe that, when given a stack of resumes, a recruiter will be more attracted to a sophisticated design than to one that is ordinary or visually unappealing. The truth is somewhere in between, and the key is readability. Your approach to design may also depend on the sector you're targeting. For example, in defense contracting, recruiters are adamant about eschewing design in favor of text-based resumes.

In some other fields, a small measure of eye-catching design will not hurt a resume submitted to a recruiter as long as it is not overpowering or distracting, and as long as the recruiter can easily and quickly zero in on the information he or she needs to screen the candidate. The majority of resume samples in Chapter 7 of this book are too elaborately designed for most recruiters, at least for electronic submission, though you could bring them to an interview with a recruiter. See instead the samples at the end of this chapter, which illustrate simpler, recruiter-friendly layouts. Remember also, as discussed in Chapter 2, that you can prepare an eye-catching resume to appear in print for interviews and networking but convert that same resume to a text version for online submission, including electronic submission to recruiters. Of course, in fields related to design and creativity, a design-intensive resume is a plus.

A well-written resume is compelling: Recruiters note that they spend more time reading resumes that are well written. Recruiter Alice Hanson notes that "meaty, well-written and impeccably spelled resumes are the most recruiter-friendly."

Provide a strategic vision of what you can do for the client employer: Because recruiters are so focused on very specific searches, they want candidates to capture their imaginations (and the imaginations of their client employers) by conveying exactly what they can do for the recruiter's client employer. They want to be able to envision and help their clients envision the future by grasping how you've made things happen for your former employers. "I'm looking for the impact this person has made in the companies they have worked for and I want to know how that tees them up for my job," says Shawn Slevin, president of P3HRConsulting (New York City).

Give the complete picture and tell the full story: Even more than other hiring decision-makers, recruiters want to see career progression, scope of what your past jobs involved (without getting bogged down in duties and responsibilities that read like a job description), a bit of information about the companies or divisions you worked for if they are not well known (especially company size), reporting relationships, products and services with which you've worked, budget authority in terms of dollars, and appropriate credentials/degrees.

Getting referred can grease the resume wheels: One of the best things you can do for the relationship between your resume and recruiters doesn't even relate to the resume itself, but to getting referred to a recruiter, a connection best accomplished through networking. If you can get a recruiter's trusted contact to shepherd your resume to that recruiter, your resume will get much more than the usual attention. "To me, networking is the most powerful thing you can do to help yourself. Come to me through someone whose opinion I trust and value and you will get more than the 20-second scan. I am prepared to be dazzled," says Doreen Perri-Gynn, associate vice president of human resources at Yang Ming (America) Corp.

Sample resume specifically targeted to recruiters: Here is a sample resume that would work well with recruiters because the design is fairly simple, it contains a summary statement and keywords, and the candidate includes a brief description of his employers.

JAMES KESSLER

13 Weeping Willow Lane • Albany, OR 97321 • Phone: 541-555-0426
E-mail: jobseeker@bellsouth.net

IT VENDOR VERTICAL CREATIVE BRANDING AND MARKETING EXECUTIVE
Branding | Segmentation | Positioning | Marketing | Primary Research | Business Value Impact

SUMMARY

Innovative consulting manager with a proven record of boosting bottom line in highly competitive and fluid client environments. Acknowledged strategic advisor to and integral team member of myriad IT vendor organizations. Equipped to expand sales and drive margins for a strategy/consulting firm by creating, selling, and delivering strategic consulting engagements. Recognized by clients as key contributor to their strategic marketing and sales successes.

— Areas of Expertise within IT Vendor Vertical —

- → Brand strategy for front-office software solutions
- → Global branding, packaging, and pricing strategies for outsourcing services
- → ROI validation, assessment, and reporting for applications software solutions
- → Value tools, calculators, and sales training for server hardware solutions
- → World-wide positioning and branding for systems integration services
- → Account management strategies for desktop and mobile computing sales

- → Competitive positioning practices for enterprise software solutions ·
- → Market segmentation for storage hardware solutions
- → Competitive differentiation for client software solutions
- → Vertical industry strategies for enterprise applications solutions
- → Value quantification for systems integration and governance/compliance services

PROFESSIONAL EXPERIENCE

Senior Vice President, Consulting, Alpha Research Analysts (ARA), Foster, OR, 2003 to Present
  ARA is a $140M IT advisory, research, and consulting firm providing market guidance, strategy evaluations, and technology recommendations to Fortune 1000 firms and IT vendors serving them.
- Develop new solutions, direct divisional operations, manage sales and marketing, and spearhead consulting services portfolio targeted at IT vendors.
- Grew practice from start-up phase to $10 million run rate with average consultant realization $350K+ annually and gross margins in excess of 50 percent.
- Direct 20+ research, analyst, delivery, business development, and marketing executives.
- Deliver quality, client satisfaction, and executive relationships with IT vendors.
- Manage division P&L, including sales operations, business development, solution development, business planning, strategic marketing, and field marketing.
- Develop and launch business impact measurement and value communications solutions.
- Enable IT vendors to position, differentiate, and sell their solutions more strategically and more closely aligned with their clients' value demands.
- Established and directed key performance metrics for sales, marketing and delivery teams.

Senior Vice President, Marketing, Alpha Research Analysts (ARA), Foster, OR, 2004

- Concurrent with Sr. VP, Consulting, position, selected by executive management team to lead strategic transformation of ARA's marketing team, function, and priorities.
- Improved global field marketing, demand generation, corporate communications, on-line marketing, events, and corporate branding practices.
- Developed new global marketing structure, field support activities, segment prioritization, branding programs, and marketing campaigns.
- Managed team of 22 marketing professionals and constructed marketing plan and budget.

Vice President, IT Vendor Practice, GBTE Group Consulting, Lebanon, OR, 2002 to 2004
    GMTE is a $140 million IT analyst and consulting firm.

- Managed team of 8 consultants to deliver $4 million+ in annual revenue, with average margins of 45 percent.
- Developed business impact calculator sales tools driving more than $1.5 million in new project revenue.
- Created new revenue stream by developing Partner/Alliance Maturity Assessment model, enabling evaluation of partnership effectiveness and improvement of business impact.
- Applied expertise in business and marketing strategy, go-to-market strategy, messaging, value measurement, market opportunity assessment, and product portfolio management.
- Played pivotal role in project scope definition, proposal generation and negotiation, management of consulting and analyst teams through successful/profitable project delivery.

Vice President, Consulting, Taylor Technology, Crabtree, OR, 2000 to 2002
    Taylor was an information and content management firm serving IT buyers and suppliers and providing publishing, IT sourcing strategy consulting, and IT vendor strategy consulting. Taylor was acquired by the Alpha Research Analysts in 2003.

- Oversaw P&L, staffing, product development, marketing, events, trade show, and sales activities.
- Doubled sales while driving net margins to 30+ percent and increasing client retention to 80+ percent.
- Managed 15 senior-level research analysts, marketing, and sales professionals.
- Secured venture-capital funding to expand research function and acted as a primary spokesperson for institutional investor road show in preparation for IPO.

Vice President and General Manager, ULB Solutions, Adverse Technologies, Corvallis, OR, 1995 to 2000
    Adverse Technologies is a $130 million provider of eBusiness services.

- Launched Application Services Provider (ASP) service in customer relationship management, which was recognized by ASP Industry Consortium "ASPire Awards" as one of four best-practices leaders in 2000.
- Developed and executed service definition plans, sales strategy, and customer fulfillment processes.
- Managed marketing, sales, and operations teams; delivered concept to field delivery in three months.
- Created branding, including AppStart and Return Preceding Investment (RPI) in support of overall business positioning.

Vice President, Marketing, eComm Communications, Junction City, OR, 1990 to 1995
    eComm is a $100 million international provider of Web and telephony-based contact center solutions.

- Led marketing team of 17 professionals and managed marketing budget in excess of $3.5 million.
- Developed corporate positioning, brand strategy, and launch plan for acquisition of eComm Technologies, an Internet-based customer interaction tools provider; acquisition closed in September 1995.
- Created strategic/tactical marketing and sales plans for acquisition of smallwondersoftworks in June 1999. Launched eComm XCalibur, a comprehensive call-center product gained from acquisition, targeted to teleservices agencies.
- Oversaw marketing functions, including market research and competitive analysis, product marketing, trade shows, advertising, direct mail, public relations, and served as industry analyst liaison.

Director, Marketing, AT&T Systemhouse, Corvallis, OR, 1993 to 1995
Senior Manager, Product Management, AT&T Business Markets, Corvallis, OR, 1990 to 1993
Manager, **Market Research**, AT&T Business Markets, Corvallis, OR, 1987 to 1990
> *AT&T Systemhouse/Business Markets is a $30 billion international provider of telecommunications services.*

- Managed marketing communications, research, and analyst relations for AT&T's $2 billion global information technology services subsidiary.
- Developed new positioning and relaunched AT&T Systemhouse as "The Network Enterprise Company," and succeeded in creating a cohesive and integrated brand image for merger.
- Oversaw marketing communications for customers, media, and industry analysts.
- Directed research and analysis of markets, industry trends, and competitors for new service development and launches, strategic alliances, and acquisitions.
- Launched go-to-market strategy for new services in e-commerce, knowledge management, and customer relationship management.
- As Senior Manager, Product Management, managed portfolio of AT&T's small business and home office products, serving over 4 million customers and generating $2 billion in annual revenue.
- Managed staff of five product managers, one reporting/analysis manager, and two analysts.
- Targeted most lucrative customers by launching five new integrated telecommunications products targeting small business and consumers through 4 sales channels (telemarketing, customer service, outside sales, and sales agents).
- Managed quarterly product and promotion launch process for all sales channels, which included business case development, marketing communications, sales collateral design/development, and sales and service programs.
- Analyzed competitive activity and developed products, features, and promotions as required to maintain competitive positioning and momentum of sales channels.
- As Manager, Market Research, directed primary and secondary research projects to support business marketing, product development, concept testing, customer retention, advertising, and direct mail.
- Managed concept development and testing for AT&T Proof Positive, networkAT&T for Business, and branding issues across several product lines.

Director, Primary Research, *HP Magazine*, Crabtree, OR, 1983 to 1987
- Managed product development, corporate communications, marketing research, market messaging, trade show strategies, and sales-management activities
- Designed, delivered, and launched C-level (CEO, CIO, CFO, CMO, COO) research programs on security, CRM, ERP, systems integration, outsourcing, governance, compliance, and identity management solutions.
- Launched partnerships with leading Wall Street firms.
- Conducted research for *Instinctive Investor* magazine on enterprise software trends that magazine cited as best market analysis in the software industry.
- Launched research activities and channel relationships in Europe and Asia.
- Developed database marketing, lead generation, and funnel management systems.

EDUCATION and CREDENTIALS

Bachelor of Arts in Business Management with Concentration in Marketing, *cum laude*
University of Oregon, Eugene, OR, 1983; Minor: English

Certified in ValueSelling, 2004

Certified Strategic Selling Instructor, 1997

Certified in Strategic Selling, 1996

Cover Letters for Recruiters

Many recruiters don't read cover letters, and the letters are infrequently entered into keyword-searchable databases, so key information must be in your resume.

Recruiters expect to be able to determine a candidate's fit with the recruiting firm's niche, as well as his or her marketability, through the resume. "If, and only if, these requirements are satisfied by the recruiter's examination of the resume—only then will he/she ever look at the cover letter," reports Gurney in *Headhunters Revealed*. "On the cover letter, they aren't interested in the candidate's self-analytical expose' of themselves but, rather, just some basic facts. The reason they don't need the candidates' elaborate ideas of themselves is that the recruiter already knows what they can sell about this person from the resume."

Ignoring the cover letter is largely a time-management issue. "Because there is so much talent on the street we just don't have time to read a cover letter as well as a resume," point out Darlene Nason, president of Miami's Nason Career Management, and Dennis Nason, president of Nason and Nason Executive Search Consultants, who receive about 30 unsolicited resumes daily.

"In all my years of recruitment, I remember only one letter that really caught my eye," says executive/technical recruiter turned resume writer/job search coach Kristen Griffin of Griffin Career Solutions. "A professional resume writer wrote it!" Osram Sylvania's Goolsby will read a cover letter only if she is on the fence about a candidate. "I read them when the resume isn't a complete match for the job," says Kristina Creed, a senior manager at a for-profit education provider. "This is the opportunity to tell me [that] while you don't have the requisite experience, I should give you a shot. I also find them a reason to reject them—spelling errors, applying for one job, but indicating another. That attention to detail is important."

For those who've labored over a cover letter to try to get the recruiter's attention, this news is a little deflating. For those who find writing cover letters to be an agonizing chore, it may be good news if indeed it's a waste of time to put a lot of effort into cover letters to these professionals.

"I advise my clients that they must write their cover letters for the one-third to one-half of employers and recruiters who will actually read them," notes Louise Kursmark of Best Impression Career Services, Inc., in Cincinnati. "Because there are many readers, particularly recruiters, who will ignore the cover letter," Kursmark cautions, "candidates should be careful not to include key information in the cover letter if it is not present in the resume."

There are, of course, exceptions in recruiter responses to cover letters. "I *love* cover letters," Maureen Crawford Hentz, manager of talent acquisition, development, and complicnce at Osram Sylvania in Boston said. Given the opportunity to upload a resume and a cover letter using a Web-based form on the employer's or recruiting firm's site so that the documents become part of the firm's applicant tracking systems, Hentz has observed that most people either don't write letters or don't upload them. "This is a huge tactical error, as it is the *one* place in our applicant tracking system where the candidate has the opportunity to answer the questions 'Why us? Why now? Why this job?'" At the Clarion Group (Placerville, California), where Joe Briand is a partner, cover letters are "an important indicator of a candidate's communication skills and, to some extent, personality. We ask for cover letters with every posting. We get them about 40 percent of the time," he says. "I read cover letters from executive/senior management candidates, and I prefer short letters," reports Miriam Torres, president of executive-search firm HRStaff Consulting (Miami Beach, Florida).

Certain differences in letters to recruiters compared to letters to direct hiring managers indicate that special care should go into recruiter letters. If you are, in fact, qualified for an opening that a recruiter is working on, your cover letter should provide crucial information that will save you and the recruiter time and aggravation down the road. Thus, it pays to attend to differences between conventional cover letters and recruiter cover letters in such areas as content, length, format, and how the letter is sent to the recruiter.

Include "recruiter-specific" content: Gurney writes in *Headhunters Revealed* that the five pieces of information that recruiters especially want to see are:

1. All contact information (true of any cover letter).

2. Reasons for leaving, why you're on the market (sometimes included in conventional cover letters, but not as a general rule).

3. Positions and industries of interest (with a conventional cover letter, you are usually applying, or at least should be applying, for a specific position).

4. Salary history and expectations (never included in a conventional cover letter unless the employer has requested the information, and sometimes not even then).

5. Locations of interest (see item 3). Variations on this theme include willingness to relocate and travel.

"Having these answers already, without having to call the candidate, allows the candidate to be put into the system immediately...without getting piled up with the hoards of other resumes needing this vital, back-up information," Gurney says.

Griffin suggests adding these items to the mix:

➤ Eye-catching intro.

➤ Brief summary of background using keywords.

On their Websites, many recruiters don't even mention wanting to see cover letters, but those that do often list the specific content they're looking for.

Keep it as concise as possible: Recruiters report that they are more likely to read cover letters if they are succinct. They point out that, these days, cover letters are often e-mailed to recruiters in the body of e-mail messages, further necessitating brevity.

Because recruiter letters also have the above-mentioned unconventional content requirements, it's not easy to align the brevity preference with recruiters' content needs. The best advice is to keep the letter as concise as possible while still including recruiter-desired content. Of course, brevity is a virtue in any cover letter.

Most cover letters to recruiters are not placed into databases, but, because some letters are, the best strategy is load your recruiter cover letter with keywords, just as you do your resume. "To 'load' your resume and cover letter," Gurney says (in *Headhunters Revealed*), "means to chock them full of all key words and phrases necessary to stand out in a database search for someone with your experience, skills, certifications, background, accomplishments, location, and even desires."

Gurney says, "Though your resume and cover letter will be seen initially by recruiters to determine whether or not you should go into the database, the only way they will see it again is if it's fully loaded with all the words and phrases that point the way to the perfect position for you."

Gurney, who is among the recruiters who do place cover letters in a database, notes, in *Headhunters Revealed*, that "on occasions, a particular word on a cover letter has popped up in a search, such as a position title or industry that the person wants but doesn't have experience in as listed on the resume." Gurney recalls a recent situation in which a young salesperson recently sent Gurney his information. "His resume stated his top-ranked experience in copier sales, whereas his cover letter mentioned that he wanted to move into pharmaceutical or medical sales," Gurney recalls. "The pharmaceutical companies are always looking for people with great sales background regardless of industry, so this would be an instance where it might help to have a cover letter databased, too."

Points out Ann Baehr of Best Resumes (Long Island, New York), "Let's not forget that keywords are also meant for the human eye. Distributing keywords throughout the cover letter, as opposed to the resume practice of listing them in groups, is still an effective strategy."

Frame your letter in terms of what you can do for the recruiter's client(s): Balancing the fact that the letter might not even get read along with the brevity aspect, include language in your letter that indicates you can solve problems, make money, save money, improve efficiency and productivity, and/or increase sales for the recruiter's clients. It doesn't take a great number of words to convey your potential value to the recruiter's clients, and one of the best ways, of course, is to briefly touch on how you've succeeded in past positions. Here are two samples of client-focused, accomplishments-driven wording:

> In addition to my strong record of solving marketing problems, my consulting background would be tremendous plus for your firm because of my exposure to a wide variety of companies instead of just one. Your client would also benefit from my unique combination of marketing expertise and knowledge of the industrial sector that is far more extensive than that of most consultants and marketers in the sector.

■

> As President of Canadiana Resort Development Inc., I supervised an international workforce and assumed all the details of daily operations, from marketing and human resources to finance, and am poised to do the same for one of your client firms.

Try reader-friendly formats, such as a bulleted list, that enables the recruiter to zero in on your top selling points: In the time-starved world of recruiters/headhunters/executive-search firms, any device you can use to bring your main selling points to the forefront without forcing the reader to wade through a lot of text will work to your advantage. "Eye-catching bullets are key!" Kristen Griffin of Griffin Career Solutions notes.

"Effective formats include a combination of paragraph and bulleted items to add clarity and impact; one or more excerpts from letters of recommendation; and the side-by-side chart-style format that answers qualification statements line-by-line (Your Qualifications/My Qualifications)," Anne Baehr says. "This format is especially effective when a job seeker's key qualifications exceed those that the recruiter or hiring company is asking for," Baehr says. "It is also easier for a busy recruiter to make a client-candidate match."

Send your cover letter in the recruiter's preferred format: Most experts say the best format is to paste both your cover letter and resume in the body of your e-mail (in ASCII text), and attach a copy of your resume in Word as well (some experts say attach both the resume and cover letter as one file). In particular, experts note that the cover letter should be in the body of the e-mail message and will rarely be opened if it is sent as its own attachment.

"The subject line of the e-mail is the critical piece," notes career transition coach and consultant Randy Block. "'Resume attached,' or 'No Subject,' result in instant deletion without looking at the resume. The subject line should say [for example], 'VP of Manufacturing,' 'CFO,' etc."

As with resumes, to find out a given recruiter's preferred way of receiving your cover letter, visit recruiter Websites. In cases where the Websites don't reveal submission preferences, you can always contact the recruiter's office and ask the how (or even whether) the firm prefers to receive cover letters.

Don't forget the other principles of effective cover-letter writing as described in Chapter 3.

Sample cover letters should be specifically targeted to recruiters: Here are two sample cover letters that provide what recruiters say they want to see in cover letters.

Although this chapter provides a snapshot of preparing executive and senior-level resumes and cover letters for recruiters, it can't convey the complete picture of working with recruiters as well as the resources in the Appendix under Working With Recruiters (page 246).

Meredith Gundersen

1050 Hudson Street
Weehawken, NJ 07086-9030
201.555.3132
jobseeker@mgundersen.com

March 12, 2008

Cheryl Boswell
Director Research
Grand Performance Recruiting
662 Madison Avenue
New York, NY 10017

Dear Ms. Boswell:

Since I've been in New York, many sources have recommended Grand Performance Recruiting as providing quality search work. If you have a client seeking someone who can play a proactive role with the **representation, operational/logistics, and management elements of high-level talent** in a range of companies from the **music industry, TV, radio**, to **film** in the world of the **performing arts**, I'd like to make a strong case for myself. Delivering that "elite" talent is what I want to do. My track record has included 12 years of international experience (15 countries in the Asia Pacific region and in Europe) in this area, with organizations ranging from direct event and client management to investment banking. I am contacting you because my husband has been promoted to New York, so I have relocated here.

I have demonstrated my strategic ability through successful involvement in international promotion and market research, promotion consultation, budget negotiations and logistics, and more. I have proven my ability to handle the details and complexities of all marketing and international promotional/advertising activities, distribution of newscasts, along with negotiations and consultation with blue-chip clients.

I have consistently contributed my leadership skills in a variety of settings, while managing the creative process, motivating and directing teams of up to 100, fine-tuning marketing plans, and juggling multiple projects in a fast-paced environment. I am a proficient top manager and profit-minded leader. My leadership has resulted in the patient, sensitive, determined, and flexible coordination of global business, where culture, business practices, and drivers often vary.

I am particularly interested in positions in the New York Metropolitan area that start at a salary range of $100K to $125K, in the **Client/Event Management** and **Marketing and Communications** categories.

I am a firm believer in first impressions, which come across in a resume in only a limited way. I would very much like the opportunity to meet and discuss my experience with you. Please review my background relative to your current search assignments and contact me at 201.555.3132 or by e-mail at jobseeker@mgundersen.com if you need additional information. Let's talk soon.

Sincerely,

Meredith Gundersen

Jonathan Herlsen

May 15, 2008

James Sawyer
RealEstateRecruit.com
611 South Palm Canyon Drive, Suite 7571
Palm Springs, CA 92264

Dear Mr. Sawyer:

My solid sales background and success with management and client service make me an ideal candidate for a sales management or executive management position in real estate/new homes with one of your client firms. Throughout my 20-year entrepreneurial career, I have proven my motivation, sales expertise, management, and operational skills. During that time, I:

- Operated a series of successful businesses and partnerships;

- Achieved more than $16 million in real-estate and new-home sales;

- Sold $10 million+ in property/casualty insurance.

If you have a client looking to engage a proven sales/management executive who can deliver excellent results, I'd like to present my qualifications. My sales and management success results from a finely honed ability to analyze a marketing/selling situation and develop an innovative program that leaves the competition behind.

Most of my professional experience has been in my own companies or partnerships in which I've successfully built teams to achieve a common purpose. The tools and techniques I have developed from this background apply directly to the skills that a sales manager or executive management professional needs: selling, concept development, strategic management, relationship building, ability to resolve tough client and personnel issues, and a visionary approach to growth needs.

With bottom-line results, I can deploy significant resourcefulness, persist in getting the job done, as well as network and interact with both clients and employees, understand their goals, win their trust quickly, and effectively persuade them. I am also adept at virtually all aspects of business operations in the real-estate, new-homes, and property/casualty insurance fields.

I am particularly interested in positions in **California**, **Arizona**, and **Washington state** in the **real estate/development/new home building** and **sales** fields with a **salary range beginning at $175K**. I am interested in leaving my current employment to advance my career. I am **very willing to travel and relocate**.

Please review my background relative to your current search assignments and contact me if you need additional information. You can call 302-829-9274 or e-mail me at jherlsen@cfl.rr.com. I appreciate your consideration.

Thank you for your time and consideration.

Sincerely,

Jonathan Herlsen

19 Hummingbird Lane, Claymont, DE 19703 ~ 302-555-9274 ~ Cell: 302-555-7620 ~ E-mail: jobseeker@cfl.rr.com

Chapter Six

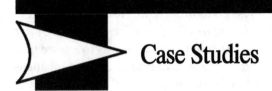

Case Studies

Because the path to an executive-level position is not always smooth, it's helpful to examine case studies of candidates whose routes to the executive suite are not clear cut. Although this chapter doesn't illustrate every obstacle or tricky situation a would-be executive might face, it presents three common situations and shows how the candidates used their resumes and other documents to position themselves. These three complete case studies are derived from real examples of job-seekers aspiring to executive/C-level positions. Each case details the scenario the job-seekers faced, describes the strategies they developed to market themselves (provides before-and-after samples of their resumes and their cover letters), and reveals the outcomes of their searches.

Case Study One: Mid-career Job-Seeker Adds New Credential (MBA) and Aspires to the Executive Level

Background: Melinda Carrollson was a Ph.D.–trained chemist who had begun her career in a researcher capacity for a chemical company and then become interested in the Environmental Health and Safety (EHS) field, advancing to the director level in the aerospace, electronics, and printing industries. As she progressed in industry, she became increasingly fascinated with the business and management sides of her field. She left her last EHS job in 2000 to obtain an MBA to better position her for a senior-level business role in EHS, leaving a one-year gap in her work history that represented the period in which she was earning the degree. Following graduation, she took a job in a company completely unrelated to EHS so she could gain management experience. After nearly two years there, she went out on her own as an EHS consultant but now is seeking an executive position in the EHS field.

Her resume needed to explain the career change, the employment gap created by her MBA program, and the post-MBA job that was unrelated to EHS. In looking at the first page of her original resume (see page 158), the reader could not tell that Melinda had been in the EHS field and wanted to return there. Though the resume did a good job of conveying her business savvy, it did nothing to position her for her planned return to EHS. Her three degrees were impressive but did not belong on page one of an executive-level resume.

Strategy: The headline atop Melinda's revised resume (page 160) made her career goal as an EHS executive clear. The Professional Profile section told her story, positioning her as an aspiring executive with both an MBA and an applicable educational and experiential background in chemistry and EHS. The profile also painted a picture of what she could do for a future employer: Develop cost-effective EHS programs that align with business goals and create sustainable change. A challenge with her resume was to *show her to be currently employed following completion of her MBA*, which she was able to do through consulting projects. Another challenge was to *ensure that some of her EHS experience appeared on the first page of her resume.* Despite her many business accomplishments in the job she had taken outside the EHS field, the portrayal of that job was significantly reduced on her resume to make way for moving her last major EHS job to page one of her resume. To further tell the story of her career progression and how she stepped back from it to obtain her MBA, Melinda used descriptive italicized statements under the listings of her last four positions. Melinda moved her Education section to nearly the bottom of her resume; yet page one of the document still clearly conveyed her MBA and Ph.D. credentials. She also packed her resume with quantified achievements. To be sure her resume would turn up in keyword searches, she included a keyword section, which, for layout reasons, was placed at the end of the resume.

Melinda tailored her cover letter to each job for which she applied. She highlighted her Unique Selling Proposition—that she offered the strong EHS background that would enable her to minimize risks and solve problems. She highlighted other strengths in three bullet points and stressed her educational qualifications. In the letter's third paragraph, she quoted from the job listing and indicated that she had the qualifications to do what the employer needed. She closed with a proactive paragraph that told the employer she would follow up.

The following job posting is typical of those for which Melinda applied with her new resume:

Vice President, Environmental, Health and Safety—[name of company]

Create strategies for environmental health and safety that are aligned with broad organizational business goals, facility needs, and EHS external forces. Provide leadership across business units, functions, and regions on the translation of these strategies to consistent and coordinated EHS programs, policies and practices. Build strong relationships which enable individual to influence and partner successfully with business leaders to drive change in every business unit, region, and function to ensure that [name of company]'s global initiatives related to EHS matters are embedded in the organization, organizational barriers to effective sustainable execution of EHS initiatives are eliminated, and key issues relating to shifts in EHS matters are addressed. Assume responsibility as the point person on EHS updates to board of directors. Recommend and implement initiatives that minimize potential risks, are aligned with long and short-term business strategies, and that maintain [name of company]'s position as a leader in EH S programs and practices. Build strong relationships and networks outside of [name of company] to remain current with global EHS practices. Effectively represent [name of company] EHS programs to external audiences and promote appropriate public position for [name of company] that maintains [name of company]'s outstanding external reputation as it relates to EHS. Partner with all senior business leaders within the function to create a culture that motivates employees, exhibits companies shared values, supports development of employees, and attracts and retains human talent. Directs the development of appropriate measures of EHS performance which identify needs for program changes and /or corrections to EHS programs. Uses the results of these measures as well as appropriate data on external factors to influence key stakeholders on any needed strategy corrections.

- -

Job Requirements: Graduate degree in an EHS field and plant experience preferred. Minimum 7–10 years' experience leading a global organization. International experience is required. Established record of successfully leading and building effective cross-functional, multi-site and multi-business teams. Excellent analytical ability, communication, negotiation, problem solving and strategic leadership skills. Ability to evaluate risks and business strategies and drive appropriate change initiatives on complex EHS strategies. Ability to present to senior management and board level with confidence and authority. Ability to influence senior management in a highly matrixed organization and to drive sustainable cultural/organizational change. Results orientation with proven ability to execute on plans. Familiarity with legal requirements relating to EHS.

Resume and Cover Letter: Melinda's before and after resumes and her cover letter are shown on pages 158–162.

Outcome: Based on her clear presentation of her accomplishments, qualifications, and business experience, Melinda quickly landed a job as Vice President for EHS.

Case Study Two: Candidate Seeks to Change Industries

Background: Although Albert Van Hees had majored in public policy in college, graduating in the mid-1990s, a financial-consulting internship between his junior and senior years whetted his appetite for the world of investments and trading. His first job out of college combined his business and public-policy interests in a position he described as "quasi-management consulting." After two years, however, he followed his fiancée to the Midwest and veered off his chosen career path by taking what he felt would be a more lucrative job in telecom sales so he could buy a house, marry, and start a family. He spent 10 years in telecom sales and was regularly promoted. He especially hit his stride in his most recent job as a program manager for service operations, in which he engaged in negotiations, managed risk, generated new business, and made strategic decisions.

Despite his success, Albert longed to return to his roots in investments. Paralleling his professional success, he excelled with his own investments portfolio. His challenge was to position himself for a significant career change back into the investments field.

Strategy: Albert sought executive jobs such as the one that follows:

Vice President, Trade Finance—[name of company]

Integrated full-service investment bank seeks VP in sales role responsible for achieving revenue growth targets and provide product-specialist support and international business advice to relationship management.

- Identify and develop profitable business opportunities and client relationships.

- Generate profitable, structurally sound trade finance transactions.

- Assist clients and relationship management with structuring the finance and mitigation of risk related to complex trade transactions.

- Maintain high quality risk analysis.

- Discover innovative ways of using trade finance products and services.

- Travel required.

- 5–10 years of relevant work experience.

- Bachelor's degree, MBA desirable.

- Strong negotiation, sales/marketing, public-speaking, and interpersonal-communication skills.

- Knowledge of international trade practices and transactions.

- Knowledge of global business environment.

Melinda Carrollson Resume Before

Melinda, Carrollson, Ph.D.
324 Butcher Street
Milwaukee, WI 53201
414-555-5627 (h) 414-555-7653 (c) jobseeker@earthlink.net

Senior executive in operations and general management with expertise in corporate, multi-site, and start-up organizations. Skilled in evaluating and improving efficiency of systems, equipping organization with tools for growth, and measuring results. Experience includes finance/budgeting, client service, and building and leading high performance teams.

Increased company revenue 26% based on 2003 YE projections.
Led seven teams to deliver new, online educational product for Asia-Pacific client—on time and under budget.

Reduced annual labor costs 9% by restructuring relationships with corporate partners and clients.
Simplified lines of communication and eliminated inefficiencies in reporting and technology transfer.

Implemented a company-wide, online training delivery system for 28 locations.
Conservative NPV of projected savings estimated at $7.8 million for 5 years.

EDUCATION

M.B.A, Madison Graduate School of Management, Northeastern University, Boston, MA
Ph.D. Chemistry, University of Southern California, Los Angeles, CA
B.S. Chemistry, Loyola College, Baltimore, MD

PROFESSIONAL HISTORY

UFirst, LLC   1/01 – 10/03
Start-up online education company offering executive business programs, undergraduate and graduate degrees

Director, Operations and Client Relationship Management Madison, WI
- Established operational infrastructure for division, including billing, program profitability evaluation, performance reviews, resource allocation, and space planning.
- Developed and managed division's $18 million budget. Mentored directors in budget analysis and control.
- Facilitated two departmental reorganizations and one site closure, reducing headcount (47%) and cost (63%), without loss in productivity.
- Hired and led seven parallel teams (35 employees) of media designers, programmers, editors, academics, and instructional designers to build new product line.
- Established clear communication and reporting processes for global virtual teams and senior executives that ensured on-time delivery.
- Exceeded client expectations by identifying cost-savings opportunities of $223,000.
- Improved internal staff's approach to improve customer service and redirected resources to core business.
- Led cross-functional strategy team and contributed analytical support that resulted in three successful rounds of funding.
- Prepared business plan proposal for new product line. Developed financial and staffing models for alternative products.
- Proactively selected and implemented time and project tracking system. Cost and resource allocation analyses were used to measure productivity, establish resource needs, and calculate product profitability.
- Generated additional $144,000 revenue by writing proposals and coordinating on-time delivery of four custom-build products.
- Sole point of contact between external clients and internal departments. Maintained positive relationship with Korean client while enforcing previously ignored contractual terms.

PROFESSIONAL HISTORY (continued)

Independent Consultant   7/00 – 12/00 and 10/03 – present
General management consulting, strategic planning, risk assessment

- Retained by Asian-owned manufacturer to evaluate an acquisition assessment performed by a major consulting firm. Identified knowledge gaps and recommended changes in strategy that allowed client to successfully obtain transaction funding despite prior rejections.

- Hired by clothing retailer to sell business to large, Chicago-based, fine-clothing retailer. Client received an acceptable offer of purchase. Analyzed client's business, conducted business valuation, prepared selling memorandum, identified potential buyers, prepared presentation, and coached client on delivery.

Directory Services   11/96 – 7/00
$5.2 billion global printing, information systems, and logistics company with 34,000 employees

Director, Corporate Environmental Engineering   Chicago, IL
- Managed 19 engineers, 22 consultants, and a $3.5 million budget. Team provided environmental engineering services to 44 global manufacturing plants.
- Saved $750,000 in labor and $118,000 annually by outsourcing lab and engineering tests.
- Obtained $1.2 million unbudgeted funding to implement a company-wide, online training in five months; conservative NPV of projected savings estimated at $7.8 million for five years.
- Reorganized corporate engineering team to improve service to plants, resulting in increased internal customer focus and cost-savings.
- Reduced compliance violations (62%) by defining success factors and metrics to increase accountability.

Motorola Electronics Corporation   1/96 – 11/96
Former $1.5 billion manufacturer of televisions and electronics; company declared bankruptcy in 1999

Director, Environmental, Health, Safety, and Workers' Compensation   Chicago, IL
- Established company-wide environmental and safety organization for five Mexico and four U.S. plants during turnaround crisis.
- Negotiated a $1.2 million reduction in regulatory fine with legal team and avoided litigation. Improved confrontational relationships with regulators, allowing Zenith to obtain required operating permits.
- Represented company in discussions with NGOs on NAFTA and Zenith's work practices in Mexico.

Fulmer Corporation   10/94 – 11/96
$200 million plastic film manufacturer with 1300 employees, nine U.S. and three Mexico plant sites

Director, Environmental, Health, Safety (EHS) and Workers' Compensation   New York, NY
- Developed M&A integration plan for acquisitions in Mexico and Brazil. Closed or divested five U.S. facilities.
- Reduced workers' compensation cost (77%), OSHA recordable rate (31%), lost workday case rate (62%).

Fiddler Aerospace   10/89 – 10/94
$3.3 billion manufacturer of satellites, nuclear weapons, microelectronics

Manager, Environmental, Health and Safety (10/90-10/94) New Brunswick, NJ
Compliance Assurance Manager (10/89-10/90) New Brunswick, NJ

- Promoted three times during tenure at company.
- Nominated for GE Crotonville's Change Agent Leadership program. Developed and used cross-functional business best practices to implement a key manufacturing initiative across 13 plants.
- Managed the installation of EHS systems (48% below budget) for 2 simultaneous plant start-ups.
- Reduced hazardous waste costs by 53%.

Melinda Carrollson Resume After

MELINDA CARROLLSON, PH.D.

17 E. BUTCHER STREET #2, MILWAUKEE, WI 53201

414-555-4186 ◆ Cell: 414-555-9898   JOBSEEKER@EARTHLINK.NET

SENIOR ENVIRONMENTAL, HEALTH, AND SAFETY EXECUTIVE

PROFESSIONAL PROFILE

- Accomplished EHS professional with global experience in corporate, manufacturing, and start-ups.
- Motivated achiever with Ph.D. in chemistry, MBA, and strengths that include developing cost-effective EHS programs that align with business goals and implementing sustainable cultural/organizational change through creating partnerships and buy-in.
- Strategic leader with proven track record of building and leading effective cross-functional, multi-site/multi-business teams, driving change initiatives, and implementing EHS strategies.
- Proficient problem-solver with the analytical skills to evaluate risks and business strategies.
- Influential interpersonal communicator, negotiator, and presenter.

PROFESSIONAL EXPERIENCE

Independent Liability-Management Consultant, Milwaukee, WI, July to Dec. 2000 and Oct. 2003 to present
Retained by top-50 law firm to consult on environmental and liability-management issues.
- Evaluated acquisition assessment conducted by major environmental consulting firm for Asian-owned manufacturer; identified knowledge gaps and recommended strategy that allowed client to obtain funding despite prior rejections.
- Hired as expert for major food-products company in legal action to compel Fortune 500 company's cleanup of hazardous waste migrating to client's property; collaborated with client and legal counsel to prepare regulatory action and comprehensive negotiation plan.

Director, Operations and Program Management, *UFirst, LLC*, Madison, WI, Jan. 2001 to Oct. 2003
Following completion of MBA in 2000, enhanced business-management experience through position with start-up online education company offering executive education, undergraduate and graduate degrees.
- Increased company revenue 26 percent through on-time, under-budget delivery of new, online educational product for Asia-Pacific client.
- Developed and managed division's $18 million budget; coached directors in budget analysis/control.

Corporate Director, Environmental Technology and EHS Compliance, *Directory Services*, Madison, WI, Nov. 1996 to July 2000
Recruited to improve company-wide EHS performance and lead environmental engineering department of $5.2 billion global printing company with 34,000 employees.
- Supervised 19 direct reports in 28 domestic and international plants; oversaw $3.1-million budget.
- Benchmarked EHS programs; conducted company-wide needs analysis; assessed risk; developed strategic plan and obtained executive support to execute.
  - Formed leadership team to identify barriers to change and align action plan with division resources, manufacturing plant loads, and company performance targets.
  - Developed auditing and training programs, metrics, and performance measurements in line with business strategy to drive accountability and change.
  - Reduced compliance violations 47 percent over two years by defining success factors and metrics to increase accountability.
- Delivered $7.8 million in projected savings (estimated net present value) by implementing online EHS training delivery system for 24,000 employees worldwide.
- Persuaded business-unit executives to provide $1.2 million unbudgeted funding.
  - Assembled company-wide, cross-functional, vertically integrated team for implementation.
  - Reorganized corporate engineering team to align with business units and improve service to plants, resulting in increased internal customer focus and cost savings.
- Established global EHS auditing program and developed risk-ranking system to prioritize audit-site selection.
- Attained projected annual savings of $372K by playing key role as program manager for installation of enterprise-wide, relational database for EHS data management.

Corporate Director, Environmental, Health, and Safety, *Motorola Electronics Corporation*, Chicago, IL, Jan. to Nov. 1996
Hired into newly created position to manage Mexico and U.S. multi-site remediation and develop company-wide environmental compliance programs for former $1.5 billion manufacturer of televisions.
- Prepared status of 16 US and Mexico air, water, soil, and asbestos remediation sites and $13 million estimated remediation strategy proposal for CEO and senior executives.
- Negotiated $1.2 million reduction in regulatory fines with legal team and avoided litigation.
- Improved confrontational relationships with regulatory agency, allowing Motorola to obtain operating permits.

Corporate Director, Environmental, Health, and Safety, *Fulmer Corporation*, New York, NY, Oct. 1994 to Nov. 1996
- Reduced workers' compensation cost 77 percent, OSHA recordable rate 31 percent, and lost-workday case rate 62 percent for $200-million plastic-film manufacturer with 1,300 employees in 12 plant sites.
- Saved $180K in initial and $40K in annual expense on pollution-control equipment by negotiating with environmental regulators to obtain more favorable permit conditions after review of competitor's air permits.
- Led environmental due-diligence consultant teams for Mexico and Argentina acquisitions and five U.S. plant divestitures; functioned as project manager for Phase I and II assessments.

Manager, Environmental, Health and Safety, *Fiddler Aerospace*, New Brunswick, NJ, Oct. 1990 to Oct. 1994
Compliance Assurance Manager, *Fiddler Aerospace*, New Brunswick, NJ, Oct. 1989 to Oct. 1990
- Established auditing program, conducting 13 multi-media compliance and management-systems audits annually for $3.3 billion manufacturer of satellites, nuclear weapons, microelectronics; assisted facilities in developing corrective action plans.
- Transferred from NY site to remediate multiple EHS issues at four NJ Aerospace manufacturing facilities with 2,200+ employees.
- Managed 13-member team, $300K operating budget, and $1.5 million groundwater remediation project.
- Promoted three times during tenure at company.

ADDITIONAL PROFESSIONAL EXPERIENCE

Chemist and Senior Research Chemist, *Atlas Incorporated*, Dover, DE
- Delivered $2 million in annual sales for $3.6 billion specialty chemicals company by leading R&D, analytical, technical service and pilot-plant manufacturing teams to produce Atlas' first new commercial furniture lacquer in 25 years in record time.
- Delivered presentations to customers, politicians, community organizations, and trade groups on environmental impact of company's products.

EDUCATION

- Master of Business Administration, Kellogg Graduate School of Management, Northwestern University, Evanston, IL
- Ph.D. in Chemistry, University of Southern California, Los Angeles, CA
- Bachelor of Science in Chemistry, Loyola University, New Orleans, LA

AREAS OF EXPERTISE

- EHS legal requirements
- EHS liability analysis
- EHS training programs
- Project management
- Compliance and management-systems audits
- EHS strategies and initiatives
- EHS benchmarking
- Risk management
- Risk ranking
- Cost reduction
- Remediation strategies
- EHS programs, policies, and practices
- EHS performance measures, metrics
- Compliance violation reduction

Melinda Carrollson Cover Letter

MELINDA CARROLLSON, PH.D.

17 E. BUTCHER STREET #2, MILWAUKEE, WI 53201

414-555-4186 ◆ Cell: 414-555-9898   JOBSEEKER@EARTHLINK.NET

Jan. 18, 2008

Judson Parker
Plastipak Holdings, Inc.
Global Business and Technology Center
41605 Ann Arbor Road
Plymouth, MI 48170

Dear Mr. Parker:

During my solid career in environmental, health, and safety, I've made it a priority to develop my skill set with an eye toward an organization like yours. Serving in senior-level environmental, health, and safety leadership positions for global corporate, manufacturing, and start-up organizations has provided me with extensive experience in minimizing risks and solving problems. I would like to bring these skills to Plastipak Holdings, Inc., in the VP, Environmental, Health and Safety position you are currently advertising, specifically contributing the following:

- A finely honed strategic sense that makes me a value-added and innovative solution-provider, combined with the ability to sell and implement cost-effective EHS programs at all levels;
- A solid EHS background and the savvy to develop, assimilate, and troubleshoot the processes and practices that form the underpinnings of an effective EHS program;
- The adaptability and solution-driven mindset that enables me to delve into complex EHS issues and respond to changing priorities.

I've enjoyed progressive advancement in my career, developing and implementing EHS programs that identified and controlled exposure and risks. My background includes the chemical, printing, aerospace, electronics, plastics, and online education fields. My Ph.D. in chemistry and my MBA further bolster my qualifications, enabling me to apply extensive business knowledge to developing and driving EHS strategies that are consistent with business goals.

As a strong team leader with a proven EHS track record, I can hit the ground running in the advertised position. With great productivity, I can provide leadership, build strong relationships and networks, remove barriers to EHS initiatives, serve as the point person on EHS issues, recommend and implement initiatives, contribute to creating a culture that motivates employees, influence key stakeholders—and much more. I'm a highly motivated, results-driven achiever, as any of my previous employers can tell you.

The combination of my experience and motivation provides a solid foundation upon which to make an immediate and meaningful contribution at Plastipak Holdings. I would like to meet with you to further discuss my qualifications for the advertised position, and I will contact you soon to arrange an interview. If you'd like to reach me in the meantime, please contact me using the information atop this letter. Thank you for your time and consideration.

Sincerely,

Melinda Carrollson

Although Albert mentioned his career change in a blurb at the top of his previous resume (page 164), the blurb did not stand out. The resume, though attractive, did little to show his qualifications in the investments field. Given how long it had been since Albert graduated college, he had retained unnecessary information (GPA, coursework, extracurricular activities) in his Education section. He had buried important information about accomplishments and awards at the end of his resume.

Strategy: Albert added a headline to his revised resume (page 166) to target this job (and tweaked the headline for other jobs for which he applied). He added a branding statement touting his knowledge of financial markets, risk management, and the effects of global events (he had studied abroad during college and maintained an avid interest in international financial news). His branding statement also acknowledged his career change. He added a keyword section emphasizing his expertise in finance-related areas—keywords unlikely to appear in other parts of his resume, given his limited experience in investments. He included a statement describing the success of his personal portfolio.

He packed the description of his most recent job with bullet points describing powerful accomplishments and measurable results, framed in terms of competencies needed in jobs such as the one above—negotiation, risk management, sales/marketing, strategy. He also showed he had the interpersonal skills that would be needed for client and relationship management in the targeted job. Because he had neglected to track his accomplishments in quantifiable terms in his older jobs, the second page of his resume was not as strong as the first, but he knew the first page would garner the most employer attention.

He employed two techniques in his cover letter (page 168) to get noticed. He used the referral technique outlined in Chapter 3, page 74, because he knew his letter and resume would get more consideration if it mentioned a mutual acquaintance. He also used a two-column format (described in Chapter 3) to illustrate that his background—even though seemingly quite different from the investments field—was applicable to the requirements of the types of job he sought.

Because the scope of his career change was significant, Albert knew he could not rely on his resume and cover letter alone to break back into the investments field. Networking, his gregarious personality, and opportunities to show off his knowledge of global financial markets would be key to his success.

Resume and Cover Letter: Albert's before and after resumes and his cover letter are shown on pages 164–168.

Outcome: Albert spent four months aggressively building his network of contacts and seeking "face time" with everyone who might be influential in his search. That in-person contact was crucial for his contacts to see that he had a winning personality and the expertise to make his desired career transition. He continued to employ sharply targeted two-column referral cover letters and targeted resumes, also depending on his network to help him land interviews. He knew that he could win over hiring managers once he met them face-to-face. His networking campaign paid off, and he was hired in an executive position similar to the previous one.

Case Study Three: Professional Desires Change to Business Emphasis

Background: Peter Gilmore was a physician who had also been closely involved throughout most of his career with educating aspiring physicians in hospital-based leadership positions. He had established himself as an entrepreneur by founding a practice group of four physicians and doing consulting work. As a result, he had developed an interest in management and administration. His next goal was to apply this background to a leadership position in either a clinical department with a position such as chair of a department of medicine/internal medicine, program

Albert VanHees Resume Before

ALBERT G. VANHEES

14 Peachtree Lane • Adrian, MO 64720 • jobseeker@gmail.com • 816.555.3401

Intuitive, creative, and results-oriented business manager seeking a career change into a fast-paced trading environment where I can leverage my knowledge of global events and financial markets, risk-management techniques, and communication skills to maximize trading profits and grow business relationships.

PROFESSIONAL EXPERIENCE

PROGRAM MANAGER, SERVICE OPERATIONS, SERVICE OPERATIONS, 2004-Present
AT&T Wireless, Oregon, MO

- Developed and executed on strategy to manage inventory risk; enacted plan reducing on-hand inventory from $12M to $4M over the 2008 fiscal year and created amortization schedule for use of future reserves.
- Drafted and led urgent response to unexpected buildup of in-field units; saved AT&T over $500k in replacement expenses and minimized impact to brand.
- Structured pricing programs for two top customers incentivizing increased purchasing while maintaining departmental margin goals.
- Designed ROI Template enabling quick assessment of costs and risks for secondary sales channel opportunities.
- Projected and prepared department for shifts in business climate by analyzing customers historical patterns and monitoring real-time market events.
- Achieved new business by identifying markets, negotiating pricing, and closing on revenue opportunities.
- Coordinated in-field inventory audit; offered Excel-based tools and solutions improving customer tracking.
- Created forecasting and tracking processes reducing replacement unit expenses by 43% over 2007 fiscal year.
- Managed orientation and training program for new business analysts on Global Business Strategy team.

CORPORATE ACCOUNT EXECUTIVE, 2000-2004
Nextel Communications, St. Louis, MO

- Managed Missouri sales territory for Fortune 500 telecommunications company with specific focus on large corporate and government accounts.
- Generated new business by conducting on-site presentations for multi-level executives within large corporations, w emphasizing state and federal agencies.
- Maintained customer base by deploying strong relationship marketing techniques and outstanding customer service to drive recurring business; leveraged existing relationships with state and federal agencies by providing exceptional support and implementation plans.
- Collaborated closely with sales management and Corporate Account Managers to develop the parameters of Major Account Executive role in assigned territory.
- Attained President's Club status.

ACCOUNT EXECUTIVE, 1997-2000
Nextel Communications, St. Louis, MO

- Focused on selling Nextel products and services in privately owned business sector.
- Identified new sales opportunities through combination of cold calls, referrals, and qualified leads.
- Employed consultative selling approach and relationship marketing to close sales and exceed monthly sales objectives.
- Developed strategies for ongoing sales while maintaining existing customer base and high levels of customer satisfaction.
- Achieved President's Club status.

RESEARCH ASSOCIATE, CORPORATE STRATEGY, 1995-1997
Corporate Executive Panel, New York, NY.

- Consulted for senior corporate strategists at Fortune 500 companies on issues including M&A trends, globalization initiatives, and strategies for competing in consolidating industries.
- Authored strategy brief on business process reengineering (BPR); offered solutions to achieve BPR success and was a top-two requested project amongst the Strategy Board membership.
- Researched and evaluated innovative corporate strategies, tools, and dashboards to monitor and manage projects, portfolios, and initiatives.

FINANCIAL CONSULTANT, INTERN, Summer 1994
Pricewaterhouse Coopers, Adrian, MO

- Identified and researched target client markets and analyzed stocks and securities; provided support to senior consultant and organized client-advisor meetings.

EDUCATIONAL BACKGROUND

TULANE UNIVERSITY, Durham, New Orleans, LA

Bachelor of Arts, Public Policy, GPA: 3.3/4.0 (1991-1995)

Relevant Coursework: Accounting, Microeconomics, Statistics, Economic Analysis of Public Policy, Ethics

Leadership: Director of Student Services (1994), Senator (1991-1992)

OXFORD UNIVERSITY, Oxford, England

Comparative Economics and Politics, Study Abroad (Fall 1994)

HONORS AND AWARDS

- Returned 46% in personal investment options portfolio Jan-Sept 2007; Returned 57% in 2006.
- Ranked in top five percent of AT&T in annual performance review (2006 & 2007).
- Honored with three AT&T 'Gold Key' awards for new business development, management of new-hire training program, and leadership in response to unexpected field crisis.
- Selected to represent AT&T at industry-specific tradeshow in 2006 and 2007.

Albert VanHees Resume After

ALBERT G. VANHEES

14 Peachtree Lane • Adrian, MO 64720 • Phone: 816.555.3401 • E-mail: jobseeker@gmail.com

VP TRADE FINANCE

Equipped to leverage knowledge of global events and financial markets, risk-management techniques, and communication skills to maximize trading profits and grow business relationships upon career change into fast-paced trading environment

SUMMARY

Intuitive, creative, and award-winning business manager who drove tremendous cost savings and became trusted go-to employee for high-profile projects, initiatives, and presentations of action-oriented/solution-based plans to CEO and other top executives.

—Areas of Expertise—

Personal investing: Returned 46 percent in personal investment options portfolio Jan-Sept 2007; returned 57 percent in 2006.

→ Business Analysis	→ Investor Presentations	→ Risk Management
→ Business Development	→ Market Analysis & Assessment	→ Stock Exchange (NYSE)
→ Commodities Market	→ Productivity Improvement	→ Strategizing Trading Needs
→ Cost Analysis	→ Negotiations	→ Technical Indicators
→ Financial Portfolio Development	→ P&L Responsibilities	→ Trade Movement
→ Financial Research	→ Relationship Building	→ Trading & Trading Practices
→ Investment Advice	→ Research & Analysis	→ Options
→ Investment Strategizing		→ Stocks

PROFESSIONAL EXPERIENCE

Program Manager, Service Operations, AT&T Wireless, Oregon, MO, 2004 to Present

Promoted from Business Process Analyst role to Program Manager role, skipping over Business Process Analyst, Senior, step. As sole departmental Program Manager, oversee 40 direct reports and report dually to department's Senior Manager and Director. Quickly learned complex business model—Service Operations at a Telecomm company—and made compelling strategic, data-supported recommendations adopted by division heads.

- Reduced on-hand inventory from $12M to $4M over 2008 fiscal year by developing and executing strategy to manage inventory risk and created amortization schedule for use of future reserves.
- Saved AT&T $500k in replacement expenses and minimized brand impact by drafting and leading urgent response to unexpected buildup of in-field units.
- Structured pricing programs for two top customers, incentivizing increased purchasing while maintaining departmental margin goals.
- Designed ROI Template, enabling quick assessment of costs and risks for secondary sales channel opportunities.
- Projected and prepared department for business-climate shifts by analyzing customers' historical patterns and monitoring real-time market events.
- Generated new business by identifying markets, negotiating pricing, and closing on revenue opportunities.
- Earned multiple AT&T Gold Key awards for new-business development; ranked in top five percent of AT&T in 2006 and 2007 annual performance reviews.
- Coordinated in-field inventory audit; offered Excel-based tools and solutions, thus improving customer tracking.
- Reduced replacement-unit expenses by 43 percent over 2007 fiscal year by creating forecasting and tracking processes.
- Managed orientation and training program for new business analysts on Global Business Strategy team.
- Quickly became a department leader by reaching out to members of other teams at all levels, listening and identifying inefficiencies in processes or programs, offering constructive solutions, and gaining employee buy-in.
- Took initiative and actively sought out projects, innovations, cost-savings, and business improvements beyond scope of assignments and conventional thinking; enhanced business by standardizing processes and driving communication and teamwork among departmental divisions.
- Selected to represent AT&T at industry-specific tradeshow in 2006 and 2007.

Corporate Account Executive, Nextel Communications, St. Louis, MO, 2000 to 2004
- Managed Missouri sales territory for Fortune 500 telecommunications company with specific focus on large corporate and government accounts.
- Generated new business by conducting on-site presentations for multi-level executives within large corporations, emphasizing state and federal agencies.
- Maintained customer base by deploying strong relationship marketing techniques and outstanding customer service to drive recurring business; leveraged existing relationships with state and federal agencies by providing exceptional support and implementation plans.
- Collaborated closely with sales management and Corporate Account Managers to develop the parameters of Major Account Executive role in assigned territory.
- Attained President's Club status.

Account Executive, Nextel Communications, St. Louis, MO, 1997 to 2000
- Focused on selling Nextel products and services in privately owned business sector.
- Identified new sales opportunities through combination of cold calls, referrals, and qualified leads.
- Employed consultative selling approach and relationship marketing to close sales and exceed monthly sales objectives.
- Developed strategies for ongoing sales while maintaining existing customer base and high levels of customer satisfaction.
- Achieved President's Club status.

Research Associate, Corporate Strategy, Corporate Executive Panel, New York, New York, 1995 to 1997
- Consulted for senior corporate strategists at Fortune 500 companies on issues including M&A trends, globalization initiatives, and strategies for competing in consolidating industries.
- Authored strategy brief on business process reengineering (BPR); brief offered solutions to achieve BPR success and became one of the top two studies that Strategy Board members requested for download.
- Researched and evaluated innovative corporate strategies, tools, and dashboards to monitor and manage projects, portfolios, and initiatives.

Financial Consultant, Intern, Pricewaterhouse Coopers, Adrian, MO, Summer 1994
- Identified and researched target client markets.
- Analyzed stocks and securities.
- Provided support to senior consultant and organized client-advisor meetings.

EDUCATION

Bachelor of Arts in Public Policy
Tulane University, New Orleans, LA, 1995

Study Abroad
Comparative Economics and Politics
Oxford University, Oxford, England, Fall 1994

Albert VanHees Cover Letter

ALBERT G. VANHEES

14 Peachtree Lane • Adrian, MO 64720 • Phone: 816.555.3401 • E-mail: jobseeker@gmail.com

Dec. 30, 2007

Art Paulson
Morgan Stanley & Co.
440 South LaSalle St., Suite 3800
Chicago, IL 60605

Dear Mr. Paulson:

Your colleague Joe Pinnell suggested I contact you about your opening for a VP Trade Finance and my desire to apply my highly applicable background to transition into this career. As I read the description of this position, I couldn't help noticing how well your requirements align with my background and skills, and especially how closely the position parallels my most recent position as Program Manager, Service Operations for AT&T Wireless. While my enclosed resume provides a good overview of my strengths and achievements, I have also listed some of your specific requirements for the position and my applicable skills:

You require:
- Someone who can identify and develop profitable business opportunities and client relationships.

- A VP who can maintain high quality risk analysis.

- Strong negotiation and sales/marketing skills.

- Knowledge of international trade practices and transactions, as well as global business environment.

- Interpersonal-communication skills.

I offer:
- Proven track record of generating new business and responding to customer needs; earned several awards for new-business development.

- Experience in managing risk, especially in inventory. Also analyze and manage risk in personal investment portfolio.

- Ten-year history of progressively successful sales and marketing success, bolstered by strong negotiation experience in current position.

- Exceptional expertise in global financial markets and business environment.

- Among many examples, outstanding performance in developing training program for Global Business Strategy team and communicating effectively with new hires.

With these qualifications, I am confident I am an excellent match for the VP Trade Finance position at Morgan Stanley. I am most eager to implement my experience and contribute to your organization. I am convinced it would be worthwhile for us to meet. I will contact you soon to schedule an interview. If you have any questions, feel free to call me at 816.555.3401. Thank you for considering my qualifications.

Sincerely,

Albert Van Hees

director or division chief, or a hospital/office-based administrative post such as a medical director, vice president of medical affairs, or chief medical officer, preferably in a teaching hospital.

Like most physicians, Peter had always used a curriculum vitae (CV) to seek jobs in the past, and had never developed a resume for use on the business side of medicine. His document was characterized by minimal formatting and writing that was a bit wordy and not as reader-friendly as it could be.

Strategy: Peter placed a headline atop his revised resume stating his career goal. The branding statement underneath the headline emphasized his medical background, as well as his entrepreneurial qualifications. His Professional Profile section clearly spelled out the areas of his expertise that applied directly to hospital administration. His Experience and Education sections emphasized the administrative (as opposed to clinical) aspects of his background while still revealing his medical qualifications. He offered strong, quantified performance metrics to show his business savvy.

Peter targeted each cover letter to the requirements of the jobs he pursued and emphasized his combination of administrative, clinical, medical-education, and business qualifications.

Among other jobs he sought out, Peter applied for the following job with the new resume:

Chief Medical Officer. [Name of hospital] is a 237-bed acute-care hospital located in [city, state] and is the area's only community-oriented, not-for-profit hospital with a special relationship and a special commitment to provide for the health and wellness of the community. The hospital has approximately 300 physicians on the medical staff and offers a broad range of medical, surgical, diagnostic, and therapeutic services on both an inpatient and outpatient basis.

The Chief Medical Officer reports to the President and Chief Executive Officer of [name of hospital] and is a key leader among the senior leadership team. This position will assist the medical staff and the leadership of the hospital in fulfilling their responsibilities to patients for the provision of quality care. Successful candidates will have licensed medical physician with clinical training, board certification and the ability to gain licensure in [state]. An advanced degree in healthcare administration or business would be highly desirable and prior experience as a full time Chief Medical Officer would be ideal. Candidates with part-time Chief Medical Officer and/or other professional medical director experience will also be considered. The successful candidate will have experience with designing effective clinical practice patterns with physicians to decrease utilization and/or enhance quality of outcomes in service lines.

Resume and Cover Letter: Peter's before and after resumes and his cover letter are included on pages 170–176.

Outcome: Peter had moderate success obtaining interviews by responding to ads and job postings, but his success increased when he began cold-contacting hospitals and healthcare recruiters. Several hiring managers told him that most applicants submitted traditional CVs for the type of leadership position Peter sought, and Peter's business-oriented resume distinguished itself, not only because of its business-results content, but also because of it unusual appearance. A few hiring managers even admitted to being startled by the look of the document, but they could not deny that it stood out in the pack of CVs and offered information that portrayed Peter as an effective hospital leader. Peter took his time in the job-search process. He was not unhappy at the hospital that had employed him for nearly 18 years; he was simply looking to take the next step. After six months of searching, Peter found a position as Vice President of Medical Affairs at a community hospital in a neighboring city. He took the time to determine that the hospital was an excellent cultural fit for him before accepting the position.

Peter Gilmore Resume Before

Peter Gilmore, M.D., M.S. Ed, F.A.C.P., C.P.E.
jobseeker@gmail.com

Business Address
304 Rose Garden Lane
Oceanside, CA 92049
(760) 555-8370
jobseeker@ocean.rr.com

Home Address
1502 Servilla Place
Oceanside, CA 92049
(760) 555-9085
jobseeker@gmail.com

Professional Experience

Oceanside Medical Center, Oceanside, California   **1991-present**

Director of Medical Education   **2001-present**

Lead department of 12 individuals and responsible for all administrative aspects of the department including residency coordination and oversight (7 ACGME-accredited programs, 100 residents and 70 medical students), research, CME, medical library, grants and applications, and budgeting comprising a budget of approximately $600,000 in a 222-bed teaching hospital.

Developed Department of Medical Education as educational resource for hospital-wide initiatives to improve compliance with quality indicators including conscious sedation, restraints and delinquency of medical records improving compliance with each of these indicators by 15-20%.

Led effort to obtain departmental input and critically analyze library holdings and acquisitions in the medical library saving approximately $7000 in costs and have developed opportunity among community hospitals for sharing of CME and library services leading to additional cost savings by all parties.

Led a team that developed a housestaff manual. This hundred-page document was based on input obtained from each clinical department, the legal department and the Department of Medical Education

Developed the Resident Advisory Council to improve communications with hospital administration consisting of peer-selected housestaff. This group was instrumental in decreasing new housestaff orientation from 5 days to one day, resulting in an annual savings of approximately $50,000

Maintained and expanded structure to offset cost of Graduate Medical Education at Oceanside Medical Center, a county facility using revenue from relationships developed with affiliated medical schools.

Have maintained full ACGME accreditation for all programs since assuming position.

As part of role, maintain active participation in committees having to do with hospital operations such as bed prioritization, efficient discharging practices and IT initiatives such Web Portal project for improved access to patient information

Lead effort to develop network of community based teachers for undergraduate and graduate medical education.

Chief of Staff   **2001-2002**
Facilitated a process that restructured hospital bylaws and committees, reducing by greater than 50% the number of committees and length of the bylaws.

Served as mentor and sounding board for faculty during a period of difficulty encompassing compensation changes and staff turnover

Advised the Chief Medical Officer on personnel issues

Residency Program Director, Internal Medicine   **1997-present**
Direct all aspects of a 24-resident UCLA affiliated Internal Medicine Residency Program, with ACGME accreditation, evaluation, educational development, recruitment and tracking as major activities

Associate Residency Program Director, Internal Medicine   **1994-1997**
Served as advisor to Program Director on recruitment, scheduling and evaluation serving as ward attending and prepared accreditation documents

Director of Primary Care Education   **1991-1994**
Worked under Department of Health and Human Services Grant for resident training in General Internal Medicine (1D28PE19209) implementing new didactic conference schedule emphasizing Primary Care and developing a "firm" system to ensure patient care continuity in the residency program

Part-Time Private Practice Experience

Internist, Oceanside Faculty Medical Group   **1990-1993**
Practiced Internal Medicine in a multi-specialty group practice

Internist and Founder, Vista Medical Group   **1993-2001**
Established a 4-physician group, which grew to include 6 physicians and three midlevels in an environment with 50% capitation working with a local independent IPA that grew to 70,000 lives. Helped develop a physician compensation system in a heavily capitated market and developed proposal for hospitalist services in a capitated environment.

Internist, Oceanside Faculty Medical Group   **2001-present**
Returned to limited private practice (6 hours per week) as hospital administrative responsibilities grew while maintaining position as Director of Medical Education and Residency Director.

Administrative Activities
Utilization Review, Managed Care Systems of San Diego County   **1998-present**
Provide professional service in subspecialty referral authorization and interpretation of health plan guidelines approximately 1-2 hours per week to this local IPA.

Physician Reviewer, Network Medical Review, Rocky Mount, NC   **2001-present**
Provide professional service in disability review and medical necessity review to private company specializing in evidence-based physician reports. This has included medical necessity review, short and long-term disability determinations based on medical record review, and determination of appropriate care and treatment of claimants seen in Latin America from review of medical records in Spanish.

Education

California State University Channel Islands, B.A Biological Sciences   1981
Internship and Junior Assistant Residency, Department of Medicine,

Meriden Hospital Health Center, Meriden, CT, Yale University
School of Medicine (PGY I-II), New Haven, CT   1987 to 1989

Internal Medicine Residency, Oceanside Medical Center, California   1989-1990
UCLA School of Medicine (PGY III)

Chief Resident, Oceanside Medical Center, Oceanside, CA (PGY IV)   1990-1991

University of California – Los Angeles, Master of Science Degree in   1994-1996
Medical Education

American College of Physician Executives, Certificate   1998-2002
Program in Medical Management (completed 210 CME
hours of medical management courses).

Certifying Commission in Medical Management Award   2002
Certified Physician Executive

University of Alabama Professional MBA program   2003-2008

Professional Organizations

Fellow, American College of Physicians
Association of Program Directors in Internal Medicine
American College of Physician Executives
National Associates Competition Review Board ACP-ASIM
National Association of Inpatient Physicians
American Board of Quality Assurance and Utilization Review Physicians

BOARD CERTIFICATION: American Board of Internal Medicine 1990
Recertification ABIM 1997 (Valid until 2010)

American Board of Quality Assurance and Utilization
Review Physicians 2002

PETER GILMORE, MD
MS Ed., FACP, CPE
1502 Servilla Place, Oceanside, CA 92049 • Phone: 760-555-8123 • FAX: 760-555-7546
E-mail: jobseeker@ocean.rr.com

CHIEF MEDICAL OFFICER
Offer unique perspective as healthcare humanist who is also an entrepreneurial realist

PROFESSIONAL PROFILE

- Board-certified, licensed MD with master's degree in medical education, Certified Physician Executive designation, current MBA training, clinical background, and 14+ years of administrative experience.
- Motivated achiever who maintains contact with patients and offers expertise in credentialing, medical staff relations and coordination, quality initiatives and processes, continuing medical education, medical management, programmatic leadership, and program improvement.
- Exceptional verbal and written communicator who excels in physician training in preparation for accreditation site visits and conveys information effectively to inspection personnel during site visits, resulting in excellent accreditation record; praised upon accreditation for solid and competent work in leading medical education programs to new heights.
- Skilled physician teacher, motivator, mentor, and coach who counsels residents and other colleagues.
- Innovative problem-solver and change agent who has initiated new ideas, radically changed residency program, and developed new community-based training experiences, resulting in remarkable program-performance improvement.
- Persuasive leader cited by colleagues and superiors for program refinements, team-building, cohesiveness among residents, efficiency, improved results in training programs, identifying problems, devising innovative and creative solutions, competent managerial skills, the ability to command respect, political sensitivity, taking on funding/operational challenges, receptiveness to ideas/concerns, achieving a balanced approach, effecting changes, long-range vision, as well as sophisticated, excellent leadership as administrator, educator, physician, community leader, and role model.

PROFESSIONAL EXPERIENCE

Director of Medical Education, *Oceanside Medical Center*, Oceanside, CA, 2001 to Present
- Lead 12-person department and oversee all departmental administrative aspects, including residency coordination of seven ACGME-accredited programs, 100 residents, 70 medical students, research, CME, medical library, grants and applications, and $600K budget in 222-bed teaching hospital.
- Collaborate with various departments to develop Department of Medical Education as educational resource for maintaining accreditation and for hospital-wide quality initiatives regarding conscious sedation, restraints, and delinquency of medical records, improving compliance with each of these indicators by up to 20 percent.
- Reduce costs and limit FTEs; led departmental effort to critically analyze medical library holdings and acquisitions, saving approximately $7K.
- Enabled community hospitals to share CME and library services, resulting in additional cost savings by all parties.
- Spearheaded cost-savings efforts and quality-improvement projects; played instrumental role in decreasing new house-staff orientation from five days to one, resulting in annual savings of approximately $50K.

Residency Program Director, Internal Medicine, *Oceanside Medical Center*, Oceanside, CA, 1997 to Present
- Direct all aspects of 24-resident, UCLA-affiliated Internal Medicine Residency Program, and oversee ACGME accreditation, evaluation, educational development, recruitment, and tracking.
- Successfully recruit residents through National Resident Matching program.
- Increased board passage rates for residents.

Chief of Staff, *Oceanside Medical Center*, Oceanside, CA, 2001 to 2002
- Facilitated process that restructured hospital bylaws and committees, reducing by greater than 50 percent the number of committees and length of bylaws.
- Served as mentor and sounding board for faculty during difficult period encompassing compensation changes and staff turnover.

Internist, Oceanside Faculty Medical Group, *Oceanside Medical Center*, Oceanside, CA, 2001 to Present
- Practice on a limited basis while maintaining positions at Oceanside Medical Center as Director of Medical Education and Residency Director.

Associate Residency Program Director, Internal Medicine, *Oceanside Medical Center*, Oceanside, CA, 1994 to 1997
- Advised Program Director on recruitment, scheduling, and evaluation while serving as attending physician.

Internist and Founder, *Vista Medical Group*, Vista, CA, 1993 to 2001
- Established part-time (while maintaining positions at Oceanside Medical Center) four-physician group, which grew to include six physicians and three midlevels in an environment with 50 percent capitation in collaboration with local independent IPA that grew to 70,000 lives.
- Assisted in developing physician compensation system in heavily capitated market and developed proposal for hospitalist services in capitated environment.

Director of Primary Care Education, *Oceanside Medical Center*, Oceanside, CA, 1991 to 1994
- Implemented new didactic conference schedule emphasizing primary care and developed firm system to ensure patient care continuity in residency program under Department of Health and Human Services Grant for resident training in General Internal Medicine.

Internist, Oceanside Faculty Medical Group, *Oceanside Medical Center*, Oceanside, CA, 1990 to 1993
- Practiced internal medicine in multi-specialty group practice part-time while maintaining positions at Oceanside Medical Center.

CONSULTING EXPERIENCE

Utilization Reviewer, *Managed Care Systems of San Diego County*, San Diego, CA, 1998 to present
- Provide professional service in referral authorization and interpretation of health plan guidelines up to two hours weekly to this local IPA.

Physician Reviewer, *Network Medical Review*, Rocky Mount, NC, 2001 to present
- Provide professional service in disability review and medical necessity review to private company specializing in evidence-based physician reports.
- Make short- and long-term disability determinations based on medical record review, as well as appropriate care and treatment determinations of claimants.

EDUCATION and POSTGRADUATE MEDICAL TRAINING

- Professional MBA, University of Alabama, Birmingham, AL, expected 2008
- Certified Physician Executive, Certifying Commission in Medical Management Tutorial, 2002
- Certificate Program in Medical Management, 210 CME hours of medical-management coursework, American College of Physician Executives, Tampa, FL, 2002
- Mentor, Fellowship Program in Medical Education, Department of Medical Education, University California Los Angeles, Los Angeles, CA, 1998
- Master of Science in Medical Education, University California Los Angeles, Los Angeles, CA, 1996
- Chief Resident, Oceanside Medical Center, Oceanside, CA (PGY IV), UCLA School of Medicine (PGY III), Los Angeles, CA, 1990 to 1991
- Internal Medicine Residency, Oceanside Medical Center, Oceanside, CA, UCLA School of Medicine, Los Angeles, CA, 1989 to 1990
- Internship and Junior Assistant Residency, Department of Medicine, Meriden Hospital Health Center, Meriden, CT, Yale University School of Medicine (PGY I-II), New Haven, CT, 1987 to 1989
- Bachelor of Arts in Biological Sciences, California State University Channel Islands, Camarillo, CA, 1981

BOARD CERTIFICATIONS

- Recertification, American Board of Internal Medicine, 1997 (valid until 2010)
- American Board of Quality Assurance and Utilization Review Physicians, 2002
- American Board of Internal Medicine, 1990

PROFESSIONAL AFFILIATIONS

- Fellow, American College of Physicians
- Member, Association of Program Directors in Internal Medicine
- Member, American College of Physician Executives
- Member, National Associates Competition Review Board ACP-ASIM
- Member, California Medical Association
- Member, National Association of Inpatient Physicians
- Member, American Board of Quality Assurance and Utilization Review Physicians

HONORS and AWARDS

- California Legislature (Assembly) Resolution and Commendation for Service, 2003
- Humanitarian Award, California Medical Association, Oceanside Chapter, 2003
- Diplomate, American College of Physician Executives, 2003
- Award for Excellence in Internal Medicine, 1991

Peter Gilmore Cover Letter

PETER GILMORE, MD
MS Ed., FACP, CPE
1502 Servilla Place, Oceanside, CA 92049 • Phone: 661-555-8123 • FAX: 661-555-7546
E-mail: jobseeker@ocean.rr.com

Feb. 29, 2008

Roger Simpson, MD, CEO
Torrey Pines Community Hospital
10000 Torrey Pines Blvd.
San Diego, CA 92130-6669

Dear Dr. Simpson:

As an experienced physician, administrator, and director-level medical educator, I am eager to provide my skills and qualifications in the position of Chief Medical Officer that you recently advertised. I offer a background of leadership and dedication to quality care that would be essential in the advertised position.

Having spent nearly 15 years in various leadership and administrative positions at Oceanside Medical Center, I am especially well prepared to design effective clinical practice patterns with physicians. I offer all the appropriate licensure and board certification you seek.

I am convinced that my background in clinical, medical-education, and business settings equip me well to guide your medical staff and hospital leadership in fulfilling their responsibilities to patients and provide quality care. I've also demonstrated my initiative by implementing a number of cost-saving, quality-improvement, and compliance strategies.

My business acumen is an additional asset. Even while excelling in my positions at Oceanside Medical Center, I undertook the entrepreneurial venture of founding and operating a group practice. I have also earned the Certified Physician Executive designation and expect to complete an MBA later this year.

Dr. Simpson, I would like to arrange an interview to review the contribution I can make in this position. I appreciate your time and consideration and will contact you to discuss this opportunity in the near future.

Sincerely,

Peter Gilmore, MD

Chapter Seven

Resume and Cover Letter Samples for Aspiring Executives

And now, the meat of this book: resume and cover letter samples. These samples are fictionalized versions of the resumes and cover letters of real executive candidates, so some of them represent imperfect careers. All these job-seekers have employed strategies to deemphasize career flaws and showcase executive results.

Use these samples as models of keyword-rich resumes with a sharp focus, broadcasted accomplishments, clear and consistent branding, unique quality, and sophisticated appearance. As noted in the Introduction, resumes and cover letters are extremely subjective, so choose a style that fits your personality, strategy, and goals; take bits and pieces from several resumes. Experiment to discover the best kind of resume for you—and the one that works best.

- ➤ **Resumes and Cover Letters for Executives in Sales, Marketing, Business Development, and Public Relations (1–9)**

- ➤ **Resumes and Cover Letters for Executives in Management, Human Resources, and Project Management (10–14)**

- ➤ **Resumes and Cover Letters for Operations Executives (15–17)**

- ➤ **Resumes and Cover Letters for Executives in Engineering, Science, and Information Technology (18–23)**

- ➤ **More Resumes and Cover Letters for Executives (24–34)**

Michael L. Blumenthaal

32 Waterfall Lane, Adrian, MI 49221 • 517.555.0678
E-mail: jobseeker@comcast.net

Senior Corporate Sales Representative

Top-producing sales executive successful in outselling competition through development of long-term, high-profit client relationships; poised to contribute abundant skills and successful track record to your Columbus-area organization.

Professional Profile

- Accomplished senior-level sales rep with consistent history of closing profitable contracts with executive decision-makers in computer-manufacturing and channel-partner sectors.
- Award-winning achiever and Six Sigma Green Belt whose numerous recognitions attest to exemplary motivation; awards include 15+ annual 100 percent club awards, four president's club awards, and numerous national sales representative awards.
- Instrumental catalyst in developing revenue-recovery strategies leading to collection of $2 million in accounts receivable.

Areas of Expertise

- Account Management
- Strategic Alliances
- New Business Development
- Contract Negotiations
- Customer Needs Assessment
- Fiscal Controls
- Profit Maximization
- Distribution Management

- Proactive Marketing Concepts
- Niche Markets
- Internet Marketing
- New Business Launches
- Forecasting Market Trends
- Networking
- Competitive Analysis

- Channel Distribution
- Creative Sales Techniques
- Sales Team Management
- Sales Forecasting
- Exceeding Sales Quotas
- Revenue Growth
- Growth Strategies
- Competitive Profiles

Professional Experience

National Account Manager, *Phoenix Corporation*, Deerfield, MI, Jan. 2003 to Present
- Serving as manager of East Coast Channel Sales, revived failing partnership with Data Solutions, one of company's largest accounts, elevating it to one of Phoenix's top performers.
- Doubled sales in first quarter and oversee subsequent steady growth.
- Earned "2003 Storage Vendor of The Year" award.
- Facilitated Phoenix's reengagement with C. L. Higginbottom.
- Restored discipline and consistency in marketing programs.
- Manage $200K+ annual marketing budget.
- Establish internal team objectives, resulting in enhanced support structure and more concentrated focus on sell-through revenue objectives.
- Ensure adherence to top- and bottom-line objectives.
- Maintain open avenues of communication through clear job descriptions and provide regular communication and productive feedback.
- Function as corporate spokesperson who proficiently delivers detailed presentations of unique offerings to corporate clients during sales consultations.
- Develop and implement effective sales strategies that achieve targeted marketing objectives.
- Organized and supervised production-facility tour, tour of a solar installation, and presentation on power-management system software for 200+ sales reps from one of firm's sales channels.

Senior OEM Business Development Manager, *Foxit Software, Inc.*, Deerfield, MI, Oct. 2000 to Jan. 2003
* Developed relationship with Microsoft Business Line management and successfully unseated competing product line.
* Negotiated and amended Statement of Work contract.
* Landed business across LeapLearn and SurfNet product lines for Foxit TrueRecord mastering application and Simple Backup for OBI, DVD R/RAM drives providing more than $4 million in potential revenue.
* Championed specific Microsoft-requested product features for inclusion in Foxit products.
* Strategized priorities with engineering professionals to close on critical technical issues and meet aggressive client schedules.
* Developed marketing plan to promote up-sell and cross-sell programs.

Senior Corporate Sales Representative, *Eastern Digital, Inc.*, Onstead, MI, Oct. 1997 to Oct. 2000
* Presented new hard-disc-drive qualification process to senior management, convincing them to proceed with $150K+ initial investment.
* Maintained better than 50 percent market share for high-end disc drives.
* Boosted market share by convincing senior-management team to support new kitting operation with on-site team.
* Calculated accurate forecasts and placed 450K+ units quarterly in 25+ warehouses worldwide – 100+ SKUs.
* Completed Six Sigma Green Belt training.

Senior Sales Representative, *Eastern Digital, Inc.*, Onstead, MI, Feb. 1994 to Oct. 1997
* Excelled as top performer in Mideast, serving key accounts and acquiring company's first billion-dollar client.
* Facilitated changes in strategies and processes to improve firm's competitive position in the marketplace.
* Maintained majority market share in accounts through turbulent period of acquisitions.
* Earned President's Club Awards.

Area Sales Manager, *LaCie Corporation*, Onstead, MI, 1990 to 1994
* Recognized as LaCie's East Coast revenue producer for consistently producing in the top 10 percent.
* Effectively restored profitability to Latin American division, increasing sales by 50 percent in six months.

Education

* *Bachelor of Science in Marketing*, Michigan State University, East Lansing, MI

Jonathan Herlsen

Sales Management | Executive Management | Project Management

REAL ESTATE ~ NEW RESIDENTIAL CONSTRUCTION ~ INSURANCE

▶ Resourceful sales-management executive with strengths in sales/marketing and proven ability to sell real estate and insurance, as demonstrated by $10 million+ in property/casualty insurance sales and more than $16 million in real-estate and new-home sales.

▶ Hold Delaware Real Estate and Brokers Licenses.

PROFESSIONAL EXPERIENCE

NATIONAL SALES MANAGER – ASSOCIATE BROKER, Country Log Homes, Middletown, DE, 2004 to present

▶ Manage portion of National Distribution network in the field, specifically developing Delaware market.

▶ Sell custom log homes and real estate associated with high-end golf-course development.

▶ Collaborate with clients, designers, and architects to develop complete design criteria and construction documents required for permitting and construction of high-end custom homes.

▶ Coordinate with designers/architects and construction crews in new-home construction to develop complete architectural programs, including floor plans, elevations, and selection of siding, windows, doors, flooring, and other components.

MANAGING OWNER/BROKER, Mortensen Real Estate, Middletown, DE, 2002 to 2004

▶ Functioned as independent real-estate salesperson and managing broker for long-time New Castle County real-estate firm.

▶ Oversaw financial and sales management.

▶ Conducted residential, commercial, and vacant-land sales.

▶ Developed and implemented property management division.

BROKER/OWNER, Delaware Development, Inc., Hockessin, DE, 1995 to 2002

▶ Planned single-family, multi-lot new development.

▶ Negotiated property transfer, secured funding, and consulted on building and pricing.

▶ Developed market plan and personally sold majority of development.

VICE PRESIDENT, James and James Financial Advising, Elsmere, DE, 1990 to 1995

▶ Owned 50 percent and oversaw every phase of independent insurance agency and financial services firm, including strategic planning, sales planning, personnel, company/supplier agreements and relations, financial management, sales and service of individual and large commercial accounts.

▶ Conceived, developed, and implemented sales campaigns.

▶ Completed risk-management surveys and implemented risk-management techniques.

▶ Managed accounting and accounts payable/receivable, as well as financial and estate planning.

▶ Effectively handled client relations and difficult claims.

▶ Conducted licensed insurance and securities sales.

SALES ASSOCIATE, Altor Real Estate, Elsmere, DE, 1987 to 1990

▶ Sold real estate on commission basis.

EDUCATION

▶ Bachelor of Science in Geological Oceanography, Wilmington University, Rehoboth Beach, DE; Minor: Public Policy

19 Hummingbird Lane, Claymont, DE 19703 ~ 302-555-9274 ~ Cell: 302-555-7620 ~ E-mail: jobseeker@cfl.rr.com

JONATHAN HERLSEN
19 Hummingbird Lane, Claymont, DE 19703
302-555-9274 ~ Cell: 302-555-7620
E-mail: jobseeker@cfl.rr.com

==
Sales Management I Executive Management I Project Management
==

....
REAL ESTATE ~ NEW RESIDENTIAL CONSTRUCTION ~ INSURANCE
....

o Resourceful sales management executive with strengths in sales/marketing and proven ability to sell real estate and insurance, as demonstrated by $10 million+ in property/casualty insurance sales and more than $16 million in real-estate and new-home sales.
o Hold Delaware Real Estate and Brokers Licenses.

===========================
PROFESSIONAL EXPERIENCE
===========================
NATIONAL SALES MANAGER - ASSOCIATE BROKER,
Country Log Homes, Middletown, DE, 2004 to present
o Manage portion of National Distribution network in the field, specifically developing Delaware market.
o Sell custom log homes and real estate associated with high-end golf-course development.
o Collaborate with clients, designers, and architects to develop complete design criteria and construction documents required for permitting and construction of high-end custom homes.
o Coordinate with designers/architects and construction crews in new-home construction to develop complete architectural programs, including floor plans, elevations, and selection of siding, windows, doors, flooring, and other components.

MANAGING OWNER/BROKER, Mortensen Real Estate, Middletown, DE, 2002 to 2004
o Functioned as independent real estate salesperson and managing broker for long-time New Castle County real estate firm.
o Oversaw financial and sales management.
o Conducted residential, commercial, and vacant-land sales.
o Developed and implemented property management division.

BROKER/OWNER, Delaware Development, Inc., Hockessin, DE 1995 to 2002
o Planned single-family, multi-lot new development.
o Negotiated property transfer, secured funding, and consulted on building and pricing.
o Developed market plan and personally sold majority of development.

VICE PRESIDENT, James and James Financial Advising, Elsmere, DE, 1990 to 1995
o Owned 50 percent and eversaw every phase of independent insurance agency and financial services firm, including strategic planning, sales planning, personnel, company/supplier agreements and relations, financial management, sales and service of individual and large commercial accounts.
o Conceived, developed, and implemented sales campaigns.
o Completed risk-management surveys and implemented risk-management techniques.
o Managed accounting and accounts payable/receivable, as well as financial and estate planning.
o Effectively handled client relations and difficult claims.
o Conducted licensed insurance and securities sales.

SALES ASSOCIATE, Altor Real Estate, Elsmere, DE, 1987 to 1990
o Sold real estate on commission basis.

==========
EDUCATION
==========
o Bachelor of Science in Geological Oceanography, Wilmington University, Rehoboth Beach, DE; Minor: Public Policy

DALE HASTINGS

601 Desert Rd. • Boulder City, NV 89005 • Phone: 702-555-5947 • E-mail: jobseeker@aol.com

VICE PRESIDENT, SALES AND NEW BUSINESS DEVELOPMENT

*Education • Financial Services • Telecom & Wireless • Healthcare • Information Management
Marketing, Channel and Direct Sales Programs • Technology Education • Partner Management*

PROFILE

Top-producing sales and marketing executive with 20+-year proven track record. Consistently deliver a ten-fold growth in sales. Developed six highly profitable businesses providing commercial as well as consumer products and services. Strong executive leader offering cross-functional management background.

Extensive experience creating and implementing solution selling and vertical selling programs that support field and channel sales organizations, particularly for global enterprise solutions. Broad knowledge of technology marketplace, from high availability platforms through networking and software solutions.

CORE COMPETENCIES

Solution selling to C-level executives	Online and offline marketing integration
Revenue growth and P&L management	IT investment roadmaps and ROI analysis
High-margin value-added services	Customer relationship management systems
Competitive strategies and scenario planning	Electronic bill presentment and payment
Joint ventures and strategic alliances	High-volume online order entry and fulfillment
Matrix management and team mentoring	Call center and e-commerce platform integration
Distribution channel design and optimization	Wireless online access/mobile data technologies
New product and service market launch	MBA in marketing

PROFESSIONAL EXPERIENCE

Vice President, Sales and New Business Development, *HBIT LIGHTING,* Blue Diamond, NV, Nov. 2006 to present

- Recruited by this leading provider of next-generation electronic billing and online financial services.
- Plan, fund, staff and direct multiple business and technical initiatives aimed at developing compelling and synergistic applications, acquiring new subscribers, and driving expanded and repeat usage.
- Acquired 25,000+ new subscribers by conceiving, launching and completing two pilot programs.
- Negotiated strategic partnerships and sponsorships with leading financial institutions, insurance companies, and retailers.
- Increased average monthly revenue per subscriber by 150 percent.

Vice President, Education, *LEAPFROG LEARNING PROGRAMS*, Tall Pine, NV, June 2002 to Oct. 2006

- Developed Leapfrog Learning organization and oversaw all aspects of training sales and technical individuals for both internal groups and partners on products and solutions.
- Deployed Leapfrog Learning Management System, enabling global tracking of both partner and internal training efforts.
- Implemented "virtual" classroom capability that successfully enabled Web-based global learning activities.

Vice President, Solutions Marketing, *LEAPFROG LEARNING PROGRAMS*, Nye, NV, Oct. 2001 to June 2002

- Built solutions marketing organization focused on building value while selling commodity LAN/WAN products to enterprise customers and channel communities.
- Enabled shift of marketing from direct sales, technology-based activities to channel, value-based programs by creating tools and programs.
- Trained channels on benefits and selling points of Leapfrog solutions.
- Initiated Leapfrog vertical marketing programs and launched to channel with collateral, training, and seminar program support.

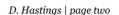

Senior Director, Merchant Ventures, *AT&T WIRELESS*, Las Vegas, NV, Jan. 1996 to Oct. 2001
- Focused on opening new markets for emerging category of telecom services, enabling financial transactions using third-generation cellular (3G) phones.
- Identified and researched key strategic business partners and technology suppliers for a wide array of high-margin e-services.
- Conceived several mobile e-commerce applications for banking, retail, and healthcare niches.
- Proposed and structured multiple strategic alliances and partnerships.

Director, Marketing Programs, *APPLE COMPUTERS*, Cupertino, CA, April 1993 to Jan. 1996
- Launched and managed Business Critical Solutions Marketing (BCSM) group to accelerate sales growth from solution selling.
- Researched, created, developed, and produced marketing products and programs for Apple's internal and external sales channels.
- Built tools and programs with goal of identifying and qualifying new sales opportunities for Apple and partner while enabling increased system revenue.
- Developed Solution Advantage Kit Program, a joint effort between Apple marketing organization and partner marketing organizations, to provide sales channel with information and programs to accelerate point-solutions known to justify sales.
- Raised awareness among Apple's direct and indirect sales channels of key solutions and product offerings for Apple high-end enterprise servers.

Director, Strategy and Business Development, *COMPUTER COMMUNICATORS*, San Diego, CA, May 1990 to Dec. 1992
- Oversaw 10 multi-discipline professionals in developing and launching two pioneering technologies involving computer/telephony integration.
- Developed multiple solutions utilizing these new technologies in tradeshow industry.
- Played instrumental role in acquiring and servicing Consumer Electronics Show as key account.

Advisory Analyst, *GATEWAY COMPUTERS*, San Francisco, CA, Feb. 1987 to May 1990
- Played key role in designing new solutions, integrating adjunct processor services with System Control Point (SCP) applications.
- Collaborating with call-center organization, functioned as subject matter expert in sales opportunities supporting US-based Customer Relationship Management (CRM) sales.
- Supported State of California data centers and various state agencies on multiple projects, including Drivers License database redevelopment, Department of Real Estate, and Office of Emergency Services.

Program Manager, *AT&T WIRELESS*, San Diego, CA, Oct. 1984 to Feb. 1987
- Led team of five professionals in managing all aspects of designing, rolling out and maintaining company's first business-to-business CRM initiative on time and within budget.

Development Manager, *CPU-INTERACTIVE SYSTEMS,* San Jose, CA, Aug. 1982 to Oct. 1984
- Developed programs to support CPU-Interactive's largest US-based customer, Pacific Phone.
- Provided sales support, including answering RFPs and writing development specs.
- Managed technical staff.
- Facilitated sales efforts and interfaced with operating groups within Pacific Phone.

EDUCATION

MBA in Marketing and Finance, Cornell University, Ithaca, NY
Bachelor of Science in Computer Science, University of California, Berkeley, Berkeley, CA

Christopher Jacobs

62 Apple Tree Hill, Damascus, VA 24236 • 276-555-4597
E-mail: jobseeker@comcast.net

Senior-Level Alternative Energy Executive

Eager to lead innovative strategic marketing and operational initiatives that aggressively increase SolarBright's market share, sustain growth, and maximize profitability.

Professional Profile

- Strategy-driven marketing and operations professional with more than 10 years of progressively responsible experience; proficient in accurately identifying potential markets and employing targeted business-development methodologies to capture them.

Areas of Expertise

- Defining/planning/meeting strategic goals and objectives
- Policies and procedures
- Staff supervision and evaluation
- Leadership
- Adapting to change in business, markets, and competition

- Wind power
- Photovoltaic energy
- Monitoring progress
- Ensuring maximum profit
- Financial plans
- Operating budgets
- Activity reports
- Financial statements

- Building collaborative, trusting relationships
- Creating productive working environment
- Maintaining positive communications
- Developing relationships with key customers

Professional Experience

Director of Business Development, *Alternate Technologies Inc.*, Damascus, VA, Jan. 2003 to Present

- Led sales team in generating $45 million in sales and more than 5MW in solar installations in first full year of production.
- Increased profit margin 5 percent and reduced sales cycle to 3 to 4 months by suggesting strategy to target Virginia School Districts instead of large retailers with sales cycle of 12 to 14 months.
- Collaborated with founder and inventor of Clean Power Research to develop comprehensive Web-based sales tool to generate proposals and financially accurate reports for prospective solar clients.
- Developed set of solar costing spreadsheet templates that enables sales team to accurately cost out projects, propelling company to profitability after barely breaking even on first project because firm lacked specific way to determine project profitability.
- Implemented Web-based tool in conjunction with detailed solar costing spreadsheets to generate accurate, cost-effective tool set for estimating and proposing solar solutions for client projects.
- Played key role in ISO 9001 and 9004 certification by developing process, procedure, flow charts, sales manual, and quality policy documentation for components of quality management system.
- Single-handedly train all sales personnel, independent agents, and channel partners, covering solar technology, selling, company policies and procedures, as well as proposal development; trained 250+ sales representatives from major sales channel in two-day event.
- Created comprehensive sales-training program, including sales-training manual and policies and procedures for all aspects of sales-cycle training.
- Function as corporate spokesperson who proficiently delivers detailed presentations of unique offerings to corporate clients during sales consultations.
- Develop and implement effective sales strategies that achieve targeted marketing objectives.
- Organized and supervised production-facility tour, tour of a solar installation, and presentation on power-management system software for 200+ sales reps from one of firm's sales channels.

Strategic Account Consultant, *T-Mobile*, Damascus, VA, Oct. 1998 to Nov. 2002
- Negotiated with corporate executive decision-makers on domestic/international multi-platform data design and initiated collaboration on development and implementation.
- Managed high-profile client module generating more than $15 million annually.
- Achieved "Master" level account consultant ranking for consistently meeting or exceeding objectives, as well as mentoring and training new account consultants.
- Enhanced corporate profitability by collaborating with clients' senior management to develop global voice and data solutions that enabled companies to improve internal and external communications, reduce costs, and improve service to customers.
- Oversaw high-profile accounts such as UltraLight and Sphere One based on experience and high level of expertise in solution consulting.
- Played key role in assisting Sphere One in designing new Internet-based global network that secured T-Mobile a three-year contract totaling more than $3 million.
- Delivered problem-solving solutions for customers that included:
    - Managed and Non-Managed, domestic and international Private Line, Frame Relay and ATM Networks.
    - Managed and Non-Managed IP Service Offerings.

Director of Operations/Sales, *Spherion, Inc.*, Clinchburg, VA, Oct. 1997 to Aug. 1998
- Managed and coordinated all intra-company activities in collaboration with client services, creative design, engineering, and sales departments for startup Web-development and Internet product-development firm.
- Wrote majority of business plan, including cash-flow analysis—costs, profits, break-even point—as well as detailed marketing plan—product, pricing, promotion, media strategy, and public-relations strategy.
- Developed sales and marketing strategies in concert with advertising, media, and public-relations partners while establishing and implementing project pricing.

Account Manager, *T-Mobile – Voice/Website Services*, Clinchburg, VA, Sept. 1996 to Oct. 1997
- Collaborated with telecommunications managers on solutions to optimize telecom services.
- Created initial Website.

National Account Manager, *Clerical Construction Inc.*, Downey, CA, April 1993 to Aug. 1996
- Supervised national account sales in 11 western states, and consulted with architects and engineers on behalf of clients, including HP, Powell International, Airbus, and Allied Alliance Materials.
- Developed comprehensive informational analysis materials on all competing single-ply manufacturers and implemented use by entire sales force.
- Trained local and regional sales representatives.

Education

- *Bachelor of Science in Business Administration*, Rutgers University, Camden, NJ; minor in Marketing

Christopher Jacobs

62 Apple Tree Hill, Damascus, VA 24236 • 276-555-4597
E-mail: jobseeker@comcast.net

Feb. 15, 2008

Richard Williams, Managing Director
Energy Recruiting Associates
15301 K Street NW
Washington, DC 20036-5390

Dear Mr. Williams:

Thanks so much for providing me with additional information about the VP, Alternative Energy, position with your client company, SolarBright. I'm excited about contributing my executive contacts, along with my strategic abilities in the alternative-energy field, to SolarBright. I've enjoyed significant success delivering bottom-line results throughout my career and would like to make a major impact for your client.

My senior-level management experience is extensive, diverse and includes startups. My experience in building a solar sales program from inception to execution aligns well with SolarBright's need for someone who can launch a new business division in a similar field. My relationships with numerous executive contacts at many of the solar and some of the hydrogen companies in SolarBright's target market would strengthen the company's position in securing new and recurring business.

I am a proven, goal-driven executive and a strong interpersonal communicator who interacts well with everyone from subordinates to boards of directors. I am particularly known for identifying the right target market to reduce the sales cycle and increase margin. For example, at Alternate Technologies, we originally targeted large retailers with a sales cycle of 12 to 14 months as the CEO directed. However, as Director of Business Development, I suggested we redirect our sales efforts toward Virginia School Districts. The new strategy resulted in reducing our sales cycle to 3 to 4 months with a 5 percent increase in profit margin.

I have unfailingly demonstrated my strategic ability, resulting in positive cash flow and significant growth. I have consistently deployed my leadership skills while fine-tuning sales and marketing, as well as juggling multiple initiatives. I have an excellent reputation for coaching, training, and motivating high-performance sales teams.

My dual understanding of sales and operations means that I truly grasp company capabilities. My track record in increasing the bottom line speaks for itself, and my operational skills range from generating revenue to strategic planning. To put it concisely, I get things done. I am a proficient strategic manager and profit-minded top executive. My initiatives have resulted in consistent revenue increases.

Rick, please review my background relative to your search assignment for SolarBright and contact me if you need additional information. I can be reached using the contact information above.

Sincerely,

Chris Jacobs

JANET ARTHURS, MBA

16 SNOW MOUNTAIN DRIVE ▪ AURORA, CO, 80601
jobseeker@comcast.net ▪ 303-555-5420 ▪ 303-555-9837

INTERNATIONAL SALES AND MARKETING EXECUTIVE

International Business Development | Cross-Cultural Relationship Building | Partner/Channel Programs
GLOBAL DISTRIBUTOR NETWORK BUILDING AND MANAGEMENT
MARKETING STRATEGY

QUALIFICATIONS SUMMARY

- Senior strategic leader with 15+ years of international experience in sales, marketing, and management.
- Highly trained and educated team player who understands how to control bottom line while growing top line.
- Rare mix of technical competence, sales savvy, leadership, and financial expertise with strong commitment to perfect quality, 100 percent on-time delivery, and customer service.
- Empowering motivator who seizes opportunities, drives positive change, builds consensus, improves productivity and customer satisfaction, significantly reduces operating costs, and executes plans that improve revenue and profit; cited by management for developing strategy and leading teams to improve productivity.

CORE COMPETENCIES

→ Sales Presentations and Training	→ Marketing Communication
→ Global Product Launch	→ Statistical/Quantitative Data Analysis
→ Event Management	→ Marketing Planning and Promotion
→ Budget and Expense Control	→ Fluent in English and Japanese

PROFESSIONAL EXPERIENCE

VICE PRESIDENT, GLOBAL SALES, PLT Ltd., Brighton, CO, June 2003 to Present
- Oversee $30 MM P&L for Electronic Manufacturing Services business segment.
- Grew new business segment for PLT 15 percent in first year.
- Increased new sales by 16 percent in less than 6 months through focused agreements with partners.
- Develop strategic relationships by targeting supply-chain executives.
- Manage four direct sales reports in North America, Japan, Brazil, and Europe.
- Develop sales and marketing strategy and create incentive programs; set goals, and motivate internal team and outside resellers and partners.

CO-FOUNDER, Sales Consulting Corporation, Tokyo, Japan, and Thornton, CO, January 2000 to June 2003
- Took immediate and decisive action by recruiting international partners after identifying market opportunity for foreign products in Japan; negotiated favorable exclusive distributorship with German, Israel, France, and US firms; developed joint sales support and marketing programs, and delivered presentation and training.
- Produced $1MM+ in additional sales revenue by introducing new product lines and utilizing reseller network.
- Oversaw P&L, strategic account planning, sales forecasting, pricing, hiring, training, and managing sales and 12-member marketing team.
- Generated superior brand awareness and sales-revenue growth by maximizing modest budget of $200K to orchestrate advertising, trade shows, and media campaign.

SENIOR SALES MANAGER, Kessler Automotive, Aurora, CO, November 1998 to January 2000
- Oversaw sales, cost control, schedule compliance, and proposals for $13MM/year largest key account.
- Managed staff of 12 people, including engineering, drafting, and administrative.
- Established project-management discipline within unit, which eventually expanded to entire division at request of Division Vice President.
- Enabled more effective portfolio management by initiating critical change in company business practice by showing financial results by project rather than by aggregate result.
- Increased department gross margin from 8 percent to 28 percent in three years through effective change order and contract management.
- Increased on-time delivery performance from 43 percent to 82 percent in 3 years via better project management.
- Led successful implementation of ISO 9000 for unit.
- Managed international projects totaling more than $10MM in Saudi Arabia, Japan, and Europe.

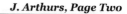

JAPAN MARKETING MANAGER, BMW Holdings Japan, Tokyo, Japan, February 1996 to November 1998
- Directed all aspects of BMW national integrated marketing campaign in Japan with annual budget of $400M.
- Managed outside ad and consulting agencies; produced award-winning advertising and product-launch events that contributed significantly to phenomenal success of new product sales, making BMW one of Japan's most famous brands.
- Successfully penetrated new customer segment by cultivating relationships with Japanese entrepreneur community and senior government officials.
- Proposed, initiated, and facilitated high-profile events such as "Future Begins with Vision," attended by four vice ministers and 150 prominent Japanese entrepreneurs; demonstrated outstanding relationship-building competency and innovative approach.
- Achieved efficiencies in marketing budget by analyzing advertising and promotional spending to identify vehicle, channels and messages that generated target ROI; coordinated and managed cross-functional international team and effectively blended requirements of diverse marketing teams.
- Edited BMW's first customer magazine featuring products, services and BMW lifestyle, a concept that was soon imitated by key competitors.

SALES MANAGER, Ace Communications, Tokyo, Japan, June 1994 to February 1996
- Initiated first international fashion show "Summer Passion at the Palace," an innovative approach that resulted in attracting world's prestige designers, such as Versace, Hugo Boss, and Givenchy, to participate for the first time in Japan; generated additional $200K in revenue without investing extra resources.
- Succeeded in meeting annual advertising and sponsorship sales goal four months ahead of schedule.
- Developed marketing programs to meet client needs and delivered creative business presentations to stimulate sales.

SALES MANAGER, Japan Media Consulting., Tokyo, Japan, July 1993 to June 1994
- Utilized various prospecting techniques such as cold-calling and presentations to establish rapport and maintain strong supportive relationships with local vendors and corporate clients.

GLOBAL PROGRAM COORDINATOR, Brightronix, Boulder, CO, July 1990 to July 1993
- Coordinated new-product development of integrated electronics systems for eight factories in five countries.
- Prepared and presented proposal for largest single program in Brightronix history, resulting in annualized sales forecast of $100 MM.
- Negotiated major program cancellations valued at $9.4 MM in three years.
- Successfully implemented new program start-ups in Ireland, Japan, Brazil, and the US.

EDUCATION

Master of Business Administration in International Business
University of Pennsylvania, Philadelphia, PA, 2004
- Conducted real client consulting project on international market penetration strategy.
- Competencies gained include industry and competitor analysis, distribution analysis, pricing strategy, financial model, market entry strategy, marketing strategy and implementation road map.
- Earned Master Consultant Award and Outstanding Award for Global Team Performance.

Bachelor of Science in Economics
Villanova University, Villanova, PA, 1990

. . .

ERICA JANSEN

11 BARRINGTON STREET • GILFORD, NH 03247
HOME: 603.555.9067 • MOBILE: 603.555.9840 • E-MAIL: JOBSEEKER@HOTMAIL.COM

CREATIVITY • BUSINESS ACUMEN • MARKETING STRATEGIES THAT FACILITATE BUSINESS GROWTH

MARKETING EXECUTIVE

Multifunctional professional with history of identifying, researching, and developing innovative marketing strategies that drive sales, build high-quality brand image, and increase consumer loyalty.

HANDS-ON MARKETING AND BRAND MANAGEMENT • SENSE OF OWNERSHIP IN ACHIEVING COMPANY GOALS

PROFESSIONAL PROFILE

- Dynamic Marketing Executive with 15 years of demonstrated success in analyzing, developing, and facilitating strategic-marketing planning process and consistent performance in both strong and volatile business climates.
- Focused, adaptable, proven leader who, with limited resources, transformed stagnant marketing function into fully functioning Marketing Department that delivers results by engaging consumers and tapping into their insights.
- Strong decision-maker with the entrepreneurial zeal to surpass company goals and objectives; for example, identified emerging US specialty coffee trend and market in 1991; created, launched, and led successful build-out of multifaceted coffee company and specialty coffee brand from concept through start-up and channel expansion to profitability and successful acquisition.

PROFESSIONAL EXPERIENCE

Director of Marketing, Burlington Foods, Inc., Laconia, NH, 2004 to Present
Lead development, growth, and re-alignment of five brands that compete in multibillion-dollar retail cereal and cereal-bar category. Position innovative products to capitalize on health and wellness, and snacking day-part trends; distribute products regionally and nationally, including Grains of Goodness™, All-Organic Grain Bars™, Field of Dreams Crunch Bars™, Bowl O'Goodness Cereal™, and Whole-Grain Wholesome Cereal, which compete with Kashi and Food for Life brands in supermarket and health-food stores across US.

- Joined company after product-launch failure cost company $500K-$1 million. Charged with developing marketing strategy to drive sales in Northeast Region and build consumer awareness—without traditional marketing tools such as advertising—as company re-launched new brand and packaging with same formulation/concept. To boost weak sales performance, deployed knowledge of emerging marketing practices and proposed word-of-mouth marketing campaign for Grains of Goodness ™ Brand targeted toward key Northeast retailers; secured leading US word-of-mouth marketing agency; co-developed and managed two $500K campaigns aimed at 4,000 highly targeted consumers; increased sales by 30 percent and positively impacted IRI by six positions over 52-week period vs. industry leader.

BRANDING INITIATIVES

- Generated $.43/lb margin increase and proper product alignment with competition in preparation for national distribution by managing project to "right-size" six SKUs from 12 oz. to 16 oz.
- Increased 2006 Retail Branded Direct Margin Contribution 21 percent vs. 2005.
- Achieved milestone in Western Region with highest ACV distribution levels in company history by targeting key consumer snacking occasions for two Field of Dreams SKUs—42 percent and 30 percent respectively.
- Created two-award winning new flavors and award-winning brand extension.
- Attained 4 percent sales increase by developing and designing "all natural" brand of retail products for Retail and Health-Food cereal categories for leading US natural and organic supermarkets.
- Analyzed, developed, and presented new marketing initiative for largest co-pack customer, Sam's Soymilk, to increase in-store cereal purchases for take-home consumption in their 300+ stores.
- Created new brand and coordinated formulation for Health-Food and Retail product line to leverage newly approved patent technology for Bowl O'Goodness Cereal.
- Establish retail pricing, promotional strategies, and POS development; facilitate initiatives and brand-development programs for private label, co-pack, and foodservice.

Director of Marketing, Burlington Foods ~ continued

STRATEGIC INITIATIVES

- Identify and analyze consumer trends, demographics, and competitive analysis; define opportunities, develop brand strategy, implement product R&D, design consumer packaging, oversee budgeting and P/L of $4 million; increased sales in retail and club channel by 8 percent.
- Collaborate with sales team, production teams, vendors, designers, and outside agencies.
- Researched, developed, and presented company's first Brand Growth Strategy Report and Retail Brands Marketing Plan.
- Facilitated two consumer-nominated "hits" by Supermarket Guru and MSNBC Today Show Food Editor Phil Lempert for Bowl O'Goodness Cereal, May 15, 2006, and June 6, 2007.
- Led and managed packaging re-design by utilizing shrink-wrap and in-mold labeling technologies for greater shelf impact.
- Led initiative to reduce packaging write-offs by 15 percent by developing Supply Chain Packaging Program.
- Developed Marketing Content Management System that collects data and analyzes emerging trends and marketing plans development.
- Attained 9 percent sales increase by harnessing consumer feedback from Marketing Content Management System and helped recapture distribution in 65 Sam's Club Northeast Buildings.
- Utilized IT resources and developed on-line consumer panel that accelerated new-product development and brand-development strategies.
- Serve as key liaison for 25 company trademarks with New York City intellectual property rights firm.
- Project revenue in three years of up to $100 million through collaboration on rollout of key company innovation to 15,000 US school systems targeting 40 million students.
- Utilized IT Web-based tools to centralize communication among sales, customer service, and 37 brokers/distributors and 272 customers.

INTEGRATED MARKETING COMMUNICATION/PROMOTION INITIATIVES

- Maximized public relations from word-of-mouth campaign for Grains of Goodness: Burlington Foods was featured in a December 27, 2006, *Business Week* article about word-of-mouth marketing and smaller, emerging brands who are using the marketing technique.
- Implemented quarterly newsletter and weekly marketing newsflashes to encourage communication and information sharing, and highlight the accomplishments of marketing, sales and production to employees, stakeholders, ownership group, brokers, and key accounts.
- Initiated and manage Website re-design to take advantage of new graphic capabilities for richer content and consumer appeal; integrate back-end interfaces for streamlining orders and leveraging greater efficiencies to achieve cost savings.
- Exceeded expectations by managing all internal/external communications previously performed by CEO.
- Orchestrated largest media event for key company brand Grains of Goodness in Hartford market, September 2007, on Yankee Cable News with approximately 7MM viewers.
- Design and implement consumer marketing initiatives and present branded product/marketing initiatives to sales team.

Marketing Consultant, Home on the Range LLC, Alton Bay, NH, 2003 to 2004

A multi-unit Cowboy-themed café and coffee roasting company located in central New Hampshire.

- Analyzed, researched and developed strategic marketing initiatives for multi-unit specialty coffee roastery with high-volume cafés, kiosks, drive-thrus, wholesale, and e-commerce fulfillment.
- Performed initial marketing research and competitive analysis, defined target consumer profile, organized new product-line development, and collaborated on marketing strategy and brand-management guidelines.
- Analyzed market trends and sales data for product-line extensions and new marketing initiatives.
- Facilitated new business relationships and prospected potential partnerships for marketing alliances; explored untapped markets and venues for specialty coffee.

President, Jansen Coffee Company, Center Harbor, NH, 1992 to 2003

Conceptualized and spearheaded creation of multifaceted business capitalizing on emerging US specialty coffee market. Researched marketing data and used financial and competitive industry analysis to assess market viability. Collaborated and directed marketing initiatives, new-product development, and brand strategies. Set business objectives and P/L success. Hired, managed, and motivated 25+ staff members.

- Propelled business through creative production, adaptive planning, marketing-strategy implementation, and brand image/awareness development.
- Targeted upscale clientele base and focused business on "platinum" customers.
- Achieved 18 percent pricing premium over competition by creating strategic marketing plan to drive brand image and product line; implemented numerous low-cost, high-impact initiatives and developed relations with major retailers such as Saks Fifth Avenue and Brentano's Booksellers to penetrate upscale quality-oriented target market.
- Created and launched 30 new products and distributed through five company-owned retail venues, specialty wholesale accounts, mail-order/e-commerce fulfillment; maximized 2,000 "platinum" customer database.
- Catalyzed slashing development costs for channel expansion and e-commerce Website by developing and integrating brand image into store design, packaging, marketing materials, e-commerce Website.
- Grew sales revenue by 17 percent through marketing initiatives tailored to sales trends, market fluctuations, competition, consumer feedback,; introduced new products into sales channel.
- Prepared business plan and delivered presentations to four regulatory agencies, resulting in approval and procurement of limited business use permits.
- Integrated positive feedback into "The Best Coffee in Center Harbor" slogan, which became tag line for all marketing materials and easy identifiable mission for associates organization-wide.
- Collaborated on "Take Home a Taste of Center Harbor" visitor-targeted coffee sales program for mail-order/ e-commerce and point-of-sale purchases of whole-bean coffees and gift packages.
- Produced additional $125K in sales by developing business relationships with Whole Foods Market, GreatFood.com, and Marriott Hotel.
- Elected to Board of Directors, Center Harbor Business Association; teamed with Boston public-relations agency to ignite midweek and off-season tourism in city of Center Harbor.
- Facilitated eight articles published in Knight Ridder Newspaper Publications with potential market penetration of up to 50 million readers and additional availability to be picked up by up to 400 wire affiliates.
- Facilitated inclusion in 2005 *Bon Appetit* Best of the Year Trip Tips and 1994 Holiday Issue of *Yankee Magazine.*
- Arranged for and participated in three live radio interviews on WRKO-Boston Radio with 5-million listener audience.
- Developed low-cost/high-impact marketing strategies, trend analysis, client/vendor relations; initiated and nurtured business relationships, analyzed potential business opportunities, and oversaw financial analysis/reporting, public relations, and governmental compliance.
- Negotiated successful company sale in January 2003; retained key personnel and assisted in ownership transition.

AREAS OF EXPERTISE

- Strategic and Tactical Marketing
- Business Analysis/Market Research
- Qualitative/Quantitative Analysis

- Brand Development/Management
- Product Development/Market Launch
- Consumer Engagement/Social Media
- Public and Media Relations

- Relationship Management
- Team Building and Leadership
- New Business Development
- Operations Management

EDUCATION

Executive MBA with Concentration in Food Marketing, Villanova University, Villanova, PA, expected 2009

Bachelor of Arts in International Business, University of Maine, Orono, ME, 1991

Professional Certified Marketer, American Marketing Association, Chicago, IL, In process

PROFESSIONAL AFFILIATIONS

- American Marketing Association

- Product Development and Management Association

- Boston Product Management Association

MOIRA MERCKELSON

2922 Colorado St. ▶ Fresno, CA 93721 ▶ Home: 425.555.1295 ▶ Cell: 831.555.4421 ▶ jobseeker@yahoo.com

EXECUTIVE MARKETING VP

STRATEGY | HIGH-TECH | MANAGEMENT
STRATEGIC MARKET PLANNING | ORGANIZATIONAL LEADERSHIP | PROJECT MANAGEMENT
MARKETING COMMUNICATIONS | BRANDING | NEW PRODUCT/SERVICE DEVELOPMENT
PRODUCT LAUNCH | CUSTOMER RELATIONSHIP MANAGEMENT (CRM) | BUSINESS INTELLIGENCE (BI) INTERNET/
E-COMMERCE

SUMMARY

▶ Visionary advertising and marketing communications professional with rich agency and client-side experience across diverse industries; recognized as highly principled, strong leader who delivers the strategies that drive millions of dollars in revenue and profit growth.
▶ Strategic thinker with know-how to position and build brands and knack for developing impactful and effective marketing communications that connect with customers.
▶ Innovative problem-solver who meets demanding project objectives on time and within budget.
▶ Exceptional communicator with passion for focused, consistent, effective communications.
▶ Highly motivated manager, planner, and organizer.

PROFESSIONAL EXPERIENCE

Vice President of Marketing, Blue Moon Interactive, Fresno, CA ▶ July 2008 to present
▶ Function as change agent leading strategic and tactical marketing efforts, including defining, building, and supporting positioning, identity, messaging, and communications strategy.
▶ Direct and complete corporate marketing projects, including Blue Moon brand strategy and marketing materials, Web content and redesign, collateral, tradeshows/conferences, and speaking events.
▶ Manage alliance program and support sales efforts with tools and targeted messaging.
▶ Define and effectively present consistent company position and message through all avenues of client contact; develop reputation in line with company business-growth objectives by:
    o Overseeing complete Website redesign and production of all new content and messaging.
    o Finalizing, producing, and delivering new collateral and sales materials, including 15 new case studies to be used in print materials and Website redesign.
    o Developing Blue Moon presence and identity at multiple tradeshows and various conferences and uncovering many leads for new business opportunities.
    o Arranging conference speakers and initiating formal speaking program.
    o Creating new Alliance Program and hiring seasoned Alliance Director effective in program implementation and forging relationships with potential clients and enterprise software partners.

Senior Manager/Director, Service Line Marketing, Braswell Consulting, Inc., Fresno, CA ▶ March 2006 to July 2008
▶ Recruited to new position based on previous business-development success.
▶ Built, developed, and managed Service Line Marketing team to meet departmental goals.
▶ Played fundamental role in increasing average sale from $50K to $300K.
▶ Defined and launched "productized" service offerings that were easier for sales personnel to articulate and for potential clients to envision.
▶ Identified and established 10+ leading partners to complement new and existing service offerings and skill sets in BI and database marketing/CRM space.
▶ Redirected Braswell's image from technical provider of individual skillsets to a manager of complete projects from start to finish; raised awareness of Braswell as a thought leader in BI and database marketing by:
    o Conceptualizing and implementing strategic marketing plans to achieve corporate business and revenue objectives for all service lines focused on CRM, BI, Internet/e-Commerce and ERP.
    o Launching overwhelmingly successful speaking program that annually secured dozens of speaking engagements that directly resulted in multimillion-dollar contracts.
    o Increasing market awareness through successfully positioning and branding new service offerings and promoting existing business lines through conference presentations.

Senior Manager, Business Development, Silicon Technology Partners, Inc., Fresno, CA ▶ Jan. 2005 to March 2006

▸ Recruited to design business-development and marketing objectives, strategies, and tactics for practice areas.

▸ Identified opportunities that resulted in new business.

▸ Negotiated and managed all partnerships for 13-state territory.

▸ Developed and implemented processes for lead generation, qualification, and dissemination; obtained leads through speaking opportunities, Silicon-sponsored and partner-sponsored marketing events, tradeshows, and campaigns; increased leads resulted in millions of dollars of new business, and raised Silicon's visibility.

▸ Planned, oversaw, and participated in executing all marketing campaigns and activities, including multi-city marketing tours, direct-mail and telemarketing campaigns, and participation at trade shows and user conferences.

Management Consultant, The ValuBrand Group, Inc., Fresno, CA ▶ Jan. 2003 to Jan. 2005

▸ Collaborated with various information-technology clients as a consultant to assist them in planning strategies to penetrate new and existing markets via market segmentation/product positioning, competitive analysis, product development/management, and channel strategy.

▸ Conducted both primary and secondary industry and market research and prepared comprehensive analyses for Fortune 1000 clients.

▸ Wrote and presented to client management teams marketing studies that reflected market-research findings related to product market positioning, competitive situation, pricing policies, distribution strategies, and ways to increase customer loyalty and market penetration.

Marketing Director, TechProgress Group, Fresno, CA ▶ Oct. 2001 to Jan. 2003

▸ Created and implemented strategic marketing plans.

▸ Developed all sales presentations and responded to proposals.

▸ Identified industry trends and practices through extensive research and analysis.

▸ Played instrumental role in starting successful new consulting division.

▸ Conducted primary and secondary research to identify offerings and relevancy in local market.

▸ Wrote proposals in response to RFPs.

▸ Increased average sale from $25K to $400K.

Director of Marketing, Brenton-Moore Krafts ▶ **Roscoe, MN** ▶ Feb. 1999 to Oct. 2001
Marketing Manager, Brenton-Moore Krafts ▶ **Roscoe, MN** ▶ Oct. 1997 to Feb. 1999

▸ Revitalized and modernized brand image of $120 million international manufacturer and distributor of floral and craft products servicing retail florists and home crafters through two-step distribution and major craft retailers such as Michaels, Jo-Ann, and Hobby Lobby.

▸ Created new brand position, ad campaign, Website and award-winning collateral material.

▸ Developed and implemented all marketing strategies and programs designed to increase sales, market share and brand equity, including advertising, trade shows, sales promotions, Website, product development, packaging, sales literature, and PR.

▸ Conceived *Idea.Krafts* magazine, a loyalty-building vehicle targeted to retail florist; tested promotional offers and introduced new products through magazine. Built and maintained retail florist database.

▸ Led redesign and relaunch of company Web site to reinforce brand leadership position by featuring innovative floral designs, in-depth product information, and business-building ideas.

▸ Spearheaded two major quantitative market-research studies that analyzed brand awareness, usage, and image vs. key competitors and provided foundation for marketing plans and brand strategies.

▸ Increased market share from 69 percent to 74 percent in a flat, mature, commodity-based industry by creating brand image campaign while largest competitor showed market-share decrease despite aggressive pricing strategies.

▸ Guided and managed advertising agency and other outside partners.

▸ Developed and managed $1 million annual budget.

▸ Managed staff of four associates.

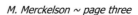

Account Director, To the Point Communications ▸ Roscoe, MN ▸ Aug. 1994 to Oct. 1997

▸ Dramatically boosted increase in agency profitability by reducing write-offs and guiding account and creative groups to collaborate more efficiently.

▸ Conceived *Building Materials Showcase* newsletter, an outreach publication that highlighted agency's specialization in building/architectural-products industry to current and prospective clients.

▸ Direct and manage largest agency accounts, including Bauer Paints and Castro Covertibles.

▸ Develop brand positioning, strategy, and marketing communications plans for clients.

▸ Oversee creative development and production of all client projects.

▸ Play key role in developing new business strategies and proposals.

Marketing Communications Manager, The Bauer Paints Company ▸ Saint Cloud, MN ▸ July 1991 to Aug. 1994

▸ Directed strategic planning, design, and launch of two Websites featuring unique interactive room-painting simulator and innovative direct-mail program designed to increase brand loyalty and sales.

▸ Successfully relaunched and repositioned Blue Signet product line as a premium paint line; reorganized this confusing line and developed new packaging and POP materials.

▸ Published *Designer's Paint Can* magazine, a twice-yearly 16-page publication featuring decorating tips and product information for consumers.

▸ Created innovative 28 ft. in-store POP merchandising program for paint department at Indoor Living, an upscale home decorating store launched by Target.

▸ Guided and challenged advertising agency to create award-winning ad campaign that garnered industry-wide attention and recognition in *Adweek* magazine.

▸ Developed and managed $2 million annual budget and supervised an associate.

Account Supervisor, Walter-Jean Advertising ▸ Saint Cloud, MN ▸ 1988 to 1991

▸ Attained unprecedented 27,000 new accounts for bank client—300 percent over projected goals—by managing creative and media planning for Free Checking promotion.

▸ Managed creative development and production of print and broadcast advertising, POP, direct mail, and sales collateral.

Account Executive, Vita & DeMatteis Advertising ▸ Saint Cloud, MN ▸ 1985 to 1988

▸ Supervised production and editing of TV and radio commercials featuring vendor's market-specific pricing.

▸ Managed planning and placement of market-specific advertising campaigns for Staples grand openings.

▸ Coordinated two-day vendor conference at which co-op funds were negotiated for client advertising programs.

Production Assistant/Junior Account Executive, Douglas James Advertising ▸ Elrosa, MN ▸ 1982 to 1985

▸ Managed creative development and production of projects, purchased printing and fulfillment, inspected jobs on press, generated print estimates and production schedules, managed traffic system.

EDUCATION

Master of Business Administration, marketing concentration, Arizona State University, Tempe, AZ
Bachelor of Science in Marketing with a minor in French, Saint Cloud State University, Saint Cloud, MN

CLAIRE HENKELTON

1632 Hunt Road Addison, MI 49220 • 517-555-6904 • E-mail: jobseeker@aol.com

Senior Organization and Project-Management Executive

Multi-talented Senior Executive who brings best business practices, clean operational strategy, and revenue-generating ideas to executing operations both locally and internationally. Highly successful in taking organizations to the next level. Excel at partnering and relationship building.

KEY COMPETENCIES

• Strategic/Operational Planning	• Partnerships and Joint Ventures	• Revenue and Profit Growth
• Project Management	• Business Development	• Research Development
• Professional Development	• Training Programs	• Marketing

PROFESSIONAL EXPERIENCE

Independent Project Management, Deerfield, MI, June 2005 to Present
- Executed international strategic-planning and business-development projects in the Northeastern United States and the Middle East, providing project management and research development on Outloud Film Festival; professional training programs for Middle Eastern women through SpecifiedSkills; and community outreach for One At a Time International, Inc.

Executive Director, *Central Michigan Film Festival,* Mount Pleasant, MI, Oct. 2003 to March 2005
- Recruited on two-year contract to revitalize and repositioning Michigan's only film festival celebrating excellence of culturally diverse talent in film/video.
- Propelled struggling, unprofitable two-year-old festival—lacking budget, official records, and means to track data—to first-time revenue generation.
- Increased revenue through aggressive client development; orchestrated television and print media campaigns and developed and actively communicated with client database.
- Overcame powerful management resistance to moving festival to downtown location and secured high-profile speakers and celebrities to increase awareness, buzz, and attendance.
- Garnered highly positive feedback from audiences, sponsors, and government agencies for festival relocation.
- Boosted audiences, press coverage, and awareness of the festival.
- Improved Board by introducing Board retreats and identifying high-profile TV industry directors for membership.
- Led planning and execution of 5-day festival under tight budget constraints.
- Introduced new programs that strategically built media-industry partnerships.
- Created first Board-approved budget, first audited financial statements, and first Annual General Meeting, thus resolving long-term budgetary issues; built complete business infrastructure, including all financial and accounting policies, operational processes, and Board policies.
- Introduced professional development to previously under-trained staff and junior board members by enlisting key speakers for meetings and organizing breakfast seminars with experts.
- Deployed techniques to partner-share within entertainment industry to build educational and training programs, thereby reducing operating and staffing costs.

Vice President, *American Women in Communications,* Deerfield, MI, Jan. 2001 to 2003
- Reporting to President, managed operations of organization dedicated to supporting advancement, professional development, and involvement of women in television, radio, film, print, and new media, including all aspects of marketing/branding, communications, strategic planning, fundraising, and revenue-driven projects.
- Dramatically improved overall quality of programs and training offered and translated improvements into increased revenue and membership.
- Promoted relationship building and training/development of 300+ active volunteers in 12 chapters nationwide.
- Introduced numerous new programs and benefits, including Mentorship Program and program to help executive women get on more boards.
- Promoted to Acting President for three months when President took time off for surgery, resolving critical budgetary issues in her absence.
- Created one of organization's most successful quarterly events entitled "Power Hour" that increased membership and awareness; organized conferences and events with high-profile experts.

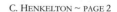

Director, Business Development and Revenue Generation, *United States Broadcasters' Association (USBA),* Hudson, MI, June 1996 to 2000

- Recruited by Secretary-General to spearhead all business facets of union of broadcasting organizations throughout United States committed to advancing broadcasters' interests at home and internationally.
- Oversaw revenue generation, marketing, communications, finance, administration, and HR, as well as staff recruitment, retention, and development.
- Raised membership from 12 member corporations to 35, bringing in almost $1 million in revenue from membership alone and provided the first surplus for next budget year.
- Increased awareness of organization internationally by raising the bar on worldwide conferences.
- Deployed diplomacy and excellent relationship skills in global role with broadcasters worldwide, including the US, South Africa, Australia, Mexico, and the European Broadcast Union.
- Created, developed, and implemented successful broadcasting conferences to reach targeted objectives and increased surplus from negative.
- Rejuvenated conference programs, introduced revenue-generating initiatives, and attracted high-profile speakers and entertainers.
- Developed and led short and long-term goals on new membership, membership retention, and revenue.
- Liaised with the World Broadcasting Unions in planning and attending annual international broadcasting/satellite conferences in Australia, Europe, South Africa, Switzerland, Mexico, and the US.
- Developed well-received sponsorship proposals that resulted in increased funding and awareness and presented Strategic Fundraising Program and Board Orientation Program.

Acting Manager, Board Secretariat, *WoodTV,* Grand Rapids, MI, 1990 to 1996

- Reported directly to Chairman and CEO while overseeing Board Secretariat operations for Michigans's Educational Network.
- Designed and implemented Board of Directors meetings, committees, and events.
- Prepared all communication reports and briefing notes for Chair.
- Recruited by outgoing Director of International Affairs to work with him at United States Broadcasters' Association.

PREVIOUS PROFESSIONAL EXPERIENCE

Communication, public-relations, and corporate-relations functions at WoodTV/MichiganMusic and Michigan Broadcasters' Corporation (MBC).

EDUCATION

Advanced Certificate in Project Management, Michigan State University, East Lansing, MI, Jan. 2008

Bachelor of Arts in English Literature, Northwestern University, Easton, IL, 1971

PROFESSIONAL AFFILIATIONS

Chair, Advisory Board, Communicators in Motion

Past Chair, Advisory Board, Making Women Leaders

Member, Michigan State Hiking Club

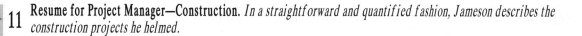

11 **Resume for Project Manager—Construction.** *In a straightforward and quantified fashion, Jameson describes the construction projects he helmed.*

RAYMOND JAMESON

19 Lake Almond Drive, WI 54909 ■ Phone: 715-555-7429 ■ Cell: 715-555-9074
Email: jobseeker@attglobal.net

Senior Project Manager – Construction

PROFESSIONAL PROFILE

- Bottom-line construction manager with more than 20 years of experience project-managing diverse, complex commercial construction projects.
- Motivational team leader skilled at leading and uniting staff, as well as collaborating fluidly among owners, architects, designers, subcontractors, and project staff with the highest level of professional ethics, respect, accountability, and personal integrity.
- Energetic, management-savvy self-starter whose core values include honesty, reliability, focus on goals, and motivation to win.

CORE COMPETENCIES

→ Delivering quality projects, on schedule, and within budget

→ Identifying critical issues and potential problems, and enacting solutions quickly and decisively

→ Assessing, organizing, and executing projects from preconstruction to close out, including:
- subcontract buyout
- budget management
- construction schedule development and maintenance
- construction ways and means
- team building and mentoring
- decisive problem solving and solution enactment

→ Managing contracts, budgets, and schedules through extensive knowledge of software applications and Internet-based management programs, including MS Word and Excel, Suretrak, Prolog, and Constructionware

→ Overseeing on-site management and construction of private and government projects such as:
- hospitals and healthcare
- office complexes
- shopping centers
- motels
- historical restorations
- education and religious facilities
- warehouses
- utilities
- garage structures

PROJECT EXPERIENCE

Senior Construction Project Manager, *Felton Construction Company*, Junction City, WI, 2005 to 2006
- ST. BARNABY'S HOSPITAL, JUNCTION CITY, WI: $16 million, 10-level structural precast parking structure with 545 parking spaces.

Senior Project Manager, *ABC Building Corporation,* Nelsonville, WI, 2000 to 2005
- UNIVERSITY OF WISCONSIN COLLEGE OF NURSING ADDITION AND RENOVATION, RICE LAKE, WI: $13 million, 98,000 SF freestanding addition to existing occupied College of Nursing and renovation of existing building.
- UNIVERSITY OF WISCONSIN NW SATELLITE PLANT, RICE LAKE, WI: $6 million utility plant tied into university infrastructure piping; Chillers warehouse producing 3,500 tons chilled water, ancillary mechanical equipment, and controls.
- RITZINGER HALL, UNIVERSITY OF WISCONSIN, RICE WATER, WI: $14 million, 110,000 SF Exceptional Student Education Facility with special equipment and design to meet specific student needs.

Senior Construction Manager, *Commercial Construction Co.,* Linwood, WI, 1998 to 2000
- FORT BROOKE GARAGE EXPANSION, LINDWOOD, WI: $11.2 million, 386,000 SF; four new pre-cast/cast-in-place levels of parking (1,200 spaces) on top of six existing levels, four new elevators, and modification and extension of four existing elevators.

Construction Project Manager, *CRA, Inc.,* Junction City, WI, 1992 to 1998
- PORTAGE REGIONAL MEDICAL CENTER, CARSON, WI: $21 million project, including:
  - o 40,000 SF 4th- and 5th-floor addition to South Wing building, including interior fit-out of labor and delivery department, exterior elevator tower, and vehicle canopy entrance.
  - o 30,000 SF radiation oncology addition, fit-out, and installation of linear accelerator and its containment structure.
  - o 11,000 SF renovation to create an emergency shock-trauma center.
  - o 3rd- and 4th-floor bridge structure connecting two hospital wings.
  - o 73,700 SF precast parking garage (540 spaces) and permanent shoring of adjacent structures.
- PORTAGE COUNTY ADVENTIST HOSPITAL, CARSON, WI: $8 million project, including:
  - o 78,000 SF three-story wing connecting to main hospital.
  - o Interior fit-out of wing for new Labor and Delivery, Emergency, Education, Physical Therapy, Same Day Surgery, and Data Processing Departments.

PREVIOUS PROJECT EXPERIENCE

Project Manager, *Chancellor Construction Company, Inc.*, Arlington, VA
- CYPRUS CHANCERY, WASHINGTON, DC: Historical and structural renovation of 19th-century building for use as Cyprus Embassy.
- B'NAI SHALOM SYNAGOGUE, BETHESDA, MD: 16,000 SF addition and renovation of existing space to double facility size.
- COLLEGE PARK SHOPPING CENTER, COLLEGE PARK, MD: New facade and arcade for a shopping center.

Construction Project Manager, *The Marcus Corporation*, Westminster, MD
- ALLEN PLAZA, RICHMOND, VA: 98,000 SF shopping center.
- AIR CARGO BUILDING, REAGAN INTERNATIONAL AIRPORT, DC: 48,000 SF customs warehouse.
- ANSELM WAREHOUSE, BETHESDA, MD: 50,000 SF warehouse.
- ARCH PLACE SHOPPING CENTER, COLLEGE PARK, MD: 30,000 SF shopping center.
- EXECUTIVE OFFICE CONDOMINIUMS, FALLS CHURCH, VA: 64 office units in four buildings.

EDUCATION and TRAINING

Associate of Arts in Architectural Construction & Technology, University of Maryland College Park, College Park, MD

Continuing Education
- o Critical Path Methods, University of Maryland College Park
- o Money and Banking, University of Maryland College Park
- o Principles of Accounting, University of Maryland College Park
- o Effective Speaking and Human, University of Maryland College Park
- o Construction Management, University of Maryland College Park
- o Human Relations in Management, University of Maryland College Park
- o Functional Spoken Spanish, University of Maryland Baltimore County
- o Dealing With Conflict, University of Maryland Baltimore County
- o Effective Communications, University of Maryland Baltimore County
- o Project Manager Workshop, University of Maryland Baltimore County
- o Construction Contracting, National Law Center, Georgetown University

- - -

KATRINA ROBBINS, PMP

52 JARED DRIVE ▪ CUPERTINO, CA, 95014
jobseeker@cox.net ▪ 408-555-7673 ▪ 408-555-8586

July 1, 2008

Jared Russell
Google Inc.
1600 Amphitheatre Parkway
Mountain View, CA 94043

Dear Mr. Russell:

Having recently earned my Project Management Professional (PMP) certification and having contributed strong interpersonal skills and cultural sensitivity during 20+ years of experience (19 of them outside the United States) in teaching/training and in management, I can make an immediate contribution to your organization on a project team involved in information systems, training, or sales.

I thrive in situations in which I can use my creativity and strong writing skills to produce positive results while working with multidiscipline/multinational project teams. Most recently I have sharpened my project-management skills while serving as a project developer/computer specialist for FEMA during the recent California wildfires. I can bring a unique set of management experience and problem-solving skills to your organization. Specifically, I can contribute the following to your bottom line:

o Experience in systems automation/conversion, having computerized personnel/training record management systems, course catalogs and schedules, registration processes and departmental correspondence;

o A solid record of establishing initial contacts and maintaining fruitful consulting and sales relationships with customers and service providers, as well as traveling to foreign destinations to meet with customers and host presentations;

o A history of designing and developing symposia and training courses to meet customer needs;

o A talent for identifying best service products within the customer's budget;

o The ability to write proposals, negotiate contracts, develop and implement marketing campaigns, as well as develop project costing models.

I am continually fascinated by such aspects of Google as Google Labs, your "technology playground." I am convinced that the creative training I will provide Google staff is an excellent fit with this innovative and risk-taking spirit.

As Manager of the Training Management Unit for the United Arab Emirates Monetary Agency, I directed the department that handled all details involved in presenting the agency's 300+ annual training courses. I can similarly develop and deliver training to your clients worldwide. As part of the agency's change management efforts, I developed a team of administrators and trained my UAE successor so that the department could operate effectively without expatriate supervision. By the end of my contract, the unit was setting the standard for efficiency and administrative excellence for the entire Institute. I would like to bring that level of managerial proficiency to Google.

I look forward to discussing how I can assist with your team's projects and will contact you soon to arrange a meeting. Thank you for your consideration.

Sincerely,

Katrina Robbins

Oscar Thorton, Ph.D.

62 East Gate Lane Adna, WA 58922 •
360/555/3961 • E-mail: jobseeker@gmail.com

Senior Manager
Transition | Business Development | Knowledge Management

Relentless innovator in thought and action.

Professional Profile

- Knowledge management professional with more than 10 years of significant experience in troubleshooting, solving problems, writing, teaching, training, research, and analysis.
- Strong leader with proven track record in business consulting, and process re-engineering, supporting strategic planning, business case development (including cost/benefit), and change implementation.

Areas of Expertise

Team Leadership	Knowledge Creation	Business Processes	Training
Case Studies	Knowledge Discovery	Change Management	Consulting
Distributed Knowledge	Knowledge Flow	Transitions	Process Improvement
Information Architecture	Knowledge Representation	Technical Writing	and Re-engineering
Information Assets	Knowledge Retrieval	Six Sigma	Customer Relationship
		ISO 9001	Management (CRM)

Professional Experience

Senior Knowledge Management Consultant – ABC Revolutions, *contract positions*, Macau, China, 2003 to present

- Negotiated pioneering Knowledge Management project valued at US$0.5M.
- Defined and designed global-transition roadmap in verticals, such as back-office payroll-account processing, technical solutions, data management, quality processes and process re-engineering, and database technology.
- Developed training methodologies and conducted training workshops on technical writing specifications for technical-documentation specialists at IT companies, as well as trained teams in quality processes, knowledge management methodologies, employee sensitivity to customer service, identifying gaps in delivery, and developing appropriate procedures to align resources and improve deliverables.
- Partnered with clients to design cross-company communication-strategy solutions.
- Implemented Six-Sigma processes and procedures and led team to implement business processes.
- Designed and deployed knowledge Communities of Practice (COP) companywide.
- Transitioned service force to sales-and-service force by identifying key factors in sales development, negotiating with clients, and implementing key workflow processes that empowered service force to contribute directly to sales.

Senior Executive – Knowledge Management, *Venture Corporation*, Spokane, WA, 2000 to July 2002

- Developed, maintained, and improved Knowledge Management (KM) Department by incorporating KM best practices at global ISO 9001-certified IT-enabled company focusing on customer-relationship management and global outsourcing needs to achieve client and operations satisfaction.
- Grew department into robust revenue-generating model while establishing cross-cultural and virtual work relationships and work procedures generating USD$5M in revenue.
- Partnered with major accounts to define and consolidate future requirements in product requirement documents.
- Traveled throughout US extensively to develop business for call center.
- Performed market segmentation, identified viable vertical segments, and created targeted messaging for business development.
- Initiated diverse analyses by assessing client needs and opportunities to determine and ramp up customer satisfaction by designing and implementing information warehouse to generate data analysis for coherent customer relationship management.
- Spearheaded global transition of KM Department's US procedures to China offices.
- Initiated technology-supported workplace E-learning solutions to support task-oriented training under time pressure; project-managed growth of KM tools in close partnership with technical department.

Executive Manager, Quality Control and Customer Care, *Integrative Healthcare*, Beijing, China, 1998 to 2000

- Oversaw infrastructure development and maintenance of 100-person portal management and software development consultancy firm, providing technical management and medical-transcription services; led personnel recruitment and training, as well as operational processes, including department-wide policies and procedures, customer support, and billing.
- Identified and managed marketing organization's key external business-partner relationships.
- Initiated quality checks to streamline transcription personnel into delivering quality production.
- Structured department-wide processes guaranteeing company's achievement of American Association of Medical Transcription industry standards in process quality control.
- Designed and systemized online functionality in troubleshooting, account activation, ordering, and bill payment with new hosting and content management.
- Recommended and evaluated business development to consolidate operations, transition assignments, and frequently improvise multi-layer contingency plans.
- Assessed joint venture opportunity between company and well-established transcription company, eventually recommending merger based on projected financial returns.

Executive – Legal and Medical Transcription, *Integral Decision Services*, Beijing, China, 1995 to 1998

- Managed high-revenue-generating teams to generate consistent quality, value-added products at technical startup medical-transcription company.
- Analyzed, structured, and organized quality processes and measures to ensure client satisfaction.
- Pioneered American Association of Medical Transcription standard training programs within department.
- Formulated technical specifications based on client requirements into key processes.
- Managed operational projects, finding solutions and improvements through cost and benefits and customer-satisfaction analysis.

Education

- *Ph.D. in English*, University of Washington, Seattle, WA, 1998
- *Master of Arts in English*, University of Washington, Seattle, WA, 1993
- *Bachelor of Arts in English*, University of Mumbai, Mumbai, India, 1991
- *Six Sigma Green Belt*, Ohio State University, Columbus, OH, 2001

Brandon Teisler

73 Apple Tree Lane,
Aladdin, WY 82710
Phone: 307/555-9074
Jobseeker@teisler.com

SENIOR MANAGEMENT EXECUTIVE

Executive Management | Reorganization & Turnaround Management | Strategic Planning

Executive Summary

- Administrative Management
- Budget Development
- Business Plan Development
- Business Strategy
- Change Management
- Communication Technology Management
- Competitive Analysis
- Corporate Reorganization
- Customer Service Management
- Decision Making
- Directing High Producing Teams
- Distribution Management
- Technology Initiatives
- Inventory Management
- Market Strategy
- Operations Management
- Strategic Vision
- Turnarounds

Enthusiastic, profit-driven senior management executive offering impeccable record of success in delivering customer-focused leadership, strategic planning, and sustainable results in operating efficiency and improved profit performance.

Take-charge business analyst with innate ability to assess situations, determine key issues, and change directions when circumstances warrant.

Specialist in developing customer loyalty and retention within highly competitive consumer-products industry.

Creative problem-solver with reputation for taking on underachieving stores, quickly turning them around, and consistently meeting and exceeding performance goals for revenue and profitability.

Performance accelerator who coaxes the best from team members.

Technologically savvy innovator who oversaw ground-floor implementation of intranet system and enhancements to retail outlet scanning system.

PROFESSIONAL EXPERIENCE

Interim Vice President Western Operations, Hometown Grocery, Inc., Alva, WY, 2006 to present
- Oversaw policies and procedures for Western region of family-owned retail grocery business with 82 stores located throughout the state of Wyoming; direct reports included meat coordinator, 4 supervisors, 40 retail units, and 2,000 employees.
- Generated immediate performance improvement and return to profitability in underachieving store by deploying turnaround strategies to lead 5-member team to identify problems and develop solutions, including pricing recommendations.
- Developed plan to install internal communication system linking all 82 stores.
- Composed and implemented corporate guidelines and procedures for new store openings.

District Supervisor, Hometown Grocery, Inc., Alva, WY, 1994 to 2006
- Played key role on 16-person executive management team that provided proactive and market-driven operating leadership in competitive business market; took charge of profitability and growth of up to 10 retail units and 500 employees in 3 Wyoming markets.
- Conducted area competitor feasibility studies to determine competitive market position for long-term revenue and profit growth.
- Opened 8 new stores from ground up; designed store layouts for shelving, ordered and arranged inventory, and managed human-resource needs.
- Deployed technology-department expertise to develop advertising markdown report that enabled scanning stores to gross out weekly advertisements and keep running total of profit.

Manager, *Hometown Grocery, Inc.*, Aladdin, WY, 1990 to 1994
- Aggressively led 50 employees in refocusing business that had been in the red for 8 years.
- Introduced customer-driven management philosophy and reinstated corporate policy to regain competitive lead after analyzing business, area clientele, and competition.
- Transformed business into profitable winner within first quarter.
- Revamped entire scanning system upon arrival; corrected numerous errors and retrained staff.

Assistant Manager, *Hometown Grocery, Inc.*, Sundance, WY, 1987 to 1990
- Selected to evaluate new competition in town and develop strategic plan to remain competitive.
- Provided leadership and support to manager for total store operation, inventory, advertising, sales, and all internal human-resource functions.

EDUCATION
Bachelor of Arts, Business Administration, Colorado College, Colorado Springs, CO, 1990

COMMUNITY INVOLVEMENT
- Wyoming Grocery Industry Association Golf Scholarship Committee
- Former Vice President, Aladdin Chamber of Commerce
- Community Betterment Committee, Aladdin, WY
- Aladdin Schools Foundation Board
- Church Pastoral Council and Finance Council
- Habitat for Humanity
- MDA Telethon Corporate Representative

ERIC JOHANSEN, MBA, PMP

1591 Kentucky Ave. ♦ Atlanta, GA 30302 ♦ 440/555-8941 ♦ Cell: 440/555-0852 ♦ jobseeker@attglobal.net

SENIOR BUSINESS SYSTEMS OPERATIONS EXECUTIVE

Competitive Strategies, Program/Project Management Disciplines, Client Satisfaction Assurance

- Technically sophisticated business leader with consistent history of business process enhancement success and outstanding record of delivering high return-on-investment results.
- Strategic visionary who has managed numerous strategic initiatives of up to $10MM and implemented project-management innovations to accelerate performance.
- Motivated achiever with sector exposure in developing systems for OEM, government, retail, utilities, financial services, education and sales/marketing.
- Operational problem-solver whose professional milestones include major project rehabilitation achievements.
- Effective communicator skilled at developing personal and strategic relationships with global executives.
- Frequent guest speaker at Outsourcing, Call Center Management, and HR Development conferences.

KEY AREAS OF EXPERTISE

Engagement Management Leadership

- Case Modeling
- Contract Negotiations
- Strategic Planning
- CMM-Based Business Analytics
- Client Liaison and Relationship Management
- Purchasing and Multi-Vendor Coordination
- RFQ/RFP Response Strategies
- Upselling and Business Development

IT Technology Infrastructure and Architecture

- COC [cost-of-computing] Reduction Strategies and Shared Services Computing
- Infrastructure Consolidation
- Internetworking and Knowledge Management
- CRM, ERP, eCom Deployment
- Data Mining/Warehousing
- B2E/B2B/B2C Portals
- Hardware/Software Outsourcing

CAREER HISTORY

Technology Account Manager, DELTA AIRLINES, Atlanta, GA, 2002 to present

- **SCOPE:** Serve as technical liaison among IT, Delta business units, and outsourced hosting providers. Provide strategic, tactical, and operational leadership of technology infrastructure services.
- **MAJOR ACHIEVEMENT:** Deliver major corporate IT cost-reduction outcome as senior team member.
- **BUSINESS LEADERSHIP:** Negotiated favorable hardware and software purchases and licensing agreements. Developed cost and service review framework to provide hard numbers for executive decision-making.
- **TECHNICAL LEADERSHIP:** Delivered $10MM+ in reduced annual IT expenses by spearheading implementation of infrastructure solution, a performance-optimized shared-services environment.

Senior Project Manager, DELL INC., Round Rock, TX, 2000 to 2002

- **SCOPE:** Directed delivery of technology consulting engagements emphasizing cost management and aggressive business metrics. Led IT infrastructure, CRM, and e-services technology management consulting initiatives on behalf of Fortune 1000 verticals. Controlled business needs analysis, customized solution development, and delivery management. Played leading role in generating proposals and program schedules articulating benchmarks/milestones, resources, and deliverables.
- **MAJOR ACHIEVEMENTS:** Generated 400-percent increase in engagement revenues, valued at estimated $6MM, by personally intervening to rehabilitate CRM project. Significantly improved client satisfaction for all projects. Crafted 100+ page business case that became the model/template for B2E projects in e-business practice.
- **BUSINESS LEADERSHIP:** Established sustainable long-term executive/client-partner relationships by responding to client needs.
- **TECHNICAL LEADERSHIP:** Identified several incremental project execution opportunities to improve enterprise performance.
- **INTELLECTUAL PROPERTY DEVELOPMENT:** Created significant portion of DELL's Portal Methodology project management approach.

Principal Consultant, BAUER CORPORATION, Austin, TX, 1999 to 2000
- **SCOPE**: Oversaw CRM, ERP, consulting, strategy development and systems integration contractor.
- **PROJECT HIGHLIGHTS**: Developed B2B CRM strategy and technology implementation for international startup CLEC [competitive local exchange carrier].
- **BOTTOM-LINE RESULTS**: Exponentially boosted client ROI by developing and implementing accelerated program schedule that produced a 25-percent speed-up while reducing COC by 15 percent.

Program Manager, EXPEDITION CONSULTANTS, INC., Fort Worth, TX, 1998 to 1999
- **SCOPE**: Functioned as solution-selling and delivery management resource in business startup context; generated requirements analysis and RFQ responses. Managed all facets of internet application development projects utilizing CMM software development processes.
- **BOTTOM-LINE RESULTS**: Increased total practice revenue by more than $4MM and profits by $1.25MM+ by building 15-person application development and design team from scratch.

Project Director, ALC ASSOCIATES, INC., Houston, TX, 1997 to 1998
- **SCOPE**: Provided strategic program leadership for corporate cost reduction initiatives resulting from merger between First Data Corporation and Western Union. Eliminated redundant systems, operations, and staff.
- **TECHNICAL AND BUSINESS LEADERSHIP**: Implemented transaction-cost model vital for increasing performance and guiding IT system consolidation. Re-designed customer contact strategy and implemented CTI [computer-telephony integration] call-center processes to streamline routing and prioritization. Instilled commitment and passion to customer service by redesigning customer contact system and procedures.
- **BOTTOM-LINE RESULTS**: Produced 15-percent cost savings. Re-engineered IT and business functions to improve customer service and reduce operational cost profile.

Acting Director/Program Manager, COMCAST TELEVIOSON, Forth Worth, TX, 1995 to 1997
- **SCOPE**: Oversaw P&L for SBU with sales of $150MM and $38MM expense budget.
- **MAJOR PROJECT**: Selected by VP to transition Comcast's Direct Marketing department into best-in-class, high-performance marketing/sales operation by designing and employing disciplined CRM approach. Provided business analytics. Built and led 26-manager team, establishing revenue, expense, quality-of-service, and net-income objectives, and liaising and coordinating multiple departments.
- **BOTTOM-LINE RESULTS**: Implemented best-in-class operational processes to achieve 400 percent incremental improvement in sales revenue with 18-percent reduction in departmental expense, valued in the tens of millions of dollars.

Senior Project Manager, COMCAST TELEPHONE OPERATIONS, Fort Worth, TX, 1993 to 1995
- **SCOPE**: Developed strategic alliance marketing plans between Comcast and partners/suppliers to pursue major voice and data service-integration business opportunities. Created and negotiated license agreements, joint ventures, alliances, and partnerships. Guided projects/programs from financial feasibility study through to market launch.
- **BOTTOM-LINE RESULTS**: Developed $20MM+ annual revenue stream.

EDUCATION

MBA in Production and Operations Management, University of Texas, Austin, TX
Bachelor of Science in Business Administration (Management), University of Georgia, Athens, GA

CREDENTIAL
Project Management Professional (PMP)

PROFESSIONAL AFFILIATION
Member, Project Management Institute, Atlanta Chapter

DIETER HUSSMAN

Rhinestrasse 60a35510 • Hamburg, Germany • Phone: +00 0000-00 00 00
E-mail: jobseeker@gmx.de

CHIEF OPERATING OFFICER

PROFESSIONAL PROFILE

- Accomplished engineering professional with more than 20 years of experience in leadership roles in plant management and process/product improvement.

- Enthusiastic performer with entrepreneurial spirit, inclusive and motivational leadership style, and solid background of performance and optimization in business and operations development.

- Confident, face-of-the-brand, C-Level and B2B liaison with passion for excellence and reputation for creating positive, highly-energized work environments that rise to levels of exceptional productivity while fully maintaining quality-assurance standards and meeting client demand and profitability goals.

AREAS OF EXPERTISE

MBA:
- Create/Execute Market Operating Plans
- Assess Growth Opportunities
- Key Account Plans
- Sales Process and Strategies
- Sales Pipeline Methodology
- Market Segmentation
- Market Share Growth
- Master Service Agreements
- Optimize Office Utilization
- Financial Management and Control
- Key Financial Metrics

Experience:
- Manage Utilization
- Client Satisfaction
- Team-building
- Organizational Strategic Plans
- Identify/Allocate Resources
- Multicultural Team and Customer Experience

- Coaching and Leadership
- Train and Develop Personnel
- State-of the-Art Manufacturing/Management Methods
- Organization/Process Management
- Develop/Implement Process Control
- Validate New Processes
- Provide New Equipment Specifications
- Cost Reduction Initiatives
- Automation Systems
- Process/Product Optimization
- Meeting Parameters
- Problem-Solving
- Identify Resources
- Leading and Coordinating multicultural construction, project, and operation teams

- Oversee Maintenance, Repairs, and Equipment Modifications
- Manufacturing Processes
- Scheduling and Budgetary Parameters
- Monitor/Debug New Methods and Procedures
- Design Concept Drawings
- Cost Estimates
- Recommend Changes to Process Documentation
- Interface with Manufacturing, Maintenance, and Quality Departments
- Resolve Engineering Issues
- Interface with Vendors and Outside Sales Personnel
- Evaluate, Estimate, and Select Purchases
- DMAIC

PROFESSIONAL EXPERIENCE

Senior Process Engineer, *GDX International,* Hamburg, Germany, Feb. 2006 to present

- Determine and specify process plant equipment and documentation for large-scale projects.

- Coordinate interdisciplinary engineering functions and provide sales support.

- Optimize equipment design and processes.

- Assess and analyze performance of existing processes and technologies, write improvement proposals, and collaborate with team-members to solve problems and implement upgrades.

- Motivate team partners by sharing knowledge of project scope and parameters, understanding of technical needs and execution, and providing team support to develop quality engineering processes and deliver projects on time.

- Assume "ownership" of large project parts, thus reducing demand on human resources.

- Submitted patent to optimize gas distribution of a Sparger.

- Participated in development process of Latex, PVC, PET, and HDPE resin technology.

The following positions held at Wolfson LTD reflect several occasions when positions and projects overlapped in scope and time.

Project Engineer, *Wolfson LTD,* Frankfurt, Germany, March 2003 to Jan. 2006

- Organized technical project team for large-scale process plants.
- Coordinated client and contractor engineering, developed schedule, and allocated resources.
- Wrote improvement proposals that saved on equipment costs and enhanced performance quality.
- Set high standard of accomplishment to deliver projects on time and within QA standards.
- Strove to ensure all management tools were used fully and effectively, including communication and goal-setting with clients and incorporating team members in integrating client contributions.
- Oversaw project scope and delivery of engineering package.
- Generated FEEP for PET bottle resin plant in Spain and for revamp of US PET bottle resin plant.
- Engineered successful startups of new plants, including successful commissioning of plant in Pakistan, producing highly satisfied customers.
- Maintained steady progression of increased responsibility from process engineer to project engineer.

Commissioning Manager, *Wolfson LTD,* Frankfurt, Germany, Nov. 2000 to Jan. 2003

- Developed and implemented organizational structure and schedule for pre-commissioning and commissioning of large-scale process plants.
- Coordinated and managed pre-commissioning, commissioning, and guarantee run.
- Analyzed and optimized plant operation, built and trained commissioning and operations teams, consistently communicated "best practice" policies, and supervised/managed site personnel.
- Orchestrated pre-commission, commission, and hand-over of large-scale process plants in Spain, Pakistan, South Korea, and Mexico.

Lead Process Engineer, *Wolfson LTD,* Frankfurt, Germany, Oct. 2000 to Feb. 2003

- Developed specification and optimization of process plant equipment and documentation for large-scale process plants.
- Provided consultation support on plant operation.
- Coordinated process team, interdisciplinary engineering functions, and quality-assurance control on specified equipment and documentation.
- Trained and developed junior engineers and operations personnel.
- Generated FEEP for revamp of process plant in USA, as well as FEEP for PET resin plants in Spain, Argentina, South Korea, Italy, and Russia.

Commissioning Engineer, *Wolfson LTD,* Frankfurt, Germany, July 1999 to Nov. 2000

- Assisted commissioning manager to lead and instruct commissioning teams.
- Supported plant operation and optimization of DCS system and process calculations; and analyzed operation data and optimization of operation.
- Orchestrated re-commissioning and commissioning of PET resin plants in Italy, South Korea, and Taiwan.

EDUCATION

- Executive Master of Business Administration, Stetson University, Celebration, FL, 2005

DIETER HUSSMAN

Rhinestrasse 60a35510 • Hamburg, Germany • Phone: +00 0000-00 00 00 • E-mail: jobseeker@gmx.de

April 25, 2008

Drusilla Portman
Yaskawa Engineering Europe GmbH
European Headquarters
Am Kronberger Hang 2
65824 Schwalbach Germany

Dear Ms. Portman:

A true leader brings about positive change in alignment with overall business objectives without negative organizational disruption. In my career, I have demonstrated this skill time and again using careful analysis, project management, and team management abilities. This experience offers you a well-rounded range of qualifications that more than meet your needs for a **Chief Operating Officer**.

Some of the attributes I offer include:

* **Organizational Change**: Initiated new ideas, proposed improvements, and implemented operational changes that resulted in enthusiastic acceptance and positive results.

* **Human Relations**: Built positive, motivational relationships with team members and customers to ensure confidence during difficult start-ups and process changes.

* **Communication**: Strong listening and speaking skills and excellent negotiation abilities.

* **Problem Solving**: Track record of finding solutions to troublesome situations through careful research, analysis, and planning.

* **Training**: Excellent reputation for delivering both formal and informal training, as well as mentoring operational personnel, junior engineers, technical support, and customers. Experience bolstered by a bachelor's degree in mechanical engineering, an executive MBA, and recent entrance into a doctoral program studying performance management in the engineering industry

Accustomed to a fast-paced environment in which deadlines are a priority and multitasking is the norm, I enjoy a challenge and work hard to attain organizational goals. Assuming that you seek a well-qualified and productive individual who views problems as growth opportunities, I am the right person to lead your team.

I look forward to speaking with you soon to discuss the ways in which my expertise can bring immediate results to your company. I will contact you soon to set up a personal interview, or you may contact me at the numbers above. Thank you for your consideration.

Sincerely,

Dieter Hussman

ALLEN EISENSTEIN

81 Center Street, Hartland, MN 56042 ♦ Cell: 507/555-9045 ♦ Home: 507/555-4802 ♦ jobseeker@gmail.com

VICE PRESIDENT, ENGINEERING

Software executive with 10+ years of experience leading diverse engineering teams from initial ideation through deployment and ongoing operations.

Hands-on, collaborative manager who fosters effective, highly loyal teams. Accomplished cross-functional analyst, problem-solver, and communicator.

CORE COMPETENCIES

- Software Development Processes
- Problem Analysis and Definition
- Budget Planning and Administration
- Talent Acquisition, Retention and Development
- Project Planning, Scheduling and Management
- Problem Solving and Change Management
- Software Patent Creation, Prosecution, Negotiation and Litigation
- Internet-based eCommerce Software
- Development and Deployment

PROFESSIONAL EXPERIENCE

General Manager, Configuration Solutions, Epitome Advancements, Hartland, MN, 2005 to Present

- **SCOPE:** Promoted to increase revenue and profitability of flagship software product line. Hold Profit and Loss responsibility for $8 million business unit. Define product direction, technical architecture, and development processes for 50-person software development and delivery organization. Develop and execute sales and marketing plans.
- **PRODUCT REVITALIZATION:** Generated new sales by defining new-product features based on perceived customer requirements to revitalize languishing product line. Assembled team to develop highly interactive web services-based product. Contributed key ideas yielding filed patent. Reviewed architecture and designs for long-term scalability and maintainability.
- **PROCESS CHANGE:** Gained buy-in for business unit's unique technology attributes in light of corporate direction to migrate development to outsourced services model. Reduced development costs by 70 percent while generating continued successful product deliveries within large, complex and volatile codebase. Created compromise solution allowing business-unit-specific contracts with vendors.
- **CUSTOMER MANAGEMENT:** Achieved 100 percent customer success through on-time, under-budget product and deployment deliveries to customer specifications, thus transforming previously negative customer relationships. Negotiated multiple multi-million dollar add-on contracts based upon successful deliveries and positive relationships.

CTO, EcommerceIT™, Epitome Advancements, Hartland, MN, 2006 to Present

- **SCOPE:** Created eCommerceIT™ program to manage creation, maintenance, and licensing of corporate intellectual property. Defined process for identifying and categorizing valuable IP. Constructed licensing program for patent portfolio.
- **PATENT PROCESS DEFINITION:** Categorized current patent portfolio, identified synergistic groupings of patents, and suggested areas of innovation to further strengthen grouping. Defined corporate process for tracking intellectual property through entire patent lifecycle from initial invention through product marking and eventual expiration. Analyze all corporate invention disclosures for originality and potential value to determine which should be filed for patent protection.
- **IT LICENSE NEGOTIATION:** Discovered potential license opportunity and negotiated multi-million dollar license agreement for key patents in corporate patent portfolio (see http://ITLicense/Ecommerce.html).
- **TECHNICAL LEADERSHIP:** Identified several incremental project execution opportunities to improve enterprise performance, along with subset of corporate patents that would increase value to open-source community. Facilitated multi-million dollar sale to appropriate intellectual property management company.

Senior Manager, Delivery, Epitome Advancements, Hartland, MN, 2002 to 2004
- **Scope:** Promoted to lead company's single largest engineering team. Oversaw all related product development and deployment efforts. Delivered monthly releases of product configuration knowledge base and application with 30-person consulting engineering team. Delivered quarterly or semi-annual releases of underlying software product with 10-person development team.
- **Process Change:** Increased quality three-fold in one year by restructuring team organization and development processes to reflect unique aspects of monthly release schedule and requirement volatility. Reduced lead time 40 percent by instituting further process changes over the next six months.
- **Team Development:** Organized transition of core team composition from highly experienced PhDs to fresh college graduates to provide more appropriate opportunities for experienced team members, resulting in team's continued highly successful deployment while simultaneously producing new products and product ideas with company's lowest attrition rate.

Development Manager, Epitome Advancements, Hartland, MN, 1998 to 2002
- **Scope:** Led multiple small-to-moderate-sized developer teams in creating, maintaining, and delivering wide variety of products. Improved quality, efficiency, and predictability of each team.
- **Product Transformation:** Identified significant technical gaps in Epitome's premier configuration product. Sponsored project to prototype updated capabilities. Defined and delivered scalable, multi-tier version as manager of small, incredibly talented group of engineers.
- **Crisis Management:** Managed transition and maintenance of majority of Epitome's existing products from original large development team to less experienced smaller one. Personally triaged issues with 30 customers for 50 products, enabling team to deliver hundreds of software releases in a single year.

Consultant, Customer Solutions Manager, Epitome Advancements, Hartland, MN, 1994 to 1998
- **Scope:** Led technical sale and implementation of account producing $30 million in revenue. Directed redefinition of consulting organization into a matrix structure. Developed consulting project methodology and software application to manage Epitome's consulting projects that eventually became the corporate standard for all engineering projects.

PREVIOUS PROFESSIONAL EXPERIENCE
Senior Associate Programmer, Microsoft Corporation, Hartland, MN, 1992 to 1994
Communications and Computer Systems Officer (Captain), US MILITARY, 1990 to 1992

EDUCATION
Bachelor of Science in Computer Science, Princeton University, Princeton, NJ
Additional 49 units of course work in Cognitive Psychology
30 units of course work toward MS in Computer Science
Instructor, TA, and section lead in undergraduate Computer Science department

ALLEN EISENSTEIN

81 Center Street, Hartland, MN 56042 ♦ Cell: 507/555-9045 ♦ Home: 507/555-4802 ♦ jobseeker@gmail.com

March 4, 2008

Thomas Denver
RW Beck
1380 Corporate Center Curve, Suite 305
St. Paul, MN 55121-1200

Dear Mr. Denver:

My leadership skills and proven track record in project management/engineering would enable me to enhance RW Beck's success in an Engineer VP position. I offer proficiency gained during almost 15 years of project-engineering experience, along a strong record of collaborative performance and leadership.

My success in bringing in 100 percent of projects on time and under budget adds to the value I can bring to your organization. I am eager to deploy my analytical, problem solving, and process-improvement skills to improve your organization's profitability.

Throughout my career, I have contributed my technical ability to developing and managing multiple multimillion-dollar projects. My diverse capabilities have enabled me to successfully meet goals, targets, and deadlines. My experience has reinforced a combination of skills that gives me a solid foundation upon which to make an immediate and meaningful contribution at RW Beck. I am also skilled at troubleshooting problems and conceptualizing innovative solutions.

My successful executive-management and project-engineering skills lend themselves well to effectively adding value and contributing to company objectives and goals. If upon reviewing my qualifications you agree that I would enhance the plans and goals of your organization, I would be pleased to meet with you to further discuss my background. I will contact you soon by phone to arrange a meeting. Should you have any questions before that time, you may reach me using the contact information above. Thank you for your time and consideration.

Cordially,

Allen Eisenstein

GARY ROBERTS

518 Palmetto Court ▪ Afton, OK 74331

jobseeker@aol.com ▪ **918-555-5220** ▪ CELL: **918-555-4566**

SENIOR TECHNICAL EXECUTIVE

Strategic Market Forecasting, Research, Planning, and Coordination
Operations |Quality Improvements | HR | Design and Development
Operations Cost Control | Project Initiation, Design, and Development | Safety

SUMMARY

Senior technical management executive with more than 15 years in automotive and power industry technology positioned to deliver innovative technology and human-centered approaches with staff, manufacturers, A/E firms, EPC contractors, and owners.

CORE COMPETENCIES

- → Global Experience
- → Superior Communication Skills
- → Proven Leader
- → Innovative Thinker
- → Multi-Disciplined Understanding
- → Solution Oriented

- → Work Patterns
- → Project Management
- → Cross-Cultural Sensitivity
- → Broad Knowledge Base
- → Equipped to Perform Across All Levels
- → Collaborative

PROFESSIONAL EXPERIENCE

SENIOR VICE PRESIDENT TECHNOLOGY AND OPERATIONS, Toyota Electric Automotive America, Inc., Afton, OK, 2005 to Present

- Constructed new $25 million facilities that established R&D capability and improved operational activities with construction on time and $1 million under budget.
- Saved company $2 million by negotiating favorable lease contracts.
- Led team in $15 million sale of new products.
- Conceived and launched quality management system conforming to ISO 9000 and TS 16949 allowing continuing customer supply and satisfaction.
- Designed research program to provide competitive intelligence for strategic planning/marketing.
- Identify and propose specific advanced technology partnerships.
- Implemented operational metrics and communications.
- Play key role in operational and advanced planning as board member.
- Founded, organized, and chaired industry automotive supplier council to cooperatively share information on common interest as subsidiaries of foreign parent companies.
- Taught staff quality principles, communication patterns and cultural differences.
- Initiated and completed new compensation and performance planning.
- Optimized production control, logistics, quality, warranty, and information systems.
- Initiated $300K in cost savings in transportation, equipment, parts, and services.

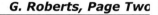

VICE PRESIDENT – ENGINEERING, Engineering Alliances, Inc., Afton OK, 2003 to 2004
- Provided technical direction, oversight, and support for global independent power producer with 20 power plants in operation or construction on six continents.
- Coordinated closely with departments to ensure safe, cost-effective work performance.
- Interfaced with and directed Owner's Engineer and EPC contractor during development, engineering, execution and commissioning of 10,000+ MW of electrical generation.

ORGANIZATION
- Restructured and managed Engineering Department to support company's changing focus from development to operations, interfacing with all departments.
- Realigned Engineering Department to support operating plants, including developing management tools to monitor global work spread.
- Formalized global approach in dealing with insurance industry, OEMs, and consultants.
- Held technical authority for all facilities, establishing and enforcing design standards.
- Coordinated technical information globally, providing centralized data to plants, reducing overall project costs while increasing security.

DEVELOPMENT
- Provided early development engineering services to diverse international power plants, including environmental impact assessments, make-up and cooling water sourcing, site surveys, and remediation.
- Established plant design.
- Played key role in obtaining more than $1.4B in international funding.
- Directed technical aspects of three gas-fired power plants totaling 3700+ MW in Turkey.

OPERATIONS
- Supported company's operating fleet, providing technical solutions, performance optimization, root cause analyses, and engineering services.
- Negotiated $5M precedent-setting claim with Latin American governmental utility.

EPC CONTRACTING
- Played instrumental role in EPC contracting for diverse international power plants, utilizing coal, oil and gas fuels.
- Evaluated all aspects of EPC bids, including subcontractors.
- Established performance guarantees/liquidated damages/bonuses during contracting and subsequently proved actual level of bonus.
- Negotiated major equipment purchases directly with manufacturers through master POs and multi-project approach to procurement, as well as individual component purchases.
- Maintained technical management from conceptual design through commissioning and acceptance testing on more than 10 power-plant projects.

DIRECTOR – ENGINEERING, Engineering Alliances, Inc., Afton, OK, 1998 to 2003
- Resolved technical EPC issues with contractor, independent engineer, and coal supplier enabling closing of +$500M construction contract in China.
- Project managed standalone natural-gas pipeline compression station in Mexico, from conceptual design, engineering, EPC selection and startup.
- Negotiated with Chinese authorities on plant design and approval, as well as offtake and supply agreements.

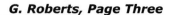

ENGINEERING DIRECTOR, AJ Control and Parts, Cardin, OK, 1996 to 1998
- Designed and developed automotive sensors and actuators worth $90 million in sales.
- Directly supervised 20 engineers and 17 technicians.
- Implemented plant resident product engineers for quality improvement and coordination.
- Spearheaded new-product programs worth $10 million, as well as cost-reduction program saving $3 million.
- Improved customer satisfaction through focus on quality, manufacturing coordination, and customer relationship management.

MANAGER, AJ Control and Parts, Cardin, OK, 1990 to 1996
- Attained contract award worth more than $10 million in direct sales through supervising activities of four engineers and one CAD operator.
- Oversaw new-products design and development, including electric parking brake, aluminum calipers, and zinc aluminum anchor plates.
- Designed reduced drag brakes with reduced operational noise.
- Developed innovative approaches to component manufacturing, saving cost and weight.

PROJECT MANAGER, Alaster Engineering Company, Peoria, OK, 1985 to 1990
- Managed multi-disciplined engineering team, providing innovative and cost-effective solutions to utility and industrial clients.
- Developed and utilized emissions compliance computational model that saved Southeast US utility more than $80M in Clear Air Act compliance costs, then oversaw program implementation.
- Coordinated cost, scheduling, and proposal development for 2400MW power and desalination plant.

EDUCATION

Master of Science in Administration
University of Oklahoma, Norman, OK

Bachelor of Science Mechanical Engineering
Massachusetts Institute of Technology, Cambridge, MA

Numerous continuing education courses in
ISO-9000, QS-9000, Quality, Taguchi, Reliability, Business, Statistics

Foundations of Leadership Program, Center for Creative Leadership, Houston, TX

CERTIFICATIONS

Certified Reliability Engineer
Certified Quality Engineer
Certified Quality Auditor
Professional Engineer, State of Oklahoma
Registered Mechanical Engineer, State of Massachusetts

PROFESSIONAL AFFILIATION

American Society of Mechanical Engineers

...

BRUCE PHILLIPS

19 CHATTERTON WAY ▪ CHENEY WA 99001
jobseeker@execnet.com ▪ 509-555-8689

EXECUTIVE-LEVEL TECHNICAL DIRECTION AND MANAGEMENT | CIO

Enterprise Computing | Information Technology | Network Operations
SOFTWARE DEVELOPMENT
EXECUTIVE MANAGEMENT | ORGANIZATION BUILDING | SYSTEMS IMPLEMENTATION

QUALIFICATIONS SUMMARY

- Technical guru qualified by 15+ years of successful experience and expertise in system, software and infrastructure design, support, and management, having progressed through the ranks from programmer to project manager to technical VP and COO.
- Proven ability to provide IT services directly contributing to revenue generation.
- Significant global business experience spanning five continents.

CORE COMPETENCIES

- Value Creation through Implementation and Development of
  - ERP
  - CRM
  - Core Business Systems and Infrastructure
- Internet Architecture, Systems, and Support
- Process Improvement

- Recruiting
- Internal and External Customer Satisfaction
- Change Creation
- Strategic Planning
- P&L
- Project Management

PROFESSIONAL EXPERIENCE

CO-FOUNDER/CHIEF OPERATING OFFICER, NextGen Software Corporation, Cheney, WA, June 2006 to Present
- Formed software-development company of next-generation, rich, interactive marketing applications to simulate traditional reading experience digitally while providing advanced navigation techniques, personalized viewing experience and reader analytics.
- Established roles; recruited for executive, promotional/product marketing, business development, and finance staff.
- Led development of corporate strategy, promotional/product marketing, competitive analysis, and product positioning.
- Negotiated and provided managed service and Web hosting to second most frequently visited individual sports franchise on the Internet.

CHIEF TECHNOLOGY OFFICER/VICE PRESIDENT, No Net Problems, Inc., Elk, WA, January 2000 to June 2003
- Oversaw integrity and functionality of full-service Internet solutions provider.
- As member of senior management team, directed all technology-related planning and operations, software/technology selection, staffing, and participation in business strategy decisions.
- Played key role in creative problem-solving in entrepreneurial environment.
- Oversaw configuration and approval of system architecture, including network services, operating systems, data communication, and Internet technologies.
- Monitored and reviewed technology developments and new products for possible application and marketing advantage, resource allocation, and long-term strategy.
- Achieve 15 percent reduction in operating costs in close collaboration with finance and CPA firms and partnered closely with CFO to achieve 12 percent budget reduction in three consecutive years.
- Directed project-design and implementation teams consisting of six direct reports and a 17-member staff, including several on-time and under budget launches.
- Designed large, Web-based on-line software repository; earned Telecommunication Award for Excellence.
- Managed teams of programmers, analysts, and Web designers, including full project cycles and staff evaluations.

CHIEF INFORMATION OFFICER, Solen Sciences, Inc., Spokane, WA, November 1998 to January 2000
- Realigned dysfunctional global Information System department at $45M software-development company to meet corporate goals and mission of specializing in complex simulation software for chemical, oil and gas industries by establishing comprehensive strategic project portfolio based on executive sponsorship and customer satisfaction.
- Attained tangible profit improvement of 4 percent by establishing and serving as executive chairman to develop new revenue channel based on PeopleSoft CRM and Lotus Notes to provide capabilities including electronic ordering and software distribution and online training; installed base support, thus provding Sales Department lead management and suggesting up-sell opportunities and software license-renewal reminders.
- Configured robust, yet cost-effective, network architecture supporting corporate offices in five continents via various network communication methods generating a savings of $.9M yearly.
- Managed development of corporate intranet utilizing Actuate and Crystal Reports and providing multi-dimensional and drill-down views and analysis based on fundamental customer, product, employee, and sales territory information.
- Saved $1.1M annually by consolidating corporate-wide telecommunication charges and services.

VICE PRESIDENT OF IT, OPERATIONS AND MANAGED SERVICES (FOUNDING), eSolutions Inc., Monroe, WA, February 1996 to November 1998
- Directed revenue generation in excess of $9M yearly for $12M Application Service Provider (ASP) for e-Business marketing solutions by providing Web-managed services to customers including Augustus Financial, Sony Entertainment, Fluid Video Electronics, Seattle Seahawks, Prada, and Nestle Foods, and encompsssing development of complex B2B, B2C, e-commerce, intranet, and data analytical sites.
- Defined, developed, and implemened Web-based solutions based on BEA, Vignette, E.piphany, BroadVision, Oracle, Microsoft and ATG software solutions.
- Played significant role in sales cycle and generating related marketing collateral supporting managed services offering; developed numerous adjunct product offerings to augment standard managed services product and data-center infrastructure.
- Developed scalable, secure, and reliable computer environment for hosting of complex e-Business applications while providing 100 percent customer renewal rate, zero incident factors related to security or virus breach, and 100 percent occurrence rate of exceeding service level agreement.
- Reduced annual costs 45 percent by managing numerous data-center relocations and consolidations.
- Developed and organized process, personnel and technology to support three-tiered Network Operations Center (NOC) providing 24/7 monitoring and escalated remediation.
- Provided specific technical guidance over system architecture, hardware standards and configuration, system monitoring, and security for ASP infrastructure.

SENIOR DIRECTOR, INFORMATION SERVICES (FOUNDING), PC Software Corporation, Wilder, WA, June 1994 to February 1997
- Founded and organized highly functional, decentralized IT organization within US and Europe for $60M supplier of real-time process-control software and devices to industrial automation market.
- Justified, selected, and implemented CRM software globally in four months utilizing internal IT and user staff for Sales and Customer Support.
- Based on data-warehousing and business intelligence tools by SQLServer, Cannons, and Aphrite, managed creation of international distributor sales network to increase customer linkage; system provided integrated remote order-entry and processing, sales management and related marketing collateral.
- Led requirements analysis, selection and implementation of Aphrite financial and distribution systems, based on Microsoft SQL Server platform on-time and within budget.
- Managed and consolidated IT entities for three corporate acquisitions.

DIRECTOR, INFORMATION SERVICES GROUP/DIRECTOR OF NETWORK OPERATIONS, MediaNation Inc., Cheney, WA, July 1993 to June 1994

- Oversaw network infrastructure, systems services and support, technology planning and strategy, financial planning, and corporate development services; recruited, managed, and motivated technology team.
- Led executive team, including HR, CEO, and Legal, to develop effective corporate IT/Internet policy, and data security, reducing hardware investment and liability costs.
- Attained 35+ percent ($240,000) cost reductions and improved SLA by renegotiating vendor contracts.
- Collaborated closely with CTO and CFO to develop financial and staffing plans.
- Assured cross-company network connectivity (necessitated by mergers and acquisitions), easy information sharing, high system security and availability, disaster-recovery planning, and capacity planning to meet growing and changing needs.
- Managed design and implementation, as well as on-time and under-budget launch.
- Coordinated e-commerce site-implementation efforts among internal staff, Microsoft Consulting Services, Cisco, and EMC engineers and facilities teams, culminating in successful and under-budget launch.
- Established monitoring systems and procedures for level 1 and 2 NOC response, assuring timely corrective action to operational issues.
- Supervised hardware and software selection and purchasing process, incorporating Cisco, Compaq, and EMC equipment on Microsoft platform, assuring a 99.999 percent SLA.

INTERIM DIRECTOR OF INFORMATION TECHNOLOGY, Euphor Corporation, Tacoma, WA, July 1990 to July 1993

- Led selection and implementation of Oracle ERP System supported by HP/UX.
- Established detailed implementation and migration plans from Appalachians to Oracle Applications.
- Managed Oracle consultants in the implementation of the Inventory, Bills of Material, GL, and AR modules.

CORPORATE DIRECTOR, MIS AND TELECOMMUNICATIONS, Keepers Corporation, Wilder, WA, March 1987 to July 1990

- Achieved standardization and commonality among 5 federate SBU IT organizations obtained through corporate mergers for $450M world leader in tape-backup storage systems.
- Reorganized and normalized IT organization in matrix structure to improve efficiency and service performance.
- Implemented IT function global reorganization, resulting in headcount decrease while improving capabilities.
- Provided overall corporate management and general IT guidance with a budget of $19M.
- Saved $1.6M annually by consolidating four regional data centers to two consolidated centers domestically.
- Cut costs $1.3M annually by standardizing all telecom and digital services.
- Generated annual communications savings of $.7M by establishing optimized global wide-area network providing support for voice, data, and fax traffic over digital lease circuits.
- Spearheaded a company-wide standardization and support of ERP system operating within IBM 3000 environment.

PREVIOUS PROFESSIONAL EXPERIENCE

DIRECTOR, MIS/TELECOMMUNICATIONS, Circuits and Conductors Incorporated, Pines, WA, 1984 to 1987

DIRECTOR OF MIS (FOUNDING), BYL Research Incorporated, Allons, WA, March 1982 to 1984

MANAGER, MANAGEMENT CONSULTING SERVICES, INFORMATION TECHNOLOGY, Mason Michael & Company, Allons, WA, March 1981 to 1982

EDUCATION

Master of Business Administration
University of Washington, Seattle, WA, 1990

Bachelor of Science in Business/Information Systems
University of Tennessee, Knoxville, TN, 1981

...

Paul David Bartholomew

632 Rose Alley Drive
Dover, DE 19901

Phone: 302-555-7940
E-mail: jobseeker@gmail.com

INFORMATION TECHNOLOGY SENIOR/EXECUTIVE MANAGER

Energetic, enthusiastic, MBA-level technology manager experienced in managing up to 40 individuals, as well as organizations with annual budgets of up to $7 million. Proven track record in staffing new organizations and focusing efforts, along with consulting experience with Fortune 500 companies and expertise in key areas of information technology, including:

- Hardware/Software
- Development
- Testing
- Production Support
- Staff Development
- Promoting Change/Improvement

- Project Management
- Database Technologies
- Customer Satisfaction
- Vendor Relationships
- Strategic Planning
- Technology Implementation

PROFESSIONAL EXPERIENCE

Management Consultant, Georgia Electrical Association (GEA), Atlanta, GA, Feb. 2003 to Present

- Reduced costs and improved productivity by establishing strategic data-management infrastructure for electrical deregulation organization, including developing storage resource management strategy.
- Researched, designed, and implemented infrastructure changes to meet market demand while reducing costs.
- Improved management and protection of data storage; reduced risks of data loss and improved storage cost management, resulting in enhanced organizational ability to predict storage needs and budget for future needs.
- Saved company $426,000 by eliminating unnecessary software purchases and avoided annual maintenance costs that would have been incurred had software been purchased.
- Created strategy documents to provide overview of direction for storage management; compiled and organized best practices in storage management and data protection.
- Produced results that include formal processes and procedures to better manage data storage and data protection, along with a dedicated group that is enthusiastic about the opportunity, the foundation to expand data storage without incurring unnecessary risks, increased confidence in data-management strategy, fewer errors; improved group morale, and generated significant cost savings.
- Implemented key storage components for environment that supports real-time, transactional, and data-warehouse processing at dual data centers requiring 200TB+ of storage.
- Cited by management for progress, impeccable work, and for providing leadership to succeed in an area where guidance was previously lacking.
- Created multiple service level agreements; deployed strong interpersonal skills to ensure cooperation and support while collaborating closely with departmental line managers to determine needs, set expectations, and reach consensus on service level agreements.

CONSULTING CLIENTS

- Boeing
- Netflix
- Sprint
- National Communications
- Anderson Wylie
- JP Morgan

- Comm-Tel
- City of Dover
- Wachovia
- Peter Pan Bakeries
- NGI Funds
- Sun Microsystems

- Verizon
- Seagate
- Hitachi
- E-machines
- Kay Jewelers
- Envision Systems

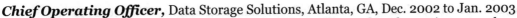

Chief Operating Officer, Data Storage Solutions, Atlanta, GA, Dec. 2002 to Jan. 2003
- Managed all daily operations and focused staff on selling and implementing network and data-storage solutions.
- Instituted turnaround strategy after co-founder departed; identified and prioritized organizational areas that needed improvement, and began process of rebuilding them; broadened product line, added new sales staff, improved technical capabilities, deepened vendor relationships, and streamlined operations.
- Maintained profitability without reducing staff during technology-industry slump when industry peers were experiencing up to 60 percent drops in sales.
- Led staff in achieving seven new technical certifications and improving firm's ability to provide new business services; increased staff professional certifications by 35 percent.
- Implemented comprehensive sales-management system that improved firm's ability to track and respond to sales leads and customer requests, resulting in improved communication and collaboration among sales staff.
- Led team to recognition as a top performance value-added-reseller for new product line.
- Supported business development and reviewed sales efforts by recruiting two new experienced salespeople, focusing their efforts on new product lines, and addressing problems with a poor-performing salesperson.
- Obtained new customers by developing telemarketing arrangement; followed up on existing customers with phone calls and surveys to determine ways to better support them.
- Managed vendor relationships; enhanced OEM relationships; expanded relationship with Microsoft and initiated new relationship with VERITAS.
- Promoted company image and communications through improved Web site reflecting organization's expanded capabilities, professional organizations, regular internal newsletters, and development/dissemination of mission statement; ensured that actions/plans aligned with mission.

Vice President, Systems Distribution, Shoebox Distribution Systems, Athens, GA, May 2000 to Dec. 2001
Assistant Vice President, Systems Distribution, Shoebox Distribution Systems, Athens, GA, May 1999 to May 2000
Contractor/Database Administrator, Systems Distribution, Shoebox Distribution Systems, Athens, GA, May 1997 to May 1999
- Established new group of professionals to provide services from Athens office overseeing $5+ million in development during tenure; hired, trained, developed, and directed staff, resulting in building new group from 11 to 25 persons.
- Promoted twice in three years to Assistant Vice President and then to Vice President for a promotion in company's top 10 percent of all staff; consistently rated highly by peers, staff, and management; recognized by division manager for key contributions that were critical to organization's success; attained highest ratings every year in 10 areas of achievement; cited for outstanding results and taking on leadership role.
- Managed diverse, productive, positive group of developers, administrators, and project managers who implemented projects using object-oriented and Oracle database skills; led group to complete $5 million+ in projects within 12 months of formation.
- Functioned as consistently high performer, willingly accepting significant responsibility, delivering on commitments, and contributing positive attitude and team-building skills that facilitated several strategic organizational changes.
- Directed staff, including development, assignments, and annual reviews; consistently rated in top 5 percent of managers.
- Earned praise from customers for group's efforts on customer projects; for example: "Our success is the result of the tremendous team spirit displayed by your group."
- Led group in key role in important project to initiate credit-card security features for 25 million cardholders; group contributed real-time update of all databases in multiple data centers to support large transaction loads.

President/Senior Consultant, Database Collaboration, Inc. Atlanta, GA, Dec. 1996 to March 1999
- Founded boutique Oracle consulting firm that provided full range of Unix/NT/Oracle services to Fortune 500 clients.

Vice President, Authoritative Computer Systems, Atlanta, GA, April 1994 to Dec. 1996
- Co-founded organization and oversaw operational management.
- Grew firm's staff from three to 85 in only 24 months.
- Increased revenues from $300K to $8.1 million in two years for 40 percent gross profitability.
- Developed or influenced entire organizational infrastructure.
- Cultivated legal and banking relationships.
- Supervised consultants and executive management.
- Determined business strategy.
- Monitored financial performance.

Senior Consultant, General Data Solutions, Atlanta, GA, Oct. 1990 to April 1994
Pre-Sales Engineer, General Data Solutions, Atlanta, GA, Jan. 1990 to Oct. 1990
- Promoted to manage outsourcing data center supporting Oracle-based clients from initial position as pre-sales systems engineer supporting sales of UNIX workstations and servers.
- Managed data center that supported 52 hospitals in five states.
- Oversaw $2M annual budget and staff of eight.
- Expanded business to include additional clients and supported sales efforts.
- Improved efficiency and monitored systems performance to service level agreements.
- Managed staffing and schedules.
- Interacted with clients to resolve issues.

EDUCATION and TRAINING

Master of Business Administration in Strategic Management, University of Georgia, Athens, GA, 2005

Bachelor of Business Administration in Statistics/Operations Research, University of Georgia, Athens, GA

Completed training in:
- Structured Development Methodology
- Guide to Project Management
- Managing Technical Professionals
- Software Project Planning and Management
- Managing Advanced Technical Projects
- Developing Complex Data Models and Designing Databases
- TCP/IP Networking
- Oracle Financials Workshop
- Oracle Database Administration
- Tune and Troubleshoot Oracle
- Professional Selling Skills III
- Dale Carnegie
- Microsoft Sales Training
- Treating People as Important Individuals
- Covey Institute's First Things First
- Adaptive Management
- UNIX System V Release 4 Administration SQL and PL/SQL using Procedure Builder
- Advanced SQL & SQL*PLUS
- ORACLE Backup and Recovery
- Developing Complex Data Models and Designing Databases
- Oracle Financials Workshop
- Application Object Library Development/Administration

LUCAS B. FULTON
762 Orange Court, Hilham, TN 38568 • 931-555-0977 • jobseeker@fultonfam.com

March 7, 2008

Henry Birnbaum
SOFT.Stats Software
2756 Edmondson Pike
Nashville, TN 37220

Dear Mr. Birnbaum:

As I read your ad for your Senior Analytical Consultant vacancy, I knew immediately that I could offer exactly the statistical analysis background you describe, along with a solid understanding of the many facets of supply-chain management.

More than 10 years in analytical consulting have equipped me with the skills to apply statistical techniques to developing supply-chain solutions to real-world problems, as well as to mentor junior-level team members. In me, you'll find someone who is unusually organized, dedicated, self-motivated, and who possesses the detail-orientation and technical prowess necessary to excel in a fast-paced environment. My master's degree bolsters my qualifications, as does my expertise with Fourier Analysis, spectral analysis, use of wavelets for anomaly detection, statistical process control, reliability models, regression methodologies, multivariate methods, and time series forecasting methods.

Throughout my career in consulting and operations in supply-chain management, data mining, and statistics, I have always been impressed with the quality of SOFT.Stats tools. I have honed exceptional skills in operations analysis/optimization, analytical methods, and SOFT.Stats procedures. My analytical skills have contributed to my ability to solve challenging problems. At Organic Farm Products, for example, the marketing department controlled promotion dollars, but information came from disparate sources, and sales quotas were not tied to financial objectives. I applied my creativity to devising a sales forecasting system in which order files could be integrated with shipments and invoicing files, and SOFT.Stats reports could be prepared to run batch mode each morning. I arranged for SOFT.Stats reports to be e-mailed to each sales unit so all parties could see the sales status daily, ensured that the system tied sales quotas to financial objectives, and added a trend projection expert system to forecast which products would not make their objectives. This report was a major contribution to the startup of the Organic Options product line.

I would also bring to your Analytical Consultant position the finely honed oral/written communication/data presentation skills that enable me to translate complex research data into comprehensible language and then effectively present actionable results.

I am confident that my qualifications and your needs are an excellent fit, and it would be in both our best interests to meet. I can make myself available for an appointment at your earliest convenience. I will contact you soon to arrange a meeting. Should you wish to reach me before then, please feel free to call me at 931-555-0977.

Sincerely,

Lucas Fulton

GAVIN MICHAELS, CPA

12 Empire Street, Oxbow, NY 13608 ❖ Cell: 315 555-8491 ❖ E-mail: jobseeker@attglobal.net

CHIEF FINANCIAL OFFICER
SENIOR FINANCE and ACCOUNTING EXECUTIVE
*Self-motivated, flexible, bottom-line-oriented financial executive recognized
for building teams and implementing corporate plans.*

AREAS OF EXPERTISE

- Budgeting/Forecasting
- Financial Reporting/Planning
- Modeling/Financial Analysis
- Working Capital Management/Cash Generation
- GAAP
- Monthly Income Statements
- Balance Sheet
- Cash Flow
- Capital Improvements
- Quarterly Board Meeting Reports

- Risk Management
- Cost Reductions/Process Improvements
- Development of Accounting Polices/Procedures
- Strategic Planning
- Monthly Ratios and Statistics
- Forecast and Project Cash for Ownership
- Budgets and Variance Analysis
- Tax and Regulatory Filings
- Excellent Customer Service
- Cost Control and Revenue Opportunities

PROFESSIONAL EXPERIENCE

Chief Financial Officer/Vice President, JEFFERSON COUNTY ATHLETIC CLUB – Oxbow, NY, 1997 to present

- Oversee financial functions for multimillion-dollar athletic club and tennis center, ranked in Top 100 revenue-producing athletic clubs nationwide for the last five years; handle finances of partnerships, private, public, corporate, government entities, and LLCs.
- Promoted from Controller to Vice President in 2000.
- Convert various cost centers into profit centers and consistently exceed performance to budget.
- Spearheaded computer upgrades, as well as financial planning for multiple high-value facility upgrades.
- Increased revenue per member and revenue per square foot every year for last four years.
- Decreased accounts-receivable days by 87 percent over last two years.
- Saved significant expenses through persuasive contract and pricing negotiation; serve as corporate expert for contract reviews.
- Played major role in selling privately held athletic club to municipal entity.
- Coordinate and support annual audit by outside accounting firm.
- Provide individual financials and integrate financials for two separate facilities and operations.
- Ensure overall performance and productivity of Accounting Department by implementing department-wide employee performance program.
- Provide financial direction for long-term strategic planning and key financial objectives for annual plan.

Staff Accountant for two local CPA firms – Great Bend, NY, 1990 to 1997

- Performed all degrees of audit and review services; planned, prepared, and projected taxes.
- Recruited staff and interacted with clients.

EDUCATION and CERTIFICATION

Bachelor of Science in Accounting, magna cum laude, New York University, NY; emphasis in Computer Systems

Certified Public Accountant, State of New York

❖ ❖ ❖

GAVIN MICHAELS, CPA

12 Empire Street, Oxbow, NY 13608 ❖ Cell: 315 555-8491 ❖ E-mail: jobseeker@attglobal.net

March 1, 2008

David Norwood
Highland Meadows Country Club
24201 State Route 342
Watertown, NY 13601-5155

Dear Mr. Norwood:

My leadership experience in multiple roles in financial planning, business-growth planning, financial controls, and profitability maximization along with my ability to deliver high performance through prioritization, cash management, information systems and human-resources optimization identify me as a powerful, cross-functional contributor equipped to perform proficiently as Chief Financial Officer for Highland Meadows Country Club.

A background in a similar setting, coupled with the ability implement corporate plans, place me among the top candidates. It's my drive and determination that especially make me stand out.

More than 15 years of accomplishment in financial performance assessment, managing overall financial health, stabilizing alignment with strategic priorities, and defining future expectations have provided me with a comprehensive expertise that assures my continuing career success. In me you will find someone who upholds high performance standards with unsurpassed integrity and solid work ethic, fosters proactive working relationships with internal/external cross-functional teams, applies unusual dedication and self-motivation, and offers the focus, drive, and leadership skills to excel seamlessly in a high-pressure, fast-paced environment.

My strong organization, presentation, and problem-solving skills, coupled with my top-tier financial savvy, enhance my ability to benefit Highland Meadows Country Club.

I would greatly appreciate the opportunity to meet with you to discuss the contribution I can make to your organization. I will contact you soon to arrange an interview. Should you wish to speak to me before then, you can reach me using the contact information atop this letter. I thank you for considering me and look forward to meeting with you.

Sincerely,

Gavin Michaels

BARRY STEELMAN, CFA

1621 E. 93RD STREET ♦ ARLEE, MT 59821 ♦ 406-555-8520 ♦ JOBSEEKER@YAHOO.COM

CORPORATE FINANCE DIRECTOR

Corporate Finance | Mergers & Acquisitions | Client Satisfaction Assurance | Real Estate | Structured Financing | Capital Markets

MBA- and CFA-credentialed financial professional with successful, proven track record of 13 years of business results and experience; strong written and verbal communicator.

KEY AREAS OF EXPERTISE

- Balance Sheet Review
- Business Analysis
- Business Development
- Capital Market Financing
- Contracts
- Credit Analysis
- Debt & Equity Analytical Tools

- Mergers & Acquisitions
- Due Diligence
- Negotiations
- Research & Analysis
- Relationship Building
- Fixed Income Products
- Forwards
- Futures

- Investment Management
- Foreign Exchange
- Mutual Funds
- Options
- Securities
- Stock
- Swaps

PROFESSIONAL EXPERIENCE

Manager of Land Banking, HOMEBUILDERS USA, Big Arm, MT, 2003 to present
- Manage $1.3 billion (16,952 lots) land-banking portfolio for nation's 12th largest homebuilder.
- Place real-estate deals, structure off balance sheet financing and collaborate with investors and attorneys to close land parcels.
- Work with corporate management as well as operating divisions on asset management to restructuring and negotiating our portfolio of real estate deals to maximize profit and ROI.
- Placed and financed $2 billion (27,453 lots) of residential real estate with various institutional land bankers as well as private investors across the US over the past four years.
- Decreased average spreads from 10 percent over Libor to 8 percent over Libor, resulting in significantly lower carrying costs by successfully negotiated lower option rate spreads on land bank deals.
- Created and standardized the Homebuilders USA Land Acquisition submission process by:
  o Playing key role in building Excel-based proforma model that measures acquisition's gross margins, RONA, and IRR on build out scenario.
  o Compiled required due diligence material and acquisition summary templates that divisions and regions need to use to submit their land acquisitions to corporate asset committee for approval.
  o Collaborated with corporate accounting to create monthly report to track and ensure that land bank deals are FIN-46 compliant, and that company receives proper deposit credits when due.

Financial Analyst, HOLLIS MATERIALS, Arlee, MT, 2000 to 2003
- Played key role on Strategy & Development team that helped Hollis Materials, one of the largest heavy building material companies in the US, successfully acquire several major building material companies nationwide that significantly increased company size.
- Provided economic and competitive information and analysis that managers used to run their businesses as well as to help in the valuation process of acquisition targets.
- Performed financial modeling and valuation analysis of acquisitions utilizing various financial measures—IRR, NPV and RONA.
- Co-produced and updated quarterly market forecasts that senior management used to set performance targets for operating units.
- Played key role in developing and creating annual five-year strategic plan.
- Produced quarterly competitor benchmarking paper for Board of Directors comparing Hollis Materials' operating performance by division to other major US and regional competitors; provided commentary and insight explaining variances in performance.
- Created and maintained in-depth reports on major competitors, including information and analysis on where each competed, strategies employed, as well as implications for Hollis Materials.

Analyst, JOHN-JACOBS INVESTMENT MANAGEMENT, Big Arm, MT, 1995 to 1999
- Performed wide range of economic and financial analyses in both US and international markets for portfolio managers of $6 billion international mutual fund company.
- Managed $500 million Canadian money-market composite portfolio, investing in various short-term Canadian money-market fixed-income instruments.
- Authored articles in *The New Century Investor*, a publication sent to mutual-fund shareholders.
- Conducted macro and micro economic research and analysis on regional and global economies.
- Performed fundamental analysis and cash-flow modeling for international equities held in global portfolios.
- Promoted from Junior Analyst after a year.

Financial Representative, UNITED HOME FINANCE, Charlo, MT, 1994 to 1995
- Performed credit analysis on applicants and ranking overall creditworthiness for one of nation's largest consumer finance companies.
- Collected and negotiated delinquent accounts.
- Sold ancillary life and disability insurance at loan and mortgage closings.

EDUCATION

MBA with concentration in Finance, University of Montana, Missoula, MT, 1996
Bachelor of Science in International Economics, University of Montana, Missoula, MT, 1992

LICENSURE AND CREDENTIALS

CFA (Chartered Financial Analyst)
Montana Real Estate Sales License (SL 2370038)

PROFESSIONAL AFFILIATIONS

Member, AIMR (Association for Investment Management and Research)
Member, Financial Analysts Society of Montana

Annika Sorensen

547 W. 145th St
New York, NY 10039-4120

Cell Phone: 212-555-4257
E-mail: jobseeker@gmail.com

March 20, 2008

James Fichter
JP Morgan Chase
270 Park Ave.
New York, NY 10017

Dear Mr. Fichter:

A successful, 10-year, high-caliber career in banking, along with a master's degree in business administration, has brought me to a moment of extraordinary opportunity and has prepared me fully and completely to lead JP Morgan Chase's efforts in Scandinavia. As an accomplished sitting CEO with highly specialized knowledge of Scandinavian banking practices and region regulatory bodies, I am uniquely positioned to head the team and advance the effort's growth and management by providing sound examples and financial infrastructure methodologies. Let me describe for you what sets me apart from other candidates for the advertised Scandinavian Director position:

- 10+ years of executive leadership experience conducting business in 60 countries spanning four continents.
- Expertise in capital markets, financial services, commercial banking, and business consultancy, establishing more than 20 new business start-up companies, and transitioning all successfully to IPOs.
- Comprehensive knowledge of the Scandinavian region and regional regulatory bodies, as well as fluency in Danish. Norwegian, Swedish, and English.
- Knowledge of regional etiquette through extensive personal experience in direct interface with the region's prominent political figures and royals.
- Experience managing fast-paced, multimillion-dollar projects from start to fruition.

I am eager to put this highly specialized, combined expertise to work for JP Morgan Chase to help build sound banking and financial systems, mobilize domestic savings, attract foreign investment, deepen international trade linkages, and create conditions that promote lasting economic opportunity.

Motivated by my passion to help developing countries reach for independence, build sound financial infrastructure, and attain financial prosperity, I can manage all aspects of the organization's program, including business development, strategic planning, client management, program reporting, and financial management. Additionally, I will recruit and hire a staff and direct and oversee their daily operations.

A proven track record in managing multiple large-scale financial projects simultaneously locks me in as a front-runner for the advertised position. Throughout my career, my employers have consistently and quickly come to depend on my expertise, demonstrated initiative, organizational skills, and writing ability. I am convinced that you will, too.

I know you won't regret talking to me about this position. I will contact you soon to schedule a time to talk. If you have any questions before then, you can contact me through the information atop this letter. Thank you for considering me.

Sincerely,

Annika Sorensen

BARRY JEPPESEN

416 ARCHWAY STREET, APOPKA, FL 32703 • PHONE: 407-555-7163 • E-MAIL: jobseeker@gmail.com

RESOURCE ORGANIZATIONAL DEVELOPMENT ~ CHANGE MANAGEMENT

MANAGEMENT CONSULTING

Consistently meet each project's objectives and deliver results to each corporate client that include cost savings, change in culture, reengineering of operations systems, organizational development, executive team-building, cohesion among senior management, implementation of appropriate supervisory and management skillsets, and behavioral change management.

PROFESSIONAL PROFILE

- Results-driven management consultant who deploys exceptional consulting skills to design/develop learning and organization training initiatives in corporate environments, resulting in reduction of operational costs, enhanced management effectiveness, optimized employee involvement, measurable performance improvement, better service, and increased profitability.
- Skilled project manager who has successfully managed and directed multiple, concurrent projects for dozens of corporate clients in Europe and North America in industries including telecommunications, manufacturing, bottling, retail, insurance, healthcare, hospitality, cruise-lines, food processing, and fast food.

AREAS OF EXPERTISE

- Creative learning approaches and techniques for participative performance optimization
- Cross-functional team utilization
- Eliminating change resistance
- Interactive employee involvement practices
- Time recovery and utilization interventions
- Senior executive team-building, encounters, coaching, and counseling

- Self-directed-team-building encounters
- Workflow system simulations
- Needs-assessment
- Employee involvement programs
- Management development workshops
- Continuous improvement processes
- Production system flows
- Quality and customer service initiatives
- Sales relationship workshops

- Dimensions in leadership
- Senior management diagnostic interviews
- Corporate culture profiles
- Departmental climate and team surveys from initiation through feedback process
- Corporate goal-setting and goal-roll-down processes
- Management and organizational restructuring
- Management/supervisory skills educational programs

PROFESSIONAL EXPERIENCE

All engagements except The Brevard Group were conducted under the auspices of own consulting firm, SMP Consulting Group, founded in 1987 (see page two).

Corporate Advisor, Collateral Associates, Orlando, FL, 2006 to Present
- Assist Managing Director and senior staff in formulating organizational strategic plans and launch of executive-coaching practice that provides professional executive coaches with corporate experience and motivational skills to help owners of small- to medium-size companies improve their odds of success.
- Conduct skills-development programs to enrich Coaching Associates' coaching/sales staff.

Director Resource Development, The Brevard Group, Cocoa Beach, FL, 2003 to 2006
- Engaged in multi-location project with $450-million North America subsidiary of a world leader French company; developed best-practice management system for all 18 US facilities; conducted two-day "Jump Start" training in change-management and systems proficiency in all locations prior to new system installation; oversaw implementation of new methodologies.
- Realigned provider and consumer services department for national insurance company and reengineered claims-appeal process and workflow to increase efficiency and quality of appeals, resulting in $8 million reduction in regulatory backlog and appeals aging cycle; supported new systems implementation with change-management facilitation workshops and multi-level management coaching.
- Transformed entire provider and consumer services department from traditional operation process into a self-directed-teams operation, thereby reducing process cycle time by up to 80 percent.

Organizational Development Consultant, DataTel, Valdosta, GA, 2001 to 2003
- Diagnosed and facilitated reengineering of organizational communication systems, leadership, and management processes.
- Directed selection process for key executive positions, including North America VP and General Manager.
- Coached executive team members in meeting new sales challenges and market demands.

Resource Development Manager, AlphaOmega Consulting, Jupiter, FL, 1998 to 2001
- Analyzed and assessed client companies' supervisory and management skills proficiency as it manifested itself at the point of execution—the work area.
- Collaborated with client teams and assisted with organizational development and training needs, including behavioral/operational enrichment initiatives, change management, teambuilding/group facilitation, organizational assessments/design, competency modeling, conflict resolution, learning management systems design, and continuous improvement processes, resulting in measurable performance improvement, employee involvement, customer service, and total quality.
- Trained client trainers to develop enriched programs combining technical and behavioral skills to maintain highly motivated workforce, thus meeting corporate objectives.

Director of North America Training, Integrative Development Systems, Charleston, SC, 1994 to 1998
- Implemented clients' management training programs and organizational development processes.
- Oversaw facilitation of Productivity and Quality Systems Installations projects in USA, Canada, and Mexico, assisted by staff of trainers and operation engineers.
- Conducted extensive senior executive and train-the-trainer management programs (management development projects) throughout Europe.
- Facilitated results in which clients saw 20+ percent in increased productivity, uptime, service, and quality, as well as substantial reduction in cycle-time and rework, measurable results with increased supervisory, management and leadership skills, team cohesion, and organizational effectiveness.

Co-founder, SMP Consulting Group, Oviedo, FL, SC, 1994 to present
- Consulted on organizational development and resource utilization projects that focused on developing client resources and actively utilizing self-directed teams.

EDUCATION
AND
PROFESSIONAL DESIGNATION

Master of Science in Arts in Psychology, Fordham University, New York, NY

Bachelor of Arts in Psychology, Rollins College, Winter Park, FL

Master Productivity Specialist, Association of Productivity Specialists, New York, NY

AMANDA DAVIS, PH.D.

485 Trumbull Ave. • *Fairfield, CT 06824* • *203-555-1964, Cellular* • *jobseeker@fairfieldu.edu*

PROFESSIONAL PROFILE

- Strategy-driven educator with extensive background in community-college settings, along with exceptional expertise in organization/management/leadership, communication and innovation, research and planning, strategic planning, entrepreneurship and development, curriculum development, and budgeting/financial responsibility.
- Strong leader with significant education experience, marketing ability, teaching background, as well as experience in curriculum development.
- Visionary innovator who excels in developing new programs in education.
- Effective grant writer who has secured significant funding for academic programs and initiatives.
- Student-centered communicator who is adept at cultivating and maintaining productive relationships with all constituencies.
- Mission-driven administrator whose dedication to service in higher education has encompassed committee participation, including search committees.

EDUCATION

- **Ph.D. in Higher Education Administration – Research and Evaluation Concentration,** Sacred Heart University, Fairfield, CT, 2005

  COMPREHENSIVE EXAM TOPIC: The Business of Higher Education

  DISSERTATION TOPIC: Profile and Distinguishing Undergraduate Programs in the United States

- **Master of Science in Sociology – Demography-Population/Research Methods and Statistics Concentration,** Sacred Heart University, Fairfield, CT, 1993

  THESIS TOPIC: *Raising Biracial Children in the United States* presented at the 1996 Population Association of America Meetings

- **Bachelor of Arts in Business – Marketing/Public Relations,** Fairfield University, Fairfield, CT, 1991

ACADEMIC AND TEACHING EXPERIENCE

Director of Planning, Research, and Grants, *Gateway Community College,* New Haven, CT, 2006 to present

- Managed projects: Halpert Center start-up; Sacred Heart University collaboration committees; state Student Success Initiative; Higher Learning Commission accreditation Steering Committee.
- Facilitate all-college institutional strategic-planning process and assist with divisional processes.
- Performed some functions of vacant Vice President of Academic and Student Affairs position in assistance to college president.
- Serve on search committees: Dean of Halpert Center and Grants Writer.
- Develop and facilitate faculty assembly and leadership retreats.
- Play key role in departmental program review and employer advisory committee activities.
- Identified new programs for development: cyber-security, bioinformatics, geospatial imaging, and online retail and sales management.
- Assisted consultants with audit of campus information technology and assessment of new programs, which led to restructuring of college divisions.
- Serve as member of all-college Assessment Committee on student outcomes, all-college Technology Committee, and Colleague Users Group.
- Wrote and received $141K Connecticut Board of Nursing grant; $250K Allen Bowman legislative earmark; Wrote Connecticut Enterprise grant for information technology (pending $465,000).

Assistant Professor (non-tenure-track), *School of Management,* Yale University, New Haven, CT, 2004 to 2006

- Played instrumental role in developing and implementing new, online master's-degree program in community-college management.
- Taught institutional research, statistical decision analysis, and operations management.
- Served on Faculty Executive Committee and University and Campus Assessment Committees for Higher Learning Commission accreditation.
- Advised cohorts of online master's level students nationwide during and after on-campus residencies.
- Consulted in research design and analysis for institutional, programmatic, and special project research.

Project Developer, Researcher, and Editor, *Sacred Heart University, Colleges of Education and Arts & Sciences Research Centers,* Fairfield, CT, 1995 to 2004, project-based contracts

- Developed and facilitated completion of grant-funded projects in university-based centers while pursuing master's and doctoral studies.
- Facilitated teams to write contract/grant proposals for academic programs, research, and workshops.
- Supervised development and completion of research and training projects.
- Trained community groups and students in outcomes management, research, and planning models.
- Wrote, edited, and published *Grant Update* newsletter for statewide community leaders.

Founding Director, Institutional Research and Assessment, *Gateway Community College,* New Haven, CT, 2002 to 2003

Founding Director, Institutional Research and Assessment, *Manchester Community Technical College (MCTC),* Manchester, CT, 1998 to 1999

- Founded two offices under same presidential leadership at both institutions and developed processes for measuring institutional effectiveness.
- Developed research processes for strategic planning (co-chaired executive committee), decision-making, and accreditation (AQIP) review.
- Served on hiring committees for management and executive positions.
- Advised about data archival for elimination of computer system.
- Assessed institutional faculty evaluation system for changes in process and reporting of outcomes
- Created policy and procedures for institutional research function.
- Collaborated with local businesses to maintain and increase regional economic activity.

Director, Continuing Education and Manistee County Center, *Gateway Community College,* New Haven, CT, 2002 to 2003

- Managed satellite learning center.
- Collaborated with academic deans and student services representatives to develop and offer on-site and distance-education opportunities.
- Partnered with Intermediate School Districts to operate and fund shared facilities and develop articulation agreements.

Interim Assistant Director, Curriculum Development, *University of Connecticut College of Medicine at Storrs, Center for Rural Health Professions,* Storrs, CT, 1999 to 2002

- Advised students in their completion of community-based research projects and evaluated community-based curriculum for specialized medical-school track.
- Collaborated with faculty and community to develop and fund new interdisciplinary program.

Grants and Evaluation Manager, *University of Connecticut College of Medicine at Storrs, Center for Rural Health Professions,* Storrs, CT, 1999 to 2002

- Assisted inner- and inter-organizational program development through team building, proposal writing—including budgeting—and funding.
- Found and cultivated contract, government, foundation, and endowment funding opportunities working with program leaders and development office.
- Advocated for formation and funding of a National Establishment for Achievement and Growth to government and businesses.
- Advised about issues of state policy and organizational dynamics to position and manage unit.
- Developed "franchise package" to recruit hospitals to become fee-paying designated clinical sites.
- Cooperated with other institutions for recruitment of students and adjunct faculty.

Administrative and Research Assistant, *Sacred Heart University, US Census Bureau State Data Center,* Fairfield, CT, 1991 to 1993

- Retrieved United States Census Data from mainframe, CD-ROM, and published sources for use by external fee-paying clients.

Instructor of Population, Sociology, Research Methods, and Statistics classes, *Gateway Community College/Sacred Heart University,* New Haven, CT and Fairfield, CT, 1992 to 2000

- Earned excellent evaluations by focusing on applying theories and techniques.
- Created Internet-based study and testing tools in WEB-CT.

PROFESSIONAL EXPERIENCE

Market Research Analyst, *Alliance Healthcare,* Fairfield, CT, 1993 to 1995

- Guided administrators through data analysis and presentation during organizational reengineering.
- Formulated and guided implementation of models for planning of re-organization and product mix.
- Retrieved and analyzed Census, Pulse Survey, and Prizm "Cluster" data; summarized and presented original survey and focus-group research.
- Played key role on team that oversaw product and program planning and evaluation.

Owner and Manager, *Dava (retail clothing store),* Litchfield, CT, 1991 to 1994

Sales Manager, *Staples (office supply company),* Hartford, CT, 1987 to 1989

Event and Database Coordinator, *Leslie Pool (wholesale distributor),* North Haven, CT, 1983 to 1986

HONORS AND AWARDS

- Research Fellow, Center for Social Development at Yale University, 2007
- Sacred Heart University Department of Educational Administration George Morris dissertation award, 2004
- University Council for Educational Administration, Herman S. Norton National Graduate Student Research Seminar award, 2003
- Phi Theta Kappa National Honor Fraternity

SPONSORED PROJECTS AND PUBLICATIONS

- Health Services of Fairfield County, Opportunities and Threats for Health and Human Services presentation, 2001
- Fairfield Public Housing Authority grant evaluation assistance, 1999
- Fairfield School District 71 Parent Satisfaction Survey, 1998; 2001
- Community College Network Economic Impact Study, 1996
- City of Fairfield, Community Development Consolidated Plan, (US-HUD), 2000
- Community College Needs Assessments: Gateway Community College (CT), 2000 and Manchester Community Technical College (CT), 1996
- Connecticut Home Contractors, Inc. strategic planning consulting, 2006
- Connecticut Governor Jodi Rell and Connecticut Century Network, *Workforce Readiness Communication* project, 2004
- Health Resources and Services Administration, Office of Rural Health Policy: *Merging Adolescent Education and Community Health* project evaluator, 1998-2001; Grants Coach for Technical Assistance Workshop, 2002
- Connecticut Department of Commerce and Community Affair projects: *Cost-Benefit Analyses*, Small Business Division, 1999; *International Trade and Procurement Technical Assistance Centers*, 1999; *International Business Division Evaluation and Planning Study*, 1997; *Business Climate Survey* (n=4,375) & *Small Business Development Survey* (n=4,475), 1996
- Connecticut Department of Energy and Natural Resources *Home Builders Survey*, 1997
- Connecticut Rural Health Association *Funding Workshop* coordination and presentations, 2001; 2002
- Sacred Heart University's Center for Higher Education and Finance, *Assessment of Gender Equity*, 1996
- International Journal of Financial Aid; Changing Society Through Service Learning Programs, 2007
- Connecticut League of Women Voters regional meetings, *The Demographics of Connecticut Women* presentation, 1995
- Long Island CarFerry, *Economic Impact Study*, 2003
- New Haven Community School District 21st Century Undergraduate Programs annual evaluations, 2000
- Litchfield Daily News, *Teen Health Behavior Study*, 2003
- Fairfield County Chamber of Commerce, *Community Issues 1998*
- National Center for Educational Accountability, *Connecticut Best Practices Study*, 2004
- Fairfield County Community Foundation, College for Kids evaluation, 2003
- United Way community needs assessments: Fairfield County *Assessment 2000;* Southeast Area *F.O.C.U.S. 2001*
- University of Connecticut, Connecticut Center for Educational Technology, STAR On-line Program Evaluation, 2001
- Town of Fairfield, *Community Development Consolidated Plan* (US-HUD), 2000
- Eli Whitney Center for Community and Economic Development: Peace Corp Fellows Program, *Conducting Health Surveys* workshops, 1999; 2000; 2001
- University of Connecticut College of Medicine: State advisory committee member; *Merging Adolescent Education and Community Health* presentations: Community Development Society, 2000; Connecticut Rural Health Association, 1999; 2000; Society for Teachers of Family Medicine, 2001

PRESENTATIONS

- *Questions administrators ask when developing new programs.* (2007, July). Invited panel discussant, Connecticut Collaborative Conference on Bioinformatics. New Haven, CT; Yale University.

- with Mallory, J. (2007, February). Engaging with difference matters. Civic Service Research Fellows Seminar. Boston, MA: Center for Social Development at Boston University.

- with Mallory, J. (2005, November). Outcomes of participation in service learning on 37 campuses. International Conference: Advances in Service-Learning Research. Atlanta, GA.

- with Gillon, P. (2001, October). Outcomes 101: Evaluating program outcomes. Process taught at a workshop for leaders of non-profit agencies. Suffolk, NY; United Way of Suffolk County.

- (2001, August – September). Funding resources and search strategies. Presentation at three workshops conducted for Township Officials of Connecticut. Fairfield, Hartford, and New Haven, CT.

- with DeMatteis, L., Baker, K., Stiles, K., & Scott, N.J. (2001, May). Practical teen health: A partnership in adolescent education and community health. Lecture discussion presented at the annual spring conference of the Society of Leaders in Family Medicine. Cincinnati, OH.

- (2001, April – September). How can this meeting be improved? Training sessions at workshops conducted for Township Officials of Connecticut (3) and the Connecticut Rural Health Association (3). Fairfield, Hartford, Manchester, New Haven, and Waterbury, CT.

- (2001, April). Searching for grants on the Internet. Training session at workshops conducted for Connecticut Rural Health Association. Hartford and New London, CT.

- with Norem, J., & Stiles, K. (2001, March). An outreach mini-grant program: Helping teens improve their health. Program presented at the Connecticut Rural Health Association meetings. Cheshire, CT.

- with Brown, K., Stiles, K. & Pinkering, J. (2000, July). Merging adolescent education and community health. Presentation and panel discussion at the annual conference of the Community Development Society. New York City, NY.

- with DeMatteis, L., & Stiles, K. (2000, March). Merging adolescent education and community health: A collaborative model. Model presented at the Connecticut Rural Health Association meetings. Waterbury, CT.

- (1996, May). Raising biracial children in the United States. Poster session presented at the 61st annual meeting of the Population Association of America. Washington, D.C.

PROFESSIONAL AND ACADEMIC AFFILIATIONS

- Fairfield County Development Coalition, institutional member, 2006-present
- Council for Resource Development, institutional member, 2006-present
- American Educational Research Association, 2004-2006
- Society for Leaders of Family Medicine, 2000-2002
- Community Development Society, 2000-2002
- University Council of Educational Administration, 2003-2004
- Ludington/Manistee Chamber of Commerce, 2002-2003
- Association of Institutional Research, 2002-2005
- Connecticut Rural Partners, organizational member, 1996-2002
- Population Association of America, 1991-1994

AMANDA DAVIS, PH.D.

485 Trumbull Ave. • Fairfield, CT 06824 •203-555-1964, Cellular • jobseeker@fairfieldu.edu

March 24, 2008

Dr. Richard Barkwell
Chief Academic Affairs Officer
Fairfield University
1073 N Benson Rd
Fairfield, CT 06824

Dear Dr. Barkwell:

I note that your needs for the Dean for Undergraduate Programs and Academic Planning position you are currently advertising coincide with my education, skills, and experience. Your ad particularly details the core requirements of several of my positions at Gateway Community College in which I enjoyed significant success.

Further, I am uniquely qualified for this position because I offer a background in strategic planning, institutional research, and academics. I have built on my distinctive experience in higher-education settings by developing exceptional expertise in collaborating with faculty, administrators, donors, and students. The parallels between your requirements and my work, not only at Gateway, but in several other higher-education positions, are remarkable.

I am convinced that my background equips me with a significant advantage in this position because it has provided me with experience in advising, university relations, administration, fundraising, enrollment management, marketing, strategic planning, and hiring, all of which are essential in the advertised position. By implementing several start-up initiatives, I have demonstrated my facility for innovative program development.

The skillset I've developed is highly applicable to a complex and ever-changing setting where solid interpersonal skills and exceptional communication skills are an advantage. That skillset includes the ability to see the big picture and think "outside the box," as well as deal with virtually anyone in any situation diplomatically, collegially, and effectively.

In addition to the nitty-gritty work of budgeting, planning, controlling costs, and solving problems, I am committed to helping to shape students' lives. A particular strength of mine is establishing rapport with students. I am then adept at motivating them to overcome their academic and personal obstacles. I would like to personally help students set goals for their academic careers and beyond, especially in the type of undergraduate programs with which I am so familiar.

My education, skills, and experience will enable me to help address the challenges your program faces. I would like to arrange an interview to discuss the contribution I can make at the Fairfield University. I appreciate your time and consideration and will contact you to discuss this opportunity in the near future.

Sincerely,

Amanda Davis, PhD

Robert Aguilar

73 Shady Hills Blvd. Edison, NJ 08837
Phone: 201/555-9074 • jobseeker@njnet.net

PRESIDENT/EXECUTIVE DIRECTOR
QUADRANGLE COMMUNITY FOUNDATION
Executive Management | Consensus-building | Measurable Results

Accomplished doctoral-level professional offering deep familiarity of current trends in philanthropy through career-long achievement in leadership roles of university scholarship and grant programs.

Focused and dedicated coalition-builder whose strengths lie in bringing people and entities together to identify common interests, negotiate and define common goals, and develop and collaborate on joint initiatives and operational strategies that produce measurable results.

Articulate, diplomatic interpersonal communicator with customer-service skills and leadership capabilities.

Motivated achiever with career history of multiple commendations praising ingenuity, creativity, resourcefulness, aplomb, and proven management style.

PROFESSIONAL EXPERIENCE

Executive Director, *Durham Scholars Program*, Edison, NJ, 2006 to present
- Built nationally recognized merit-scholarship program from ground up and function in key management role as inaugural director.
- Achieved merger of two rival universities to collaborate on and form joint program that is unique among American higher-education institutions.
- Lead staff of six university administrators in governance of program.
- Recruit, advise, and monitor 120 participants and oversee budget in excess of $5 million.
- Earned Employee Forum Community Service Award recognizing distinguished contributions to promote cooperation and collaboration among faculty, staff, and students.
- Manage, supervise, and facilitate implementation of $50,000 annual grant program.
- Maintain contact with donors, board of directors, and university administrators; plan, arrange, and facilitate board and administrator meetings.
- Oversaw creation of support organization and new governance structure.
- Secured long-term funding commitment for program.
- Implemented multiple projects to enhance collaboration between Rider College and University of New Jersey.
- Established and oversee smooth operations of transportation system between campuses.
- Played key role in establishing national identity for Durham Scholars Program.
- Launched program development in Northeastern US.

Director, *Laurel Programs*, New Brunswick, NJ, 1999 to 2006
- Oversaw all aspects of off-campus undergraduate experiences program, including program development, budgeting, student recruitment and advising, and implemented new programs.
- Established new field-research seminar with programs in Washington. DC, Cape Town, South Africa; Dijon, France; Death Valley, CA; and Beijing, China.
- Secured faculty and administrative buy-in for program.

Assistant Professor of Political Science, *Rutgers University*, New Brunswick, NJ, 1996 to 1999
- Specialized in foreign policy and international relations.

EDUCATION
Doctor of Philosophy in Political Science, University of Massachusetts, Amherst, MA
Bachelor of Arts in Political Science, Brandeis University, New York, NY

PROFESSIONAL AFFILIATIONS
- Member, Board of Trustees, and Chair, Educational Philosophy Committee, Prince School, 2002-2005
- Member, Advisory Board, People's First Corporation, 2003-Present

ALYSSA MARTINDALE

13 East 93rd Street NW • Clio, SC 29525
Phone 842-555-7630 • E-mail: jobseeker@cfl.rr.com

ARTS ADMINISTRATION EXECUTIVE

Senior-level Arts Administrator with successful concert-management skills, proven organizational abilities, and strong diplomatic skills.

PROFESSIONAL EXPERIENCE

Executive Artistic Administrator, Marlboro County Symphony, Clio, SC, 2004 to present
- Implement and manage all programming for symphony.
- Develop programs in collaboration with Music Director, ensuring that all concerts are consistent with symphony's musical, educational, and strategic goals.
- Collaborate with operations and event staff to coordinate technical aspects of all productions, special events, and other ancillary activities.
- Negotiate artists' fees, prepare and process contracts for commissions, conductors, artists, choirs, and guests.
- Communicate artistic information to all departments; serve as staff resource in artistic matters.
- Develop and manage artistic budgets, monitor expenditures, and ensure compliance with established targets.
- Research current programming trends, evaluate artist portfolios and scores; recommend artists, repertoire, and conductors.
- Manage all on-site liaison for guest artists and conductors; supervise Artist Coordinator in booking all artists' travel and hotel arrangements.

Artistic Administrator, South Carolina Symphony Orchestra, Charleston, SC, 2001 to 2004
- Managed all aspects of engagements for 50+ guest artists and conductors yearly.
- Coordinated travel, hotel, rehearsal, and concert schedules, hospitality, and ground transportation.
- Researched immigration issues and prepared visa applications for artists.
- Monitored artistic budgets and managed accounts payable.
- Collaborated on all areas of artistic planning with executive artistic administrator, managing director, and music director; researched and prepared reports on repertoire, guest artists, recordings, and programming of other orchestras.
- Chaired Information Flow Cross Function Team, a select group of staff members charged with examining and improving process of distributing information throughout organization.
- Led strategic-planning sessions, set goals/objectives, planned and prepared staff presentations.
- Oversaw development and implementation of Orchestra Planning and Administration Software (OPAS); trained new users, established protocols, negotiated service contracts, and coordinated data-entry from all departments.

Operations Assistant, East Cost Symphony Orchestra (ECSO), Charleston, South Carolina, 1998 to 2001
- Assisted with production of all ECSO concerts, including two nationally televised concerts from Columbia Metropolitan Convention Center, pops and classics concerts at the Charleston Convention Center, and nine concerts at the Myrtle Beach Convention Center.
- Scheduled load-ins and load-outs for all concerts, coordinated production schedules, and disseminated weekly stage requirements.
- Supervised performances comprising Columbia Metropolitan Convention Center's summer Mozart Festival.
- Managed travel, scheduling, and pre-tour production of ECSO Raleigh, NC, residency.

Box Office Manager, University of South Carolina, Columbia, SC, 1996 to 1998
- Hired and supervised staff of seven; set regulations and employee guidelines.
- Prepared daily sales reports and audits; oversaw subscription and single-ticket sales for five resident companies and other performances.

EDUCATION

- **Bachelor of Science in Music Business with honors,** North Carolina State University, Raleigh, NC, 1996
    - Studies included non-profit accounting and financial management, public relations, economics, orchestra management, music theory, and history.

PROFESSIONAL AFFILIATIONS AND COMMUNITY SERVICE

- Professional Affiliate, United States Symphony Orchestra
- Volunteer, KC Cares: Mothers Against Drunk Driving, St. Jude Children's Research Hospital, Relay for Life, and MS Walk

ADRIANA BELMONT

327 CARSON STREET, ALTAMONT, UT 84001

PHONE: 435-555-7420 • CELL: 435-555-8520 • E-MAIL: jobseeker@yahoo.com

SENIOR ATTORNEY/COUNSEL

PROFESSIONAL PROFILE

- MBA/JD-educated attorney and businessperson experienced in corporate governance, drafting, negotiating, managing, problem solving, and providing corporate and departmental guidance beyond complying with SEC rules/regulations.
- Internationally experienced legal practitioner with experience on five continents.
- Legal representative of both buyers and sellers in such business-operations as procurement, marketing/sales, real estate, and facilities; experienced in advanced technology products and services.
- Skilled problem-solver who identifies issues before they escalate.
- In-house and private practice contracts expert experienced in drafting and negotiating substantial ($10 million+) contracts.
- Award-winning performer who excels in billable hours and bonuses; recognized with rapid promotions and top evaluations from management, subordinates, and clients.
- Effective oral and written communicator.

HIGHLIGHTS OF PROFESSIONAL EXPERIENCE AND ACCOMPLISHMENTS

NEGOTIATING AND DRAFTING CONTRACTS

- Established Contracts Department for Higgins Systems Network, Inc.'s new corporate Wireless Networks Business Unit; beyond this business unit, developed, drafted, and initiated first processes forms, processes, and procedures for entire corporation's contract administration; refined processes and procedures to meet ISO 9000 certification requirements.
- Optimized ability to draft/negotiate beneficial contracts by attaining knowledge of all steps for installing, testing, and commissioning wireless networks.
- Managed growth of Contracts Department from one to 11 employees; earned corporation's highest rating from direct reports in annual "reverse review" of manager performance.
- Negotiated and drafted business agreements beyond contracts, e.g., joint development agreements, teaming agreements, marketing agreements, sales agent agreements, and corporate representative agreements.
- Collaborated with client management and staff to determine then-current contract operations; reengineered processes to optimize success potential; developed and drafted procedures and forms for contract management from proposal development through contract closeout.
- Analyzed and presented to executives and management summaries of contemplated/completed transactions (sales contracts, procurements of major components and subsystems), competitor products and positioning, and other factors that could affect achievement of corporate goals.

GENERATING NEW BUSINESS

- Facilitated growth of corporate division from two contracts in one wireless telecoms product line valuing $25 million to multiple contracts in three wireless telecoms product lines valuing more than $1 billion; oversaw worldwide legal aspects of these product lines, including procurement.
- Identified ways for sales people to meet objectives and consistently brought in revenue required to support business goals.
- Arranged for international trading company to act as financier for a sale to telecoms department in country that lacked funds to pay for the system.
- Assisted in developing RFIs and RFPs for proposed undertakings; facilitated client determination of business objectives and technical solutions with respect to technology transactions.
- As member of corporate proposal teams, analyzed RFIs and RFPs; identified risks and opportunities.
- Collaborated with team members (e.g., pricing, program management, marketing) to produce responses consistent with corporate risk and revenue guidelines.

TRAINING AND PROCESS IMPROVEMENT
- Excelled as team leader and lecturer for Johnson Space Center Productivity and Quality Enhancement Seminars.
- Proposed, drafted charter for, and established corporate management alliance to improve interdepartmental communications and facilitate problem resolution.
- Established corporate-wide system to advance and sustain employee involvement in corporate decision-making, including developing and drafting procedures and forms.
- Instructed classes in employee problem identification, analysis methodology, and solution development.
- Initiated first automated systems at Harold Electronics Systems Group, Space Division, to track incoming, outgoing, and internal correspondence and contract modifications.
- Played key role on team to reduce cycle time of contract review/contact close out; collaborated on quality-improvement team at Harold Electronics Systems Group, Space Division.

INTERNATIONAL EXPERTISE
- Established corporate foreign branch and representative offices; managed support provided by domestic and foreign outside counsel.
- Counseled clients on implications of FCPA, US Export Control, and U.N. Convention on Contracts for International Sales of Goods, and other US and foreign regulations and practices with respect to the international sale and purchase of high-technology products and support services.
- Earned Best International Win of the Year, 1992, 1993, and 1994 at Higgins Systems Network Inc.

PROFESSIONAL HISTORY

- Principal, The Belmont Group, Altamont, UT, 2001 to present
- Associate, Gary Heintzelman, Outsourcing and Technology Practice Group, Salt Lake City, UT, 1997 to 2001
- Senior Contracts Manager, Higgins Systems Network Inc., Wireless Networks Business Unit, Eden, UT, 1995 to 1997
- Contracts Manager, Higgins Systems Network Inc., Wireless Networks Business Unit, Eden, UT, 1993 to 1995
- Senior Contracts Representative, Harold Electronics Systems Group, Space Division, Herrimen, UT, 1991 to 1993
- Contracts Representative, Harold Electronics Systems Group, Space Division, Herrimen, UT, 1990 to 1991
- Associate Industrial Engineer, Technologies Illuminated, Johnson Space Center, TX, 1985 to 1987
- Industrial Engineer Trainee, Technologies Illuminated, Johnson Space Center, TX, 1983 to 1985

EDUCATION

Juris Doctor, Yale University, New Haven, CT, 1990
Academic Achievements:
Business Editor, Law Review: *Journal of Technology and Law*
Research Note: "Videotaped Ceremonies of Dispursement" approved for 1991 publication.
Law Student Liaison to The American Bar Association, 1986-1998
Founding Editor, *Law Student Quarterly*, quarterly newspaper promoting law student involvement in ABA activities

Master of Business Administration, Harvard University, Boston, MA, 1982
Academic Achievements:
Assistant Editor, *The Law Case* (MBA Program Quarterly Newspaper), 1981-1982
IBM Women in Business Scholarship, 1980-1982.
International Paper Women in Business Scholarship, 1980-1982

Bachelor of Arts in Humanities, Georgetown University, Washington, DC, 1980

BAR ADMISSIONS

- State of Utah, Dec. 1990
- District of Columbia, Sept. 1991
- US Supreme Court, June 2005

HONORS AND DISTINCTIONS

AUTHOR

- Chapter 3, "Negotiating Contracts in Foreign Countries," in legal textbook *Transaction Abroad Done Right*, LIBUDL, Salt Lake City, UT, 2005.

FACULTY MEMBER

- LIBUDL Commercial Transactions in Foreign Countries Seminars, 2005-present.

AWARD WINNER

- *Best International Win of the Year* for leading team, negotiating and drafting most significant international contract for 1992, 1992, and 1994, Higgins Systems Network, Inc.
- *Gold Key Award* for dedication and service to the ABA; only law student in nation to earn award in two consecutive years, 1986 and 1987.
- *Special Award* for outstanding contributions to the corporation, United Illuminated, Inc., 1986.
- *Team Award* for significant contributions to space program, Johnson Space Center, 1984.

INTERNATIONAL EXPERIENCE

In-Country Experience

- Brazil
- Canada
- Czech Republic
- France
- Germany
- Switzerland

- Indonesia
- Japan
- Malawi
- Mexico
- People's Republic of China (including Hong Kong)

- Republic of China (Taiwan)
- Republic of South Africa
- Singapore
- United Kingdom
- Viet Nam

Legal work performed in U.S. for services to be performed in country identified

- Australia
- India
- Italy

- Kazakhstan
- Nigeria

- Russia
- Ukraine

ADRIANA BELMONT

327 CARSON STREET, ALTAMONT, UT 84001
PHONE: 435-555-7420 • CELL: 435-555-8520 • E-MAIL: jobseeker@yahoo.com

SENIOR ATTORNEY/COUNSEL

RESUME SUPPLEMENT
SELECTED TRANSACTIONS

REPRESENTED:

- Systems vendor in sales of satellite communication systems, satellite sensor systems, and related services. Contract values range from $22 million to $450 million.

- Corporation in due diligence for proposed acquisition of aerospace corporation; only attorney assigned to due diligence team. Acquisition price: $40 million.

- Systems manufacturer/service provider in sales of Space Shuttle payload processing services and other space hardware sales and services. Contract values range from $500,000 to $50 million.

- Manufacturer; negotiated and drafted $400 million worldwide agreement between multinational IT manufacturers for development, marketing, sales and after-sales support of cutting-edge wireless telecommunications product.

- Systems vendor in sales of wireless telecommunications networks. Contracts included hardware sales, provision of services, and software and other IP licensing. Contract values range from $1.5 million to $500 million

- Systems vendor in the contracted provision of maintenance and support of vendor-sourced wireless telecommunications networks. Contract values range from $10 million to $25 million.

- Global financial services provider in outsourcing its Asian and Australian IT requirements, including sale of its Australian outsourcing subsidiary to outsourcing vendor. Contract value (exclusive of sale of subsidiary) $350 million.

- Multinational hard-goods retailer in purchase of mega-terabyte data warehouse and its integration into then-current IT environment, including development and licensing of specialized software, maintenance, and support. Contract value $45 million.

- International apparel and sporting good manufacturer/retailer in full-scope, worldwide IT outsourcing transaction. Contract value $500 million.

- Multinational financial institution in outsourcing its multi-currency account processing (worldwide accounts managed in UK; daily processing performed in US). Contract value $27.5 million.

- Multinational chemical manufacturer in US desktop (hardware/software/applications/help desk) outsourcing transaction. Contract value $150 million.

- US healthcare resources organization in recruiting, training, and obtaining US employment for foreign-trained nurses.

- US patent application preparation and search organization in providing services to foreign-based IP owners.

ROLAND STROM

1365 San Angelo Blvd. Huntsville, AL • Phone: 256-555-4349 • Mobile: 256-555-5684
E-mail: jobseeker@yahoo.com

EDITORIAL EXECUTIVE

Prepared to deliver creative direction and literary expertise to high-end publishing house
in an editorial leadership capacity.

List of books authored, exhibitions managed, and exhibition catalogs published available upon request.

PROFESSIONAL PROFILE

- Highly respected literary professional with exceptional blend of experience, including more than 15 years as executive manager for two international juried literary awards.
- Accomplished publisher with comprehensive background in high-end publication authoring, editing, and production, along with experience in producing four books and numerous fine arts catalogues.
- Savvy senior-level business developer whose multiple career accomplishments in the publishing arena include successful launch and direction of art-publishing house in France and cultivation of numerous art and literary contacts worldwide.
- Globally experienced scholar with comprehensive expertise in French, Spanish, and Latin American literature.
- Exceptional verbal and written communicator who is bilingual in French and Spanish, fluent in written and spoken English and Italian, and conversant in Portuguese.
- Solutions-oriented problem-solver known for ability to consistently identify challenges and apply unsurpassed leadership and creative-direction skills, resulting in effective team collaboration and solid project management.

AREAS OF EXPERTISE

- Art Literature Publishing
- American, European, and Latin American Literature
- Editorial Direction

- Design Principles
- Defining Creative Challenges
- Conceptualization and Idea Generation
- Language Translation

- Effective Communication
- Creative Meeting Direction
- Brainstorming and Strategizing
- Team Leadership

PROFESSIONAL EXPERIENCE

Director, *Arts of Latin America,* Huntsville, AL, 2001 to Present
- Created and launched prestigious French art-publishing house and exhibitions producer.
- Conceptualize, develop, and introduce new publications and exhibition products.
- Supervise permanent staff of four and occasional staff of 15.
- Market books and exhibitions throughout Europe.

Counselor to the Secretary General/Joint Chief Executive Director, *Culture and Communications Department,*
Madrid, Spain, 1989 to 2000
- Headed department of 35-nation international, intergovernmental organization and supervised staff of 37 in 15 countries.
- Conceived, edited, and produced numerous fine-art exhibition catalogues. *List of books authored, exhibitions managed, and exhibition catalogs published available upon request.*
- Engaged in fundraising activities.
- Coordinated protocol and provided diplomatic follow-up of exclusive social and political engagements.
- Deployed strong communication skills as counselor to Secretary General for strategic matters.
- Functioned as Senior Project Manager of complex projects, leading teams of high-level scholar-experts.
- Cultivated unique international experience in nearly all important Spanish-speaking capitals.

EDUCATION

Master in Arts and Literature, Oxford University, Oxford, England, 1986
Bachelor in Arts and Literature, Oxford University, Oxford, England, 1984

Appendix

Guide for Brainstorming Accomplishments

Although resumes and cover letters should be accomplishments-driven (and should *not* focus on duties and responsibilities), many executives have difficulty pinpointing their accomplishments. This guide will help you brainstorm the accomplishments that will help sell you to your next employer.

As you work through this guide, keep the following in mind:

➤ Try to list accomplishments that are specific and measurable.

➤ Quantify whenever possible. (Example: Increased sales by 50 percent over the previous year.)

➤ Use superlatives and "firsts." Use words such as "first," "only," "best," "most," and "highest."

➤ Consider the "so-what factor." For every accomplishment you list, ask yourself, "So what?" Does the item you've listed truly characterize your abilities and your potential for contributing to your next employer's success?

➤ Make sure each accomplishment is relevant to the type of job you seek.

➤ Respond to as many of the questions as you can for each job.

1. In each job, what special things did you do to set yourself apart? How did you do the job better than anyone else did or than anyone else could have done?

2. What did you do to make each job your own? How did you take the initiative? How did you go above and beyond what was asked of you in your job description? What did you do that was new to your job function to improve what was there before? Can you attach dollar amounts to your most successful projects?

3. What special things did you do to impress your boss so that you might be promoted?

4. And were you promoted? Rapid and/or frequent promotions can be especially noteworthy.

5. How has the organization benefited from your performance? How did you/will you leave this employer better off than before you worked there? What critical strategy components did you identify to propel the organization to a better place?

6. List awards you've won, recognition you've attained, media coverage you've received.

7. What are you most proud of in each job?

8. Check your annual performance reviews for each job. Identify glowing or complimentary quotes from your reviews. Did you consistently receive high ratings?

9. Have you received any complimentary memos or letters from employers or customers? Find quotes from these communications that support your accomplishments.

10. What tangible evidence do you have of accomplishments—publications you've produced, products you've developed, new technologies you've introduced, business strategies you've deployed, programs or policies you've initiated?

11. How did you contribute to this employer's profitability, such as through sales increase percentages? How have you helped your employer to make money? How did you contribute to the firm's return on investment (ROI)?

12. How did you contribute to operational efficiency in each job, such as through cost-reduction percentages? How did you help this employer or a part of the organization to save money, save time, or make work easier? In what ways have you streamlined or automated processes?

13. How did you contribute to productivity, such as through successfully motivating your team?

14. What did you do to improve your organization's competitive advantage?

15. What did you do to foster relationships inside and outside the organization?

16. What was your role in bringing in new customers and satisfying the existing customer base?

17. What role did you play in business growth? Did you initiate mergers, acquisitions, partnerships, or operating agreements?

18. What role did you play in executing the organization's mission, goals, and objectives? What is your track record in meeting deadlines and budgets?

19. If someone asked your boss from each job to identify your most significant contribution in that job, what would your boss say?

20. Consider specific problems in each job. What were the problems or challenges that you or the organization faced? What did you do to overcome the problems? What were the results of your efforts? Did you turn plummeting sales around? Did you fix weak financials? Did you raise brand awareness? Did you launch a new product? Did you penetrate the market? Use the SAR or PAR technique, in which you describe a Situation or Problem that existed in a given job, tell what Action you took to fix the Situation or Problem, and what the Result was.

21. Imagine you are in an interview with a CEO who has 10 minutes to see you. He or she asks you to "bottom-line your impact to your current organization in 30 seconds." How would you reply?

22. Describe the result of something you did in each job as though it were a headline. Then, back in to the story to describe why your action was needed and how you executed it.

23. Consider how each accomplishment fits with your brand/target? Explain in just two sentences in what way this accomplishment will have impact on your target and reflect your brand.

24. Describe the strategic impact of each accomplishment? What was the result? How did you make it happen? What was the initial problem/challenge?

25. What would *not* have happened had you not done your job well?

26. Imagine you had to write an accomplishment on a paper the size of a business card—and get an interview from it. What would you say?

27. How is optimal performance or success in a given job or function typically characterized, and how do you measure up? What would a description be of performing this job or function successfully and at its highest level?

28. Identify skills in which you excel—far above the performance level of most people—and give results-based examples of how you've demonstrated those skills.

29. Illustrate ways that your knowledge of industry trends and governing regulations has resulted in achievements.

30. What are you most known for? What is your style or technique for consistently driving results?

Resources
Websites for Executives
Job portals and networking organizations

Quintessential Careers Job and Career Resources for Executives, Top Managers, and Experienced Mid- and Senior-Level Professionals
www.quintcareers.com/executive_jobs.html

6 Figure Jobs
www.sixfigurejobs.com
Portal for $100K+ jobs.

hundredK.com
www.hundredK.com
Center for $100K+ job search and recruiting.

futurestep
www.futurestep.com
A Korn/Ferry company providing outsourced recruitment for middle-management professionals.

BlueSteps.com
www.bluesteps.com
Online global community of senior executives and career management service that provides executives with continual exposure to search firms.

ExecuNet
www.execunet.com
Membership-based executive referral network.

NETSHARE.com
www.netshare.com
Membership-based organization that provides executives with $100K+ job listings and networking opportunities.

RiteSite.com
www.ritesite.com
Helps senior executives contact and build relationships with 485 retained executive-search firms.

Executive REGISTRY
www.executiveregistry.com/
$100K+ jobs via executive recruiters.

TheLadders.com
http://TheLadders.com
Online community catering exclusively to the $100k+ job market and offering online job-search resources and content for the $100k+ job seekers and recruiters.

FENG (Financial Executives Networking Group)
www.thefeng.org

MENG
www.mengonline.com/
National network of top-level marketing executives.

CIO.com
www.cio.com
Serves chief information officers and other IT leaders and provides technology and business leaders with insight and analysis on information technology trends and an understanding of IT's role in achieving business goals.

LinkedIn
http://LinkedIn.com
Online network of more than 16 million experienced professionals from around the world, representing 150 industries.

CEO Express
www.ceoexpress.com/default.asp
Business portal for executives.

Boardroom Insider
www.boardroominsider.com
Insights on governance, boards of directors, and the 21st century boardroom.

Executive Resumes and Career Transition Strategies
www.executive-resumes.com
Blog describing executive resume-writing and career-transition strategies.

Working With Recruiters

Quintessential Careers Recruiter/Headhunter Resources, Directories & Associations
www.quintcareers.com/recruiter_directories.html

Online Recruiter's Directory
www.onlinerecruitersdirectory.com
Online recruiters directory of headhunters, executive search firms, and executive recruiters.

Oya's Directory of Recruiters
www.i-recruit.com/about.html
Online directory of links to recruiter Websites.

Books

Executive Job Search

Executive Job Search for $100,000 to $1 Million+ Jobs by Wendy S. Enelow and Louise M. Kursmark, Impact Publications, 2006

Networking

I'm on LinkedIn – Now What???: A Guide to Getting the Most OUT of LinkedIn by Jason Alba, Happy About, 2007

Salary Negotiation

Perks and Parachutes: Negotiating Your Best Possible Employment Deal, from Salary and Bonus to Benefits and Protection by Paul Fargis, Crown Business, 1997

Negotiating Your Salary: How To Make $1,000 A Minute by Jack Chapman, Ten Speed Press, 2006

Working With Recruiters

Headhunters Revealed! Career Secrets for Choosing and Using Professional Recruiters by Darrell W. Gurney, Hunter Arts Publishing, 2000

Personal Branding

Career Distinction: Stand Out by Building Your Brand by William Arruda and Kirsten Dixson, Wiley, 2007

Brand Yourself: How to Create an Identity for a Brilliant Career by David Andrusia and Rick Haskins, Ballantine Books, 2000

Professional Executive Resume Writers
Key to Certifications

CARW: Certified Advanced Resume Writer

CCM: Credentialed Career Manager

CCMC: Certified Career Management Coach

CCS: Certified Career Strategist

CEIP: Certified Employment Interview Professional

CERW: Certified Expert Resume Writer

CFRW: Certified Federal Resume Writer

CHRP: Certified Human Resources Professional

CIS: Certified Interview Strategist

CLTMC: Certified Leadership and Talent Management Coach

COIS: Certified Online Identity Strategist

CPBS: Certified Personal Branding Strategist

CPS: Certified Professional Secretary

CPRW: Certified Professional Resume Writer

CPRWCC: Certified Professional Résumé Writer and Career Coach

CRS: Certified Resume Strategist

CTL: Certified Teleclass Leader

CTMS: Certified Transition Management Seminars

CTSB: Certified Targeted Small Business, State of Iowa

DCC: Distance Career Counselor

FJSTC: Federal Job Search Trainer and Coach

IJCTC/JCTC: [International] Job and Career Transition Coach

MCC: Master Career Counselor

MRW: Master Resume Writer

NCC: National Board Certified Counselor

NCCC: National Board Certified Career Counselor

NCRW: Nationally Certified Résumé Writer

Resume Writers Who Write Executive Resumes Exclusively

Christopher Aune
CORE Coaching
812-756-0986
lifepro@etczone.com
www.lifeskillspro.com

Wendy Enelow, CCM, MRW, JCTC, CPRW
Enelow Enterprises, Inc. & Resume Writing Academy
434-299-5600
wendy@wendyenelow.com
www.wendyenelow.com
www.resumewritingacademy.com

Meg Guiseppi, CPRW, MRW
Resumes Plus LLC
973-726-0757
megguiseppi@resumesplusllc.com
www.ExecutiveResumeBranding.com

Abby M. Locke, NCRW, CPBS
Premier Writing Solutions, LLC
202-635-2197
alocke@premierwriting.com
www.premierwriting.com

Don Orlando, CPRW, JCTC, CCM, CCMC
The McLean Group
334-264-2020
yourcareercoach@charterinternet.com

Laurie J. Smith, CPRW, JCTC
Creative Keystrokes Executive Resume Service
800-817-2779
ljsmith@creativekeystrokes.com
www.creativekeystrokes.com/

Resumes Writers Who Specialize in Executive Resumes

Georgia Adamson, CCM, CCMC, CPRW, CEIC, JCTC, MRW
A Successful Career
408-244-6401
success@ablueribbonresume.com
www.ablueribbonresume.com

Diane Burns, CPRW, CEIP, CCMC, FJSTC, CPCC, CCM, CLTMC
Career Marketing Techniques
208-323-9636
dianecprw@aol.com
www.polishedresumes.com

Jewel Bracy DeMaio, CPRW, CEIP
APerfectResume.com
800-227-5131
mail@aperfectresume.com
www.aperfectresume.com

Don Goodman, CPRW, CCMC
About Jobs
    800-909-0109
    DGoodman@GotTheJob.com
    www.GotTheJob.com

Sharon Graham, CRS, CIS, CCS, CPRW, CEIP
Graham Management Group
    905-878-8768, 866-622-1464
    info@GrahamManagement.com
    www.GrahamManagement.com

Susan Guarneri, CERW, CPBS, COIS, NCCC, CCMC, MCC, IJCTC, DCC
Guarneri Associates/Career Goddess Group
    715-546-4449/Skype: susan.guarneri
    Susan@Resume-Magic.com
    www.Resume-Magic.com

Makini Theresa Harvey, CPRWCC, CEIP, JCTC
Career Abundance
    650-630-7610
    makini@careerabundance.com
    www.careerabundance.com/

Karen P. Katz, CCM
    Career Acceleration Network (CAN)
    215-378-6685, 215-860-6869
    karen@careeracceleration.net
    www.CareerAcceleration.net

Murray A. Mann, CCM, CPBS, COIS
Global Diversity Solutions Group
    312-404-3108
    info@GlobalDiversitySolutionsGroup.com
    http://GlobalDiversitySolutionsGroup.com

Sharon McCormick, MCC, NCC, NCCC, CPRW
Sharon McCormick Career & Human Resource Consulting
    919-424-1244
    careertreasure@gmail.com

Jan Melnik, MRW, CCM, CPRW
Absolute Advantage
    860-349-0256
    CompSPJan@aol.com
    www.janmelnik.com

JoAnn Nix, CPRW, CCMC, JCTC, CEIP, CBPS, CTL
A Great Resume Service, Inc.
    800-265-6901
    info@agreatresume.com
    www.agreatresume.com

Debra O'Reilly, CPRW, CEIP, JCTC, CFRWC
A First Impression Resume Service/ResumeWriter.com
813-651-0408
debra@resumewriter.com
www.resumewriter.com

Resume Writers Whose Clientele Includes Executives

Marian Bernard, CPS, CPRW, JCTC CEIP
The Regency Group
866-448-4672/Local: 905-841-7120
marian@neptune.on.ca
www.resumeexpert.ca

Georgiana Carollus, CPRW
Resumes with Spirit
630-654-8540
gc@resumeswithspirit.com
www.resumeswithspirit.com

Laura M. Labovich, CCM, CARW, CFRW
A & E Consulting, LLC
703-942-9390
aspireempower@gmail.com
www.aspireempower.com/

Sandra Lim, CHRP, CPRW, CECC
A Better Impression
641-715-3900, ext. 19929
newcareer@abetterimpression.com
www.abetterimpression.com/

Terrie Osborn, CPRW
Resumes, Etc.
315-676-3315
tosborn2@twcny.rr.com
www.cnyresumes.com

Kris Plantrich, CPRW, CEIP
ResumeWonders Writing and Career Coaching Services
248-627-2624, 888-789-2081
kris@resumewonders.com
www.resumewonders.com

Barbara Safani, NCRW, CPRW, CERW, CCM
Career Solvers
866-333-1800, 212-579-7230
info@careersolvers.com
www.careersolvers.com

Billie R. Sucher, CTMS, CTSB, JCTC
Billie Sucher & Associates
515-276-0061
billie@billiesucher.com
www.billiesucher.com

Index

About the Author

KATHARINE HANSEN is an instructor and creative director of Quintessential Careers (*www.quintcareers.com*). Her other books include *Dynamic Cover Letters* and *Write Your Way to a Higher GPA*, written with Dr. Randall S. Hansen, as well as *Dynamic Cover Letters for New Graduates*, and *A Foot in the Door: Networking Your Way into the Hidden Job Market*, all published by Ten Speed Press. She also coauthored the *Complete Idiot's Guide to Study Skills* (Alpha Press) with Dr. Randall S. Hansen.

Katharine holds a PhD in organizational behavior from Union Institute & University, Cincinnati, Ohio, and the career certifications Master Resume Writer and Credentialed Career Manager from The Career Management Alliance.

Katharine has taught the writing of resumes and cover letters and critiqued the job-search correspondence of countless college students and other job-seekers and served as chief writer for the resume-writing service she owned for five years. Katharine also is editor of QuintZine, a career and job-hunting newsletter.

Katharine was previously writer/editor at numerous newspapers, magazines, and nonprofit organizations, and she served as speechwriter for the first woman elected to the Florida Cabinet. Katharine lives in DeLand, Florida, with her writing partner, Randall.